Battling Editor

Battling Editor

The Albany Years

Harry Rosenfeld

excelsior editions

AN IMPRINT OF STATE UNIVERSITY OF NEW YORK PRESS

Published by
STATE UNIVERSITY OF NEW YORK PRESS, ALBANY

Printed in the United States of America

EXCELSIOR EDITIONS IS AN IMPRINT OF STATE UNIVERSITY OF NEW YORK PRESS

For information, contact State University of New York Press, Albany, NY
www.sunypress.edu

Library of Congress Cataloging-in-Publication Data

Name: Rosenfeld, Harry, 1929– author.
Title: Battling editor : the Albany years / Harry Rosenfeld.
Description: Albany : Excelsior Editions, 2019. | Series: Excelsior editions
| Includes bibliographical references and index.
Identifiers: LCCN 2018021847| ISBN 9781438473758 (hardcover : alk. paper) |
ISBN 9781438473772 (e-book)
Subjects: LCSH: Rosenfeld, Harry, 1929– | Journalists—United
States—Biography. | Newspaper editors—United States—Biography. |
Knickerbocker news (Albany, N.Y. : 1975–) | Times Union (Albany, N.Y.)
Classification: LCC PN4874.R5955 A3 2019 | DDC 070.92 [B] —dc23
LC record available at https://lccn.loc.gov/2018021847

10 9 8 7 6 5 4 3 2 1

For the men and women with whom I had the good fortune to work at newspapers for more than seven decades, stalwarts of the people's liberties.

And for Paul and Rachel, forever in our hearts.

Contents

Foreword

Harry Rosenfeld was Bob Woodward's editor at the *Washington Post* during the Watergate scandal, and Woodward later characterized Harry as "a tough sonofabitch." In his new memoir, *Battling Editor*, Harry gives us a manifesto on how a TSOB behaves when he's the top editor at not one but two newspapers. He migrated from the *Post* to Albany, New York, to take command of Albany's two dailies, the *Times Union* and the *Knickerbocker News*, both owned by the Hearst Corporation. It was 1978, when print journalism was becoming an endangered species, and the *Knick*, an afternoon paper, was limping toward the chopping block before Harry arrived. The two papers would eventually merge, and the *Knick*'s final headline on April 15, 1988, was "We Say Farewell."

Harry wanted to bring the *Post*'s brand of investigative journalism to Albany, and in his years at the *Times Union* he absolutely did. He chronicles how he accomplished this, decision by decision, exposé by exposé, adhering rigorously to a journalistic code of ethics that begins in the First Amendment and blossoms into holy writ: insistence on hard, critical reporting and on "distinguishing between the false and the factual," and demanding the same of everybody in the newsroom. I remember when Harry took over—penetrating stories began to appear about the Albany political machine, whose like I had not seen in the Albany papers in many years.

Harry's book is often about tough decisions, and it stands out as a handbook on how to live an ethical life in the news business right now. Is it possible to tell the truth all the time? Sometimes. But this is an instructive narrative—especially today when the truth is such a rare commodity in the White House and Congress, and the financially beleaguered press is itself under threat as an enemy of the people. Harry and his family lived in Nazi Germany, and escaped it in 1939. A large part of his subsequent life has been an ongoing war against fascism, racism, and political criminals. This book explains how he waged that war on a daily basis in the newsrooms he managed so well, and for so long.

WILLLIAM KENNEDY
September 4, 2018

Acknowledgments

My thanks go to:

George R. Hearst III, the publisher of the *Times Union*, for his support and permission to use photographs and reproductions, and Susan Wright, his administrative assistant, for preparing manuscript copies;

Associate Editor Michael V. Spain for his constant help searching contemporary and old files as well as his prodigious memory, Will Waldron for extraordinary help shepherding photos, and Mark Losee, who yet again extracted me from serial conflicts with the computer system;

Paul Grondahl, former colleague and constant friend, first to read the manuscript and offer encouragement;

Dan Kaufman for handling legal issues and following up with a thorough error-catching read, Janice Kaminsky for her insightful comments and good catches, and Mel Damski for contributing his editing skills;

My editor, Rob Brill, whose keen eye and intense scrutiny contributed countless improvements—our collaboration will remain memorable, as will our friendship;

My publisher, James Peltz, and his staff at SUNY Press, for once again helping to make a book of mine a reality; Laurie Searl, for carefully guiding the manuscript through the production process; and Dana Foote, for thorough copyediting.

I must also thank my close colleagues throughout my retirement years, the members of the *Times Union* editorial board—Rex Smith,

Mike Spain, Tena Tyler, along with Jay Jochnowitz, the leader of this band. They insist on being knowledgeable and perspicacious and are the best company.

I thank my family for cheering me on and Anne, my wife these six and half decades, for her perceptive assessments of the work in progress. And for putting up with me.

Prologue

It took me the better part of seven hours to drive out of one world into another. After a dozen eventful years I left the *Washington Post*, a newspaper of international stature published at the nation's center of power. Awaiting me in Albany, New York, was command of two underperforming newspapers published in the capital of what remained in name only the Empire State.

The drive was the latest in a series of shuttles between Washington and Albany for job interviews, follow-up meetings, and house hunting. By my side in the car were my wife, Anne, and our youngest daughter, Stefanie. I was taking on an exciting new opportunity at the *Times Union* and the *Knickerbocker News*.

My wife and child were surely not the only ones who questioned my decision. (Our other daughters, Susan and Amy, were in college, and their lives were not as disrupted by the big change.) I was, after all, giving up a job as assistant managing editor at the *Washington Post* to head two smaller papers, albeit as no one's assistant. I was going to be a bigger fish, but the pond had shrunk considerably. Furthermore, I was departing Washington as supervisor in the newsroom management team of a paper famous in large part for exposing, against great odds, the political scandal now known as Watergate. The paper's investigative reporting earned it a Pulitzer Gold Medal for Public Service, in which I had played a key role as the editor in charge of the reporters who broke the story.

For me, though, the job in Albany was not a wrong turn. In Washington, I had been a department head with ten or so peers, but now I would be the top editor. I would oversee the editorial pages as well as the two newsrooms, which neither of the renowned editors I had worked for in New York and Washington did. The editorial pages at those papers reported directly to the publisher, not to the editor.

Far from a comedown, it was an opportunity to deploy skills and ideas developed over a quarter of a century as an editor never in charge of more than a part of the newsroom at the *New York Herald Tribune* and, after that paper died, the *Washington Post*. The publisher of the morning *Times Union* and afternoon *Knickerbocker News*, J. Roger Grier, in his announcement of my hiring, stated the mission plainly: "It is our intention to make these newspapers among the very best in the United States." I saw it as the chance to bring to Albany the kind of in-depth reporting and vitality that distinguished many big-city newspapers. I firmly believed that people living in smaller cities and suburbs would welcome and make good use of vigorous journalism.

What I did not so much as glimpse at the time were the tectonic changes lurking in the future, created by digital technology. In the years ahead, the internet would undermine reader and advertiser support of the printed word and impede the best journalism.

In the 1970s, newspapers had begun to take baby steps to revolutionize their manufacture. For more than a century, the industrial fixtures essential to print America's newspapers—linotype machines, printing presses, and other apparatus—gradually gave way to new inventions. It was the season for newspapers to reduce their high labor costs.

Over time, the number of typesetters, printers, and pressmen was reduced. Many blue-collar jobs were eventually eliminated, while advertising remained a dependable source of revenue. Readers had not yet been lured away by the variety of digital distractions that lay in wait and would soon convert what turned out to be a comparatively short-lived boom into a grave threat.

Yet it was also a good time for journalism. Radio and television already had displaced the pencil press from its exclusive role as the first bearer of breaking news. Extra editions faded into the distant past. The ubiquity of broadcasting pushed the best journalism to probe deeper and provide context and clarity, all functions that upgraded the work of the better newspapers and set higher standards for those not as good.

At the *Washington Post*, new production systems were fitfully installed over the years, as the backshop unions through contract negotiations accustomed themselves to running their operations only in theory managed by the owners. The *Post*'s publisher at the time, Katharine Graham, is famous for having stood up to the White House: Over the government's implacable enmity, in 1971 she authorized her paper to publish the Pentagon Papers in the face of an existing court order to desist. A year later she supported the publication of the Watergate exposé. The first embarrassed the government by revelations of lies told the American people during the Vietnam War; the second divulged lawbreaking that led to the resignation of President Richard M. Nixon.

Katharine Graham is not as celebrated, however, for another act of courage, which derived from a series of confrontations with craft unions that flared in 1975. The *Post* was still in the opening stages of integrating new industrial equipment while trying to deal with work rules that were accrued and embedded over the years. Featherbedding and make-work threatened the viability of the enterprise. When her newspaper was struck by the pressmen that year, it was basically over the issue of who controlled the *Post*'s production operations. The unions opposed the introduction of new devices and methods that could interfere with their control and threaten their jobs. When the strike began, the pressmen heavily damaged all the presses on their way out to the picket lines. The *Post* missed one edition and turned for help from outlying publishers as the crippled presses were restored one by one.

I was the assistant managing editor for national news during the strike and was in the pressroom the night she touched the start button on the first repaired press. For a host of reasons, it was an historic moment. The *Post* continued to publish, using newly trained nonunion labor. The strike ended after nearly five months on February 22, 1976, confirming that management not only owned but also operated the newspaper. Katharine Graham's stouthearted defiance of the worst the strikers could do surely widened the opportunity for other newspapers to modernize.

As these changes permeated the newspaper trade, I was restless. I had been a senior editor successively in charge of four news departments.

Although my work interested me, after nearly twelve years at the *Washington Post*, I was looking elsewhere.

It was no sudden impulse. For long, my goal was no higher than department head, first as managing editor of the Herald Tribune News Service, where I began my career on the editorial side of newspapering. Then I was cable editor and later foreign editor at the *New York Herald Tribune*. When that newspaper succumbed in 1966, after a series of strikes, I landed at the *Washington Post* and resumed the steep climb up the ladder as night foreign editor, then a couple of years later as foreign editor. Foreign editor was my ultimate goal, and I reveled in it. From time to time, I peeked out over the parapet of my mink-lined rut—editing the coverage of crises around the world, traveling to a dozen countries, meeting movers and shakers. I scrutinized all around me and decided I possessed the skills to aspire to be a managing editor, the person who oversees the operations of the separate departments. I also understood my limitation: I had run only rather small departments. I needed to demonstrate my ability to manage a much larger one.

The evolution of my ambition coincided with the plans of Benjamin Crowninshield Bradlee, the executive editor of the *Post*. My joining the staff in 1966 was part of the program as Ben methodically undertook his formidable assignment to upgrade the newspaper.

Early after my promotion to foreign editor, Bradlee approached me to take over running the local staff—the metropolitan operation, the largest by far—and bring it up to his standards. At first, I declined, en-joying too much my new berth begun with a tour as staff correspondent in South Vietnam during the war. On later reflection, I decided this was the perfect way for me to validate myself to others, as well as to confirm my own high opinion of my capabilities.

So I took the job to run Metro, did what was expected of me, and built up a first-class operation to match the performance of the national desk, the Style section, sports, and other departments, and managed the paper's daily coverage of Watergate. By then I knew for sure I could do more than I had ever been in place to do.

When a headhunter approached me seeking an editor for a Minneapolis newspaper, I agreed to be considered. It was now clear that having headed the foreign, national, and metropolitan staffs, as well as the Sunday Book Review and Outlook opinion sections, I had pretty much exhausted the opportunities open to me at the *Post*. My bosses—Bradlee and Howard Simons, the managing editor—stood at the head of their respective classes and showed no signs of going elsewhere.

The Minnesota job did not pan out, but the chance to make a change came in 1978, when I heard three words: "I need somebody." Roger Grier spoke them over the telephone as he explored my interest in running two daily newspapers and three community tabloids in Albany, of which he was the publisher. Although the idea of Albany did not excite me, I was primed to explore the opportunity. I knew little about the city except that it was controlled by a notorious Democratic political machine and that it was located where the New York Central Railroad, after traveling 150 miles north from Grand Central Station in Midtown Manhattan along the east bank of the Hudson River, made a sharp left turn to proceed westward across the state. The four years I rode those rails, I got off at Syracuse, where I studied at the university.

In the first phone call, and on the theory that you never say never when contemplating your future, I agreed to visit Albany. Roger had been given my name by a colleague, Richard Harwood, the deputy managing editor of the *Post*. He took that position after a tour as editor of the *Trenton Times*, owned by the *Washington Post*, where Roger was previously the publisher. Bradlee had offered me first crack at the Trenton job in 1974, when the *Post* bought the paper, and I had said no. Ben did not like being turned down, but I risked his displeasure then because of what I remembered about the capital of New Jersey, which I had I visited a couple of times while in Army basic training at nearby Fort Dix during the Korean War. The Trenton of my memory was a place of utter dreariness.

Prior to Roger's phone call, matters had evolved at the *Post* to the extent that I had changed my mind and had come to regard a move to Trenton not so much as a way out but as a way up. More than anything, I wanted to run my own newspaper. A couple of editors from the *Washington Post* had filled the Trenton job only to return without having enlarged the paper's prospects. Either they or the *Post* company had

had enough. By the time Bradlee approached Mrs. Graham, sometime around 1977, to propose me (again) for the job, she was no longer open to dispatching another *Post* editor to try to produce the results the company expected in Trenton.

Roger had recently left the *Trenton Times* to become the publisher of Capital Newspapers Group in Albany. In our first talk, he said he wanted to make a major innovation and place one editor in charge. He said neither of the editors heading the two papers were up to implementing his vision, which included hard, critical reporting.

After analyzing a bundle of the newspapers sent me, I flew to Albany. Roger and I talked at length in his office, which was on the second floor of the newspaper building where the business departments were located. We came up with similar approaches to what needed to be done. On a personal level, I perceived Roger as a man I could work for, a fact of substantial importance to me. A long interview process played out, including a session in New York with Robert J. Danzig, general manager of Hearst newspapers, before I was selected from among three finalists. I did not think turning the papers around would be easy, but that would not have interested me.

The story of my time in Albany as editor of these two newspapers recounts the final days and years of a particular golden age of newspapers and, toward its end, the portends of the profound and punishing alterations the internet would inflict. It is the story of my success upgrading the effectiveness of my newspapers by cultivating their quality. It turned out to be as well a constant effort to maintain high standards as the second floor struggled to deliver high profit margins.

Under the leadership of John Miller and Frank A. Bennack Jr., the Hearst Corporation's nationwide newspaper holdings developed reputations that supplanted the notorious Yellow Press image of preceding decades. In part, it was accomplished by bringing on board accomplished editors, including my old *Trib* boss, Jim Bellows, to be the editor of the Hearst paper in Los Angeles. Soon after I was recruited, the *New York Times*, in a March 11, 1979, article about the comeback of Hearst newspapers, reported that each paper was autonomous, apparently reflecting what the reporter had been told. Though the autonomy turned out to be less than absolute, it sufficed.

To prepare myself for the new position, I had lengthy discussions, almost amounting to debriefings, with several business executives and one editor at the *Post*. All had worked at either the *Times Union* or the *Knickerbocker News*. Their assessments of staffers alerted me to the scope of the challenge ahead. They turned out to be mostly on the mark.

In the weeks winding down in Washington I received notes of welcome and encouragement from old Albany hands. One came from Senator Daniel Patrick Moynihan, who had been an aide to Governor W. Averell Harriman and a contributor to the *Post*'s Outlook section, of which I was in charge. The speaker of the state assembly, Stanley Steingut, wrote a note of greeting as did the chancellor of the State University of New York, Clifton Wharton. Historian Barbara Tuchman, whom I had met through my work, sent best wishes. I also heard from *Post* staffers. Mike Causey, whose columns chronicled the federal workforce, wrote: "You have been a rough-and-tough editor. But you have always backed your people."

CHAPTER 1

Getting Started

During our negotiations, Roger Grier promised an increase of four or five to the editorial roster of 140. This was the opening of a constant game of push and pull between editor and publisher. As the bloom quickly faded, the pressure to hold down costs, which invariably meant staff, became the norm with occasional respites.

From the first, my task was to motivate the staff and stiffen performance standards. As I had done when I became the *Post*'s Metro editor, I met with reporters, editors, and photographers to get acquainted. I went around the two newspapers' newsrooms, shaking hands and speaking with every person in sight. The middle-level managers of both papers—to my mind, the key element to mold a successful news operation—were called to a meeting in the large second-floor conference room. Their welcome was hesitant at best, if not bordering on hostile, the latter personified by Joann Crupi, who asked barbed questions. These I considered a reflection of the anxiety of the group about what the new guy had in mind for them. Over the years, Crupi rose in the editorial hierarchy, and in time I promoted her to managing editor, the first woman to hold that rank at the *Times Union*. We developed a strong friendly relationship well into my retirement, when I continued to serve on the editorial board, of which she was then the editor in charge.

The two newspapers occupied separate sides of the first floor. The copy desk was located between the two city rooms and occupied by morning and afternoon staffs at different parts of the workday. The papers shared photo, art, features, and sports departments but maintained competing news staffs. Their rivalry was intense and unrelenting. Each paper had an executive editor, with a managing editor as second in command. The retirement of John Leary, the executive editor of the *Times Union*, gave Grier the opening to create my new post. *Knickerbocker News* Executive Editor Robert Fichenberg had wanted the top job so much that when he was passed over he began to look for another. Fichenberg transparently was disheartened by my arrival. Whenever I walked into his office he looked up at me, almost startled to see me on his turf, and quickly slid shut a desk drawer. It was a doomed relationship. His departure within my first years was good for him. He did very well as Washington bureau chief for the Newhouse newspapers. For us, it was beneficial because his discontent would not have made for an effective collaboration.

The two managing editors, William Dowd at the *Knick* and Bernard Zovistoski at the *TU*, remained in place. In the first weeks, I knew heavy lifting was to be our lot. A woeful lack of quality in the stories reflected a deficiency in curiosity. Poor work habits demanded fixing.

The *Times Union* published seven days a week. The *Knickerbocker News* did not have a Sunday edition. My strategy was to strengthen the Sunday *Times Union*, which had the larger circulation, and use it as a wedge to acquire more readers for the dailies. Easier said than done. There was little evidence among the *TU* editors about what should differentiate a Sunday story from a breaking-news story, fodder for the weekday editions. Breaking news was scarce on a weekend day while the ampler Sunday paper offered a forum for enterprise stories, those that go beyond reporting the surface of events. Attempts to reach out on topics that would display sweep and analysis mostly fell short; few reporters demonstrated they understood the concept. In the early weeks, Judy Shepard was the reporter who produced the kind of copy I sought.

Part of the problem was how the senior editors regarded their responsibilities. They worked five-day weeks, taking weekends off, not being there for the most important Sunday edition. They gave key section editors the same arrangement whenever possible. When I came on board, the Sunday paper's city desk, the hub of the operation, was in the hands of a part-timer who worked weekends. He was an experienced, old-fashioned Albany newspaperman who in retirement was doing public relations for the region's largest medical complex. Albany Medical

Center was a frequent subject of our coverage. Those in charge had overlooked the glaring incompatibility of interests implicit in the two roles.

For my office furniture, I specified a drafting table on which I marked up the papers every day in red crayon, citing the good points to be emulated and the more frequent shortcomings to be forever shunned. The markups unsettled the recipients, which was the point.

I ran into a problem that resembled what Ben Bradlee faced when he took over the *Washington Post*. The staff he found on arrival needed severe shaking up, which he did over many years. It resulted in resentment from the old-timers against the many recently enlisted. Bradlee was empowered by the carte blanche he had to hire the best people he could persuade to join him. As his regime took hold, it became evident that a lot of the existing staffers were up to the new demanding standards. They required only the leadership to free them to fully put their talents to use.

Bradlee painted on a wide canvas with a spectrum of colors. I had nothing equivalent on my palette. For practical purposes, I had to make do with the staff in place. I did not have the power to hire at will, and growth was strictly limited.

A new boss's incorrigible inclination is to move the furniture around, if for effect alone. Given what faced me, there was greater justification for implementing changes as quickly as possible. Overcoming deeply rooted habits was not an overnight affair. The editors had a high opinion of themselves for being at the helm of the biggest publications in the Capital Region. They resented and resisted the more strenuous demands I imposed. An illustrative incident occurred during a heavy snowstorm in December of the first year. I commented the coverage was superficial. I received a self-justifying response from the managing editor. With undisguised smugness, he noted Albany had up to six big snowfalls a year and this one was nothing special. I had another perspective: "The point is whether the *Knick*'s stories showed enough curiosity." The paper's coverage overlooked the difficulty of getting workers for emergency duty on Christmas Day, how many removal trucks were out on the streets and how many had to be garaged, obstacles the fire department encountered and whether firefighters refused to report to work.

Early the next year, the new regimen was put to the test with the death of Nelson Rockefeller. This was a very big story because he had been a transformative governor who imposed reform and renovation on the city and the Capital Region, as well as the state. He created the state university system (supplanting teachers colleges) and tore down a huge quadrant of a working-class neighborhood in Albany to erect a monumental government center. The Empire State Plaza was among his ambitious undertakings that made Albany stand out from even larger cities in the state of New York.

We produced comprehensive coverage for the Sunday paper. I asked one of the state Capitol reporters to write the obituary. Word came back that he did not want to do it; he had not been around during Rockefeller's terms and suggested we use the Associated Press. I thought differently. The Albany paper was not going to offer readers a news-service obit competing papers were likely to use. I instructed the reluctant writer to pull himself together and fulfill his assignment. This he did with skill. Our total presentation won praise from New York headquarters.

The self-satisfaction, alive and well at the two newspapers, mirrored the wider community. People were content with things as they were and for the most part disguised unhappiness. Albany labored under the heavy-handed administration of a long-entrenched Democratic machine, whose pervasive corruption attained the status of folklore, something to chuckle about while shaking one's head. That was simply the way it worked in Albany. Civic reform movements found their voice from time to time, inevitably to fall short. Discontent was expressed in whispers and, when probed for details, those purveying it rapidly backed off. Their tax assessments or business interests were understood to be at risk.

Under the leadership of a previous publisher, Gene Robb, twice removed from my time, the papers took on the machine, headed by political boss Dan O'Connell and Mayor Erastus Corning 2nd. As a consequence, the papers suffered legal and other harassment, all of which did not deter them from vigorous pursuit of the machine's wrongdoing. It also resulted in the newspapers shutting their offices and plant downtown to relocate to the suburb of Colonie. The immediate spur for this drastic move was the refusal of City Hall to approve acquisition of a sliver of land the papers needed to accommodate new printing presses. Corning and his minions no doubt savored the little victory for which in the not-so-long run they and the city paid a steep price. The new newspaper building anchored one end of a major suburban thoroughfare, accelerating its development as a vibrant business district, which sucked trade out of downtown. Big retailers like Macy's and Sears in the Colonie Center mall, along with other businesses on Wolf Road, sounded the knell for the family-owned department stores, downtown's major draw for decades. Not for the last time, politicians had outsmarted themselves.

Albany in 1978 had a population of 100,000-plus set in a metropolitan region of about a million. Its attractive attributes included rush-hour traffic, a pale copy of what plagued larger cities. It was easy to get around town and the surrounding communities. Lovely countryside was close by and driving there took only twenty minutes or so.

My thought on arriving was that our papers, although regional, found most readers in the city and county of Albany and should have a visible presence in the city. At first, I explored moving the newsroom operation back downtown, possibly into the long-shuttered yet still architecturally elegant Union Station. Production would remain in Colonie along with whatever business departments were more suitably located there. The idea was too much of a reach, but we did open a street-level office at the intersection of State and Pearl Streets, the crossroads of downtown.

The growth in staff was less than first promised. More than a year after my start, I finally wangled agreement for the slots for my confidential secretary and the downtown office manager not to count against reporter or editor allotments. My first reporter hire turned out a winner. Alan Miller interned in the Tokyo bureau of the *Washington Post* after earning a graduate degree and was recommended by former colleagues at the *Post*. From the time he started in 1978, he provided the kind of ambitious enterprise coverage I aspired to cultivate. His stay with us was predictably too brief—three years—as his portfolio helped him to move up to ever-larger papers. He won a Pulitzer Prize along with a colleague as a member of the *Los Angeles Times* Washington bureau.

With Miller on board, joined by other hires in the months ahead, steady insistence on hard reporting raised standards. The staff began to show a better side that indifferent leadership failed to nourish. By the spring, it was clear the two managing editors would not suffice to implement the range of changes I envisioned. An experienced topline editor was needed, and I created the position of managing editor for the Sunday *Times Union*, carving it out of Bern Zovistoski's jurisdiction.

On a visit to New York in May 1979, I met with a candidate found by a headhunter for breakfast in Peacock Alley at the Waldorf Astoria. Dan Lynch was then an editor at *Newsday*, the growing Long Island newspaper. We were there to look each other over as we weighed a decision crucial to us both. I wanted a senior editor to help elevate the quality of our paper. I was looking for someone who shared my view that a newspaper's obligation to its readership and community was to provide incisive local reporting about important matters without kowtowing to sacred cows. The new ME, along with talent and leadership skills, would need the facility to work alongside senior news executives in place.

Before becoming an editor at *Newsday*, Dan Lynch was a political writer for the *Philadelphia Inquirer*, and strong recommendations accompanied him. I liked what I saw and heard and concluded at the end of breakfast that he was the right choice. Even so, I traveled to Washington, D.C., to meet with two other prospects. They did not change my mind. Dan decided to leave his solid editor's assignment at *Newsday*, a much larger paper where his prospects were good, for wider immediate responsibilities at the *Times Union*.

His hiring made for resentment and stress I would have preferred to avoid, remembering the counterproductive aspects of Bradlee's creative tension that pitted one editor against another. Yet if we were to grow the quality of the Sunday paper, it needed the hands of an editor with broader and higher-level experience. Inescapably, Dan's hire put the two managing editors into competition, and the good and the bad of it.

CHAPTER 2

Settling In

During my first years in the job I got to know the leaders of Albany's major industry—government—while also integrating myself into the structure of the newspapers, on both the editorial and business sides. There was a lot to learn and absorb. Some fundamentals needed adjustment, if not reformation.

Early in 1979, Hugh Carey invited me for a one-on-one breakfast at the Governor's Mansion. We talked easily for a long while. That morning we began a comfortable relationship that endured through those times when he was the subject of critical stories in one or the other of our newspapers. Once following dinner out with mutual friends, we went to the Mansion for drinks. The governor insisted on showing Annie and me through the grand old house on Eagle Street. We trekked up the wide staircase to upper floors outsiders seldom visited. Our host opened the doors of one room after another for our inspection. Hugh Carey was the father of fourteen children, and of course he soon enough barged into a room in which some of them were trying to sleep with us in tow. The chief executive surely was down to earth.

Getting on well personally did not stand in the way when Governor Carey gave flight to an excess of rhetoric for which he was well known. Once he volunteered to swallow a glass of water laced with PCBs, deemed a carcinogen, to demonstrate it was safe to drink. With his marriage to his second wife (he was a widower), the Greek-born Evangeline Gouletas, he began to live a grander lifestyle. His justification was he could earn a million dollars a year, in its day a much more impressive sum, in the private sector. We decided to examine what Carey as governor actually cost the public. Alan Miller pored over every attainable record of expenditure run up by the governor, including the expense of his helicopters, numerous vehicles, and mansion staff. In short, everything paid for by the public. Then we had enough material to publish with confidence a series entitled "The Million Dollar Governor."

Another project exposed what happened at St. Anne's School, a home for troubled girls run by the Sisters of the Good Shepherd, whose spokeswoman was the governor's daughter and one of whose executives was a personal friend of mine. We found that some difficult girls, considered out of control, were mistreated, confined in a lockup for weeks. In Alan Miller's words: "We painted a portrait of a well-meaning institution that was over its head in resorting to 19th century practices to deal with 20th century challenges." When the first part was done, I wanted to know whether the state had regulations banning these stringent punishments. It did not, and after we published the story, the state finally passed such rules.

Down the road more than a bit, our newspaper found itself in a touch football league of sorts, facing the governor's men. Carey's team had a slight advantage, with a former National Football League player among his staff and on his team. The gods of chance were with us one Saturday afternoon as we met on a playing field of the State Police Academy. Somehow, we won. The governor more than graciously presented us with a handsome, beautifully wrought silver cup (commissioned years earlier for some loftier occasion). We held on to the trophy but before he finished his last term, I knew we had to return it, with thanks, to state custody. We explained how retaining it might appear to some, rightly, as inappropriate.

Not long after the breakfast with the governor I found myself lunching with Mario Cuomo, his lieutenant governor. It was the first of many encounters we had over the years. During the early ones, an aide provided a wooden back brace to alleviate an obviously painful condition. As he went on to serve three terms in the top job, he was a regular visitor to our editorial page board, expanded for the occasion to include the publisher and a complement of editors and reporters from the news side.

Early, too, I arranged to meet the widow of Gene Robb, the publisher who was forceful in unleashing the powers of the press to reveal municipal scandals. He was a legendary figure at the papers. Lee Robb was quite regal in bearing. We had lunch, and afterward she sent a note in which she expressed her enthusiasm "for the future of Capital Newspapers."

She wrote: "I feel excited once again over the possibilities of unraveling some of the intricacies of life as lived in this disturbing, apathetic, controlled, diversely constituted, wonderful old city. . . . And I do think you just may do it." Her expectations mirrored mine.

After three months at the job, I sorted out possibilities for enhancing the papers during a period of economic downturn. The technological revolution that was to overtake the national economy, and particularly newspapers, was apparent in its early forms. There was enough going on for me to propose to Roger that we get into the cable TV business. Under the next publisher, Joe Lyons, I interrupted a California vacation to make a quick visit to familiarize myself with a successful cable scrawl operation in Yuma, Arizona. We did not pursue what would have been no more than a modest step.

Early in my tenure, I was invited to speak to the advertising staff. I prepared remarks on the ambitious plans for the newsrooms. Before my turn, the ad people unself-consciously spoke out about the necessity of reporters producing puff pieces about their advertisers or prospects to help them sell ads. In their world, it made good sense. I put aside my outline. I made it plain that hype for any purpose would not be tolerated in the newsrooms, and they should understand and make peace with it. I encouraged them to explain to their clients that puffery undermined the foundations of journalism. The success of newspaper advertising, I said, relied on the credibility of the publication. If readers had ample reason to distrust the journalism, it could lead them to question the claims of advertisers.

The ad people clearly had not expected what they heard, but they were not outwardly hostile. At first glance, it appeared they might be receptive to my argument. I was mistaken; the advertising director fought back at every opportunity. His department expected the news department to avoid writing anything that might irritate an advertiser, and to not even mention businesses that didn't buy ads. When the state fined an auto dealer for misrepresentation, he expected the story would be squelched as a matter of course. He told Managing Editor Lynch that they both knew how the world worked. When Lynch filled me in, I told him to increase the size of the headline because I wanted the car dealer to easily see how it worked.

Mostly, the ad department was interested in masquerading advertiser self-promotion as news, its claims and assertions published as submitted by the advertiser or its PR firm. Restaurateurs frequently cried foul when a reviewer criticized any aspect of their operations. To counteract, ad managers proposed a special section that would rave about restaurants. When we would not go along, they said okay, transfer a couple of your experienced editors so that the ad department could handle it. I told them that if it was so important to their mission, they should hire their own editors.

Over the years, I struggled repeatedly to identify advertising supplements as such on every page. The publishers agreed, some more reluctantly than others. Despite the supposed policy, violations continued.

I did manage to end the practice of using news photographers to shoot assignments on behalf of auto dealers and realtors, in the face of pleas from the ad chieftain. He insisted competing papers did it, and for us to refuse gave them unfair advantage. I told him to hire his own photographers.

Problems with the circulation department took longer for me to recognize. At first, I tended to accept circulation's reasoning that shortcomings in local coverage were to blame because we did not publish enough news of minor events, generally called chicken dinner news, compared to what our competitors in the adjacent cities, Schenectady and Troy, gave their readers. These were mostly no more than handouts.

Slowly, I began to discern the broader issues in play, beyond what could justly be attributed to newsroom deficiencies, such as poor copy flow and missed deadlines that impacted getting the newspapers to home delivery carriers. The more fundamental problem was the high number of our papers sold at newsstands and out of street-corner coin boxes. This fact incited circulation to push for bigger, and more sensational, headlines to attract the eye of a sometime customer. Our home-delivery numbers were strikingly low, although individually each was the biggest morning and afternoon paper in the market. Single-copy sales were not nearly as steady as those sold by subscription. In large part, the reason for this was the complicated arrangements our circulation department had agreed to over the years with middlemen wholesalers. These deals with outside distributors hampered on-time delivery to thousands of homes. It took many years to untangle the problem; in the meantime, the newsroom, although not blameless, served as a handy scapegoat.

In my early days on the job, I was interviewed on a local television program. The conversation proceeded along conventional paths, when suddenly I was asked about the history of Capital Newspapers dumping bundles of papers into the river to bolster sales figures. The questioner offered no support for the allegation beyond the provocative implication that this was common knowledge. I replied I had not heard of it and while I doubted it, I would follow up at the office. I never found any validation for the claim.

In the newsroom, self-indulgent ethics were an obvious problem to me from the start. This impelled a move to draw up a code of conduct for the editorial staff to make plain the cardinal rules: We don't exploit our newspaper connection for personal gain, and we pay our own way. The word got out, long before an ethics code was ready to be promulgated. An astonished public relations chap for the state police wrote: "A cup of coffee paid for by your business editor, John Klucina, prompts this letter. The mottled world of journalistic ethics has reached its apogee of inverse rationale when a newsman buys for a public relations man. Your strictures have taken hold and the status quo is tottering."

My insistence on an ethics code was rooted in more than what I found in Albany. Freeloading had long tarnished journalism. The image of the reporter on a freebie was widely accepted and largely true. Anytime the press takes something in the form of a gift, there is the implication it's part of a payoff. In some manner, this quid pro quo would serve the interests of the party who bestows the benefit seeking special consideration of some sort. This I learned early in my career, at the *Herald Tribune*. When Christmas approached, the business editor several times filled up a large handcart, used to transport paper supplies for the newsroom, with bottles of whiskey and goodies, presented by financial houses, PR firms, and other subjects of the newspaper's coverage. It was their way of wishing him a Merry Christmas.

My own worst offense came as the *Trib*'s cable editor when the paper was invited to join a press junket to Israel for the opening of a Hilton Hotel in Tel Aviv. I accepted the invitation because it permitted me to visit our resident stringer correspondent in Israel, then as now a constant source of news, as well as to hire a stringer in Rome on the way home. The *Trib* had no budget for such travel. For the cost of the airfare and the hotel room, my obligation was to write an article for the Sunday Travel section. My first effort was rejected by the Sunday editor as too far removed from the purposes of the junket. My second try was accepted.

You could argue the applicability of situational ethics. No harm was done, and some good was accomplished in my face-to-face talk with our correspondent. In the end, this rationale is no better than all the other good reasons one could muster for being on the take, however benignly, from "You can't buy me with a free lunch or a bottle of booze" to elaborate alibis concocted by creative imagination. All excuses don't make up for the price paid in the diminished public perception of the credibility of the press. Token gifts pave the way for tolerating acceptance of valuable ones.

Credibility is a newspaper's single most important asset. Anything that enhances it—quality work and honorable behavior—makes it possible to reach more people with consequential information. Shoddy work and shabby behavior undermine it.

The Capital Newspapers' ethics code was drafted over time under the supervision of our labor lawyers. What I wanted stated unambiguously they insisted on framing in legalese, assuring me they knew what was required for the union arbitration hearings they predicted were inevitable. The attorneys and management kept the Newspaper Guild informed, invited comment on a draft, but did not negotiate its terms. The union vigorously objected, claiming work conditions were being altered without the negotiations required under its contract. Much of the upset stemmed from the need to inform a managing editor of outside activities. Absent such an obligation, reporters and editors could easily work for a competing newspaper on their days off. In addition, I could not see the moral justification for the union regarding freeloading as a perk whose proscription would have to be offset by giving members a concession, say another day or two off with pay. Without our ability to legally impose the code on the staff, we showed the code to job applicants and asked them if they had any problem with its provisions. No one ever did.

Among the rules laid down: no free passes, unless reviewing a play or film; no gifts or gratuities because of the newspaper connection; no junkets. Reporters and editors should pick up the tab for lunches and coffees. Freeload affairs were to be avoided.

No ethics code can encompass the far-reaching activities journalists encounter routinely. It would make for a handbook thicker than *Webster's* dictionary. Ethics codes help to set a tone to discourage holding a hand out for a handout.

A test of our commitment to the code occurred in 1981, when the New York State Society of Newspaper Editors held its annual meeting in Corning. The group arranged for the Corning Glass Company to underwrite two receptions and a dinner. I argued the editors should pay for these events. When the society would not budge, I restricted our editors' participation to the working sessions.

Over time, we developed a codicil to the code. The staff had to understand that rules governing news applied to the staff no less than the public. We routinely printed stories about people who broke traffic laws, specifically drunken driving. Being a staffer would not buy you a get-out-of-the-newspaper card. After an editor was arrested by Albany police on a DWI, a brief item appeared in our local section, over his strenuous protests. He cited his embarrassment in front of his children.

From the first, I made it clear to the publisher: If either the editor or the publisher was involved, the importance of these positions in the community meant that their indiscretions or worse would be front-page news. One night, Publisher Lyons drove with our friend Bernard Conners in the front passenger seat and I in the back. Joe was a little worse for wear and his driving did not always hug the roadway. Bern remembered years later that after a bit of this, I tapped Joe on the shoulder to remind him that if he caused a problem it meant Page 1 for him.

CHAPTER 3

Legal Confrontations

Besides newsroom ethics, we had to deal with judges closing their court-rooms to the press. With the leadership of our attorney, Peter Danziger, we struggled, with some success, to keep the proceedings of our local courts open to the public. Four times we went to the Appellate Division in 1979. We did not seek these confrontations. Although they always engendered large legal bills for us, we embraced the battles to forestall creation of bale-ful precedents. We had to protest so that the public could be informed about the quality of justice meted out in the people's name. In 1989, the New York News Publishers Association asked our law firm to list the cases it handled for the *TU* and the *Knick* that "made a positive contribution to media law." The firm cited nine cases.

We encountered an especially difficult problem in 1982 when an Albany County judge wanted to keep us from publishing photographs of a car in a public street. Imposition of prior restraint, which this was, is among the most drastic curtailments of freedom of the press. Prior restraint—when a court orders a newspaper not to publish information it already has—is a form of censorship.

This is what happened. Judge Joseph Harris, who was widely un-derstood to have a high regard for his intellect, at least partially de-served, was presiding over a murder trial involving a car. One of our photographers was in the corridor of the courthouse and snapped the first few frames of a fresh role of film to ensure it was correctly loaded. He pointed his camera out a window at an adjacent public parking lot, unintentionally photographing an unoccupied Thunderbird, the same make and model of the car involved in the crime. The vehicle was to be used for a demonstration to the jury in the trial. The judge heard through the grapevine that our photographer had taken the pictures and ordered us to give them up. He said the corridor and the lot had become an extension of his courtroom.

Our lawyer argued the judge had not placed the car or the lot off-limits until after the pictures were taken. Consequently, we contended he tried to expropriate our property without due process and sought to retroactively apply his order to the lot and car. We maintained the ban against publication of those photos was unconstitutionally putting prior restraint on us. We did not turn over the film. I strenuously urged that we print the photo the next day. Our lawyers opposed my position, and instead, in the next day's edition, we published only the Thunderbird's silhouette.

A hearing was set by Judge Harris for us to explain why he should not hold the photographer and our lawyer in criminal contempt of court. We appealed to challenge the prior restraint and the order of seizure and to have the contempt hearing dismissed.

Lawyers from the state attorney general's office, representing the judge, argued this was an issue of preserving the defendant's right to a fair trial. They tried to make it a conflict between the First Amendment right of freedom of the press and the Sixth Amendment right to a fair trial, which was specious because the photographs were not of the actual car. In fact, Judge Harris permitted the media to copy a photo of the murder vehicle itself. We published two photos on the front page the next day: Juxtaposed were the copy of the actual murder vehicle (by that time impounded in a North Carolina lot) and the silhouette to underline the absurdity of Harris's order.

More importantly, the jury was to look at the parking lot car a couple of hours after our photos were taken, but many hours before they would be published. So the newspaper photos could not show the jurors anything they would not already have seen. There was no way for the newspaper photo to prejudice them.

Judges routinely instruct juries not to read, watch, or listen to news media. If jurors disobey the instruction, it would be the judge's

responsibility to handle, not the press's. Or the judge could have arranged the demonstration to be conducted some place more private than
a parking lot abutted by public streets.

In time, the appellate court decided Judge Harris had given unclear
orders in an improper form. The newspapers would not have to undergo
the contempt hearing. Nothing was said about the constitutional questions that so much concerned us. Lawyers patiently explained to me that
judges routinely decide questions on the narrowest grounds.

On the surface, we won in court. We were spared more distress and
costs. There was also satisfaction because the appellate panel constrained
a fellow judge. When power is made to obey the rules, justice and the
public are served. We depend on judges for wise and humane decisions
influencing our lives and fortunes. They must adhere scrupulously to
procedures to make certain their great powers are not misused.

Another noteworthy effort by us to keep the courts open to the public involved a young reporter who developed into an admired writer on
legal matters. John Caher recalled what happened:

> There was a matter involving a raging pedophile who was retarded
> and found not guilty because of a mental disease or defect and
> confined to a mental institution. Some years later, there was a
> hearing under the mental hygiene law to determine whether this
> guy should be released.
>
> Those hearings can legitimately be closed to the public as they
> involve all kinds of medical and psychiatric testimony. However,
> the judge was asleep at the wheel and did not notice me sitting
> right in front of him. He never closed the proceeding.
>
> I got an earful. When the judge realized who I was, he chased
> after me to forbid me from publishing what I heard in an open
> courtroom. Harry went to bat for me, got lawyers involved, and
> the principle that the public cannot be barred from revealing what
> happens in an open court was upheld.
>
> After winning the right to publish the story, Harry decided not
> to print it. He thought it was an unnecessary invasion of the guy's
> privacy. I certainly did not agree at the time, but now do, and
> greatly respect Harry for his judgment and integrity. He could not
> let go unchallenged the judge's contention that he could unring a
> bell, and then exercised very sound discretion in determining that

the harm we would have done to this guy outweighed the prurient interest in the story.

My first one-on-one meeting with William Randolph Hearst Jr., one of five sons of the founder and himself editor in chief of Hearst newspapers, was a year after I came on board. At his invitation I took the train to New York to have lunch with him. I was a bit concerned because, after I arrived in Albany, I moved his Sunday column off its accustomed Page 1 spot to the Opinion section inside. Publisher Roger Grier and I had laid out our argument to Mr. Hearst to explain that his commentary got better display there than being continued, jumping, in our parlance, from the bottom of the front page after three or four paragraphs. He took it in stride, yet now I was coming face to face with him.

We walked from the Hearst building near Columbus Circle to a French bistro on Fifty-Seventh Street. On our way, we passed a street vendor offering Rolex watches for $15. Bill was intrigued by the bargain. With all the finesse I could muster, I suggested a $15 Rolex probably was not quite genuine. I envisioned him returning home that evening, showing off his purchase. Somewhere in their conversation, Mrs. Hearst was sure to ask, "Who was with you when you bought this thing?" "Oh," he'd say, "the new editor up in Albany." I foresaw a brief career with Hearst. Whether it was anything I said all so softly or his good sense, in the end Bill passed up this hard-to-believe bargain, much to my relief.

Over lunch I shared my vision of how the staff would grow to implement improvements of the newspapers. He liked what he heard and quickly said he would contact Roger Grier and fix it all up. I had to restrain his enthusiasm and urged him to let me handle it without instructing Roger. Going over the head of a publisher is not a prescription for a happy relationship.

As our association lengthened, Bill Hearst one day told me I was a Hearst editor born and bred. He said I reminded him of his mentor, long-tenured Hearst editor and publisher Edmond Coblentz, affectionately known as Cobby, of whom he had been boundlessly fond.

I learned a valuable lesson early on in Albany: the collateral damage that all too easily can accompany the best-intended editorial tactic. At the start of the Iran hostage crisis in November 1979, Roger urged us to feature on every edition's front page a box counting off the number of days our diplomats were confined in Tehran. "America Held Captive" was intended to keep the Carter administration focused on efforts to free the hostages. I readily agreed. I was caught up in the moment and wanted to influence an indecisive president. It turned out to be a major mistake. Too late, I realized the downside of pressuring the White House. On later reflection, I understood that this device, adopted by many other media, goaded President Jimmy Carter to launch a desperate rescue mission that failed. Had I considered possible ramifications more, I might have talked Roger out of it. The Americans were freed after 444 days, only hours after Ronald Reagan's inauguration as president, succeeding Carter.

Erastus Corning 2nd, America's longest-tenured mayor, dominated Albany city and county politics after the death of his mentor, Dan O'Connell, in 1977. As mayor and chairman of the County Democratic Committee, he controlled the party's majority in the county legislature. In October 1979, Alan Miller produced a penetrating examination of Corning's singular power.

The series, titled "His Honor, the Boss," laid out the reach of Corning's power embedded in a voter enrollment edge of 16 to 1 over Republicans. His word, though spoken softly, was law, and his enemies in the party or out of it were disarmed through patronage or intimidation. He and his cohort lived well off the public, through salaries or cozy contracts by one scheme or another. Corning's arrangement was his insurance agency, Albany Associates, its name a wink and a nod.

During his reporting, Alan learned of Corning's long-time confidante and close friend, Polly Noonan. Everybody in town knew about her, not just those in politics. Alan searched the newspapers' files and did not find one reference to her. He made sure she was included by name in the articles depicting her growing power and that of her daughter and son-in-law, Polly and Douglas Rutnik.

In the 1980 contest between President Jimmy Carter and Senator Edward Kennedy of Massachusetts for the Democratic presidential nomination, Alan Miller was in Albany's Democratic Party headquarters on the night of the New York primary. Corning backed Carter. When Kennedy won, the mayor's reputation suffered a major blow. Alan overheard as Polly, analyzing what had gone wrong, repeatedly said to other Democratic stalwarts, "It was those Jews." The *Times Union* led the color piece with that quote. Corning never spoke to Alan again, reportedly at Polly's bidding. I refused to remove Alan from the assignment. I told the reporter, "We are not going to let the mayor determine who covers him."

Years later, after Polly had been delicately described in our coverage as the mayor's confidante, an obituary appeared for an elderly woman who had been a friend of Dan O'Connell's. Polly read the obit and told our reporter Carol Demare: "She was Dan's confidante, and your paper knows what that means."

Despite our disagreements, Polly and I became friendly and were demonstratively glad when we ran into each other. Her granddaughter Kirsten Gillibrand inherited her aptitude for politics. She was elected to the House of Representatives and then appointed senator to fill the seat of Hillary Clinton when she became secretary of state in the Obama administration. Gillibrand subsequently easily won election and earned a national reputation taking on the Pentagon over pervasive sexual assault in the military. Her renown intensified with her leadership on the issue of confronting sexual harassment, in Congress, industry, and the media.

In the course of his coverage, Miller made what he called a "major misstep." It was about one of Corning's lieutenants in a sweetheart real estate deal with the city. Corning refused comment. It was front-page news. To our embarrassment and dismay, Alan had confused the terms lessor and lessee in a key provision of the lease. The offended party threatened to sue. The next day, we ran another front-page story correcting the mistake. This underlined how grave our error had been; corrections normally ran inside the paper.

Afterward, I talked to Alan. Three decades later, when I was writing this book, he recounted my words this way: "I can tell by looking at you that there is nothing I can say that will make you feel worse about this than you already do." In Alan's recollection, I added: "There are two lessons you can learn here: the right one and the wrong one. The right one is to be extremely careful in everything you report and to especially guard against your own assumptions or finding what you expect to find. The wrong one would be to back off on your reporting on the mayor and the machine."

Alan a year later examined the flourishing network of nepotism under the aegis of the Corning regime, and how the party faithful and their extended families studded the payrolls of various government agencies. And in 1984, reporter Ralph Cipriano detailed another aspect of the party's dominance with an exposé of the hidden costs to the city and the county of the no-bid contracts with their cronies. Our close coverage of the Corning administration set the tone, which did not dissipate after Corning's reign was over. In the absence of a viable political opposition, we alone had the resources and the will to hold those in power to account.

Corning and Co. was a Democratic Party operation. At the *Washington Post*, I was accused of being part of a Democratic legion persecuting the Republican White House. In truth, confirmed by my record in Albany, I was nonpartisan in avid pursuit of political wrongdoing, whatever the party affiliation.

CHAPTER 4

Synergy of the Cutting Edge

The *Knickerbocker News* and *Times Union* earned recognition for cutting-edge work scrutinizing business, government, and community organizations. The stories sometimes incited outrage by those who in their hearts believed they were on the side of the angels but in their workaday world did not quite attain celestial status.

Much of the investigative, enterprise, and explanatory reporting was proposed and executed by reporters and editors hired after my arrival. They came mostly with experience at smaller newspapers, and they enriched the reputation of the Capital Newspapers throughout the region and the industry as newspapers that searched behind the scenes of events instead of settling for routine reportage. The newcomers joined a core of editors and reporters whose talents were encouraged under the new dispensation. This kind of work always took time, care, and resources and produced an esprit de corps among the staff that fed on itself. The best of these demonstrate the scope of our efforts and reflect the staffs' steady progress.

The *Times Union* was among the first newspapers to report on the phenomenon of acid rain. A senior reporter journeyed to Canada in 1979 to describe how emissions wafted southward to the Adirondacks, poisoning its pristine lakes. It was an early installment in a much longer, still-running saga about the despoliation of the environment by fossil-fuel pollution.

The Winter Olympics returned to Lake Placid in 1980. Planning the coverage of the global competition in the outer reaches of our circulation area began before I joined the papers. Robert Fichenberg, executive editor of the *Knick*, proposed a lowball approach because he thought potential benefits were not worth the expense. He wanted to rely on major news services coverage, devoting no more than a part-time freelancer or one staffer to provide our newspapers with special coverage.

Although I had no knowledge of Fichenberg's prior recommendation (his memo was buried in his files that came to me after he left), I had a totally different idea for coverage. It was to plunge in with as many reporters and photographers for whom we could get press credentials. As it turned out, we got more than the *New York Times* or the *Washington Post*, arguing that we were the local newspapers. About eight staffers drawn from sports, the city desk, features, and photography made up the team, not counting day-trippers. Dan Lynch was put in charge at Lake Placid to produce copy for both newspapers. It was a huge investment. Even Roger, looking at the expense of it all, plaintively asked, "Just how good do Capital Newspapers have to be?" My answer: As good as they can be.

To hold down expenses and to make do in the limited rental space available in the overbooked Lake Placid environs, we squeezed our people into tight quarters at a motel. The stress in the accommodations was intense. Ralph Martin, sports editor and columnist, was a fitness runner; he was determined not to forgo his daily routine and jogged in place for half an hour while others tried to sleep. After four or five days, a rather brainy writer, sleep-deprived for several nights, asserted his right to repose. He threatened to tear off Ralph's head. Lynch recalled: "I sent him home that morning with a figurative Purple Heart."

The enormous payoff was worth the discomforts. It was a message to our readers and a morale booster for the staff and for nervous top management. When the American hockey team beat the heavily favored Soviet squad, our headline—"U.S. 4, SOVIETS 3"—was bannered in large, bold type across the top of Page 1. It made national TV.

In 1980, welfare payments were cut despite predictions of dire consequences. We looked into what was feared would be a crisis. We did not know what we would find and did not anticipate what we found. The series of articles reported that the reduction in stipends did not account for food stamps and other assistance, nor for Medicaid health care. In fact, we revealed, welfare benefits as a whole in New York State increased at a faster rate than the incomes of wage-earning families. The findings were controversial, violating widely accepted assumptions. They reflected a reality that time has not altered. Thirty years later, a cure for poverty remained elusive, and the *New York Times* reported similar findings for the nation, impelling the need for a more accurate measure of what constitutes poverty.

We had uncovered an illustrative finding when we searched scattered databases at various agencies to assemble accurate statewide numbers to reveal how Medicaid served the poor. Our team in 1989 unearthed and tabulated the data, which no government agencies had troubled to do. We informed not only our readers but, when it came to the data, the state bureaucracy as well. The series was entitled: "Medicaid: The high cost of poor care."

In the anxious days following the death in prison of Bobby Sands, the Irish Republican Army hunger striker, we sent the *TU*'s special projects editor to Northern Ireland in 1981. The Irish were the second largest ethnic component (after Italians) of the Albany metropolitan area, and many were first- or second-generation Americans. Robert L. McManus humanized the coverage out of that stricken land and included family of Albany residents in his interviews. Our aim was to talk to those relatives to try to see the turmoil through their eyes. By such focus premised on ties of blood, we could perhaps put a human visage on that ancient struggle and provide a graspable handle on how life is lived day by day during the worst of times.

One of Bob's telling discoveries was how frightened many of our people's relatives were. They would not talk to an American reporter, even under guarantees of anonymity. Their silence was a profound insight into the texture of their condition created by the intimidating power of the IRA, the Protestant paramilitaries, and the British. Thankfully, others did speak out, and Bob painted a picture of human endurance, some 2,900 miles from Albany yet still a local story for us.

"Suppose the bomb hit Albany" was the headline of a lead Sunday Page 1 story in 1982. It aroused a strong public response. Most praised it because the article detailed what would happen hour by hour, neighborhood by neighborhood. Others were outspokenly critical. One said we did it to distract from a recent price increase, others that we sought to demoralize Americans. A handful suggested this effort would make more sense if the Soviet people were exposed to the same kind of information. We took up the suggestion, and I wrote the editor of *Pravda*, the official Soviet Communist Party organ, explaining what we had done and suggesting he do the same for his readers. He replied politely that he did not need to. The Soviet people, he argued—unlike Americans—experienced on their own territory the horrors of the Second World War. Trying to change his mind, I wrote in my final communication with the *Pravda* editor: "I am sorry that so far we have not been able to agree on how to treat this issue. I agree with you when you say that such matters and techniques do not translate easily from one country to another. But that should serve as goad to our imagination to find ways to accomplish it, rather than to resign ourselves to our differences."

The persistence of Ron Kermani, using his reportorial skills, in 1983 exposed a nice little sideline undertaken by Exxon. Its oil tankers dumped contaminated seawater ballast out of their holds after delivering their cargo in New Jersey. They then sailed to the Hudson River and filled up with fresh water before their homebound journey to the arid Caribbean island of Aruba. Fresh water was scarce there, and some of it was sold to the island government.

The corporation fobbed off Kermani's initial articles, saying in effect the corporation did not charge Aruba for the water, only for the island's share of the cost of transporting it. Exxon used the fresh water for its refinery and sold the surplus. Ron's dogged reporting revealed that over a couple of years Exxon had made $3 million and twice as much over a longer time span. He exposed the fact that at least twenty tankers did not bother to carry cargoes to be unloaded in New Jersey. Instead they sailed north with empty hulls, headed directly to the Hudson off Hyde Park for the sole purpose of taking on fresh water.

When the story was wrapped up in 1984, Ron's reporting led to hardening of state regulations for the taking of state waters. It also resulted in Exxon settling federal and state lawsuits for $500,000 and $1.5 million.

In the midst of a fierce political debate, the *Times Union* tackled the issue of abortion. In 1984, four reporters produced a comprehensive package. The reportage provided facts to inform discussion, including illuminating who were getting abortions. Much of the public controversy focused on reasons the procedure was done, including preservation of the woman's health, defectiveness of the fetus, as well as rape, incest, or the involvement of teenagers. To the contrary, the reporting found: "The majority of abortion patients in the 1980s are, in fact, slightly older women seeking to maintain or improve their quality of life—to finish college, keep a job, remain single and financially independent or spare the potential child what they believe would be an undesirable home life." All in all, it was a useful primer shedding factual light on a raging dispute.

In July that year an incident in Albany foreshadowed events that would occur later across the nation. On the eighth day of the month, police responded to a "man gone berserk call." Four officers found Jessie Davis, a thirty-seven-year-old black man with a history of mental illness, tearing up his apartment. During the confrontation, police said, Davis held a carving knife in one hand and a long-tined fork in the other. He lunged at one of the officers as he attempted to subdue Davis. Two other officers then shot Davis five times, killing him. The Albany newspapers covered the shocking incident as it was being investigated by authorities. A grand jury in August criticized the conduct of three officers but found the shooting of Davis was justified. There was a huge public outcry and in time a suit for damages filed by Davis's sister.

The newspapers stuck with the story, our coverage persevering in the face of steady political machine attempts to quash knowledge about the encounter. The cops, the district attorney, and the judges were all part of the Democratic Party governing structure. Our work contributed to forcing the secret grand jury findings as well the names of the policemen involved to be made public. We also helped to establish a community review board. However, it had little effective power.

As all this was playing out, I was invited to address a forum of the Albany County Bar Association. I criticized the tendency of courts and attorneys to invoke the rights of defendants' privacy to keep the public from knowing what goes on in the courts. Furthermore, much of the system of justice worked behind a barrier that kept the public from knowing about it.

The way the Jessie Davis case was at first handled demonstrated what was wrong with the system. "There are no checks and balances," I said.

"Why should the public rely on a system vulnerable to such abuse? At best, you can ram a decision through and use your political power to muscle it in place."

I warned: "You are not winning hearts and minds, and you are increasing the sense of cynicism about what government really is there for." Our reporting demonstrated, and the editorials based on it concluded, that the grand jury system should be abolished. Not much later, the chief judge of the state's highest court, Sol Wachtler, delivered the memorable epithet, saying district attorneys, if they wished, could get grand juries "to indict a ham sandwich."

Years later, a photo turned up that showed Davis was not holding a knife and fork, as alleged. He was holding a key case and a toy truck.

Nearly two decades following the bloody Attica prison riots in which forty-three inmates, correction officers, and civilians died, we examined the state's prison system. Over four months, our reporters conducted nearly one hundred interviews with ex-convicts, prison inmates, correction officers, prison officials, and probation officers. Two maximum-security prisons were visited to detail how authorities maintained order and kept prisons humane enough to prevent another bloodbath like the one in 1971.

We researched racism and discrimination in our area, sponsoring a survey by the University at Albany's Center for Social and Demographic Analysis and producing a report on the underestimated prejudices against racial and other minorities. The six-part series, titled "Capital District's Dirty Secret," was published over eight days in the spring of 1989. The findings showed that despite a lower percentage of minorities in our population than in major urban areas, and a general sense of comfort with things as they were, discrimination against minorities was just as strong.

———

These enterprise projects, selected from among many others, reflected our commitment to surpass reporting the breaking news, as important as that was. Only by probing deeper into complex and sometimes divisive issues was it possible to grasp the real problem and then perhaps discern paths to likely remedies. These stories raised morale because they dignified the hard work of all the involved staffers.

CHAPTER 5

The Copious In-Basket

During the presidential campaign in 1980, I sent President Carter and Republican challenger Ronald Reagan letters of invitation to meet with our editorial boards. Carter's man, Jody Powell, responded, writing that it was a "neat idea." Neither candidate showed up, but politics on the national scale walked into our newspapers in the persons of the two vice presidential candidates, Walter Mondale and George H. W. Bush, who separately sat for questions from our editorial boards. Bush sent a note of thanks and asked for our endorsement. Mondale's camp went a bit further. One of his campaign aides wrote us, "You may not realize this, but all Editorial Boards are not as bright, well-informed and sophisticated as yours is." In one version or another, that became a refrain throughout the years. State and national figures came, all too obvious in their inclination to patronize the apple knockers in Albany only to be unsettled by the hard questions they encountered in their sessions with the editorial board. Lewis Lehrman, who had the explicit support of Hearst headquarters as he began his run for New York governor in 1981, wrote following his encounter: "After the session with your colleagues, governing New York should be easy. You ask tough questions—the ones that have gone unanswered for too long."

All the while, the *Washington Post* remained in my life. When Katharine Graham in 1979 stepped down to turn over the publishership to her son, Donald Graham, I wrote her: "It's got to be a moment of exquisite pain and joy. The great leadership you've given the *Post* stands as a monument not only in your extraordinary family, not only for the *Post*, but for all newspaperdom." To Don I wrote: "Somehow I always knew you'd make it. I hope you feel entirely secure depriving your very own mother of what probably is the best job in journalism." Bradlee phoned me one day the same year to offer the editorship of the *International Herald Tribune*, in which the *Post* had acquired a major share some years earlier. It was the second time he asked me to go to Paris. I was in the middle of my first two-year contract and we had just bought our house in Albany, so I was not enthusiastic about Paris, which on its face would have been a much more prestigious perch for me. In addition, our two older daughters, Susie and Amy, were in college and our widowed parents were of an age when they needed us to be nearby, not an ocean apart. Flattered as I was by his offer, I turned it down.

Howard Simons, the *Post's* managing editor, returned occasionally to the hometown he had left as quickly as he could after college to visit his widowed mother, who lived not far from us. Howard and I would meet one way or another, and in time our family was warmly received and overfed by his mother, Mae.

When Capital Newspapers' attorney was precluded from representing us in a legal matter because the other side was also his client, I turned to the *Post's* law firm, Williams & Connolly, and they helped us out. Roger asked me to invite Ben Bradlee to speak to the Colonie Chamber of Commerce and I had the pleasure of introducing him. He was a big hit and spent the night at our home. In 1981, Don Graham on behalf of the Reporters Committee for Freedom of the Press invited me to cochair the New York State committee to help raise funds for a cause I wholeheartedly supported—the fight to keep the courts open to the press and public.

As the years and then decades passed, contact with the *Washington Post* continued episodically, usually by telephone, on occasion by spontaneous contact. I went to Katharine Graham's office to lobby her on behalf of a project to find a substitute for trees out of which to make newsprint. I met with her for hours at her Georgetown home when she interviewed me for her book, *Personal History*, winner of a Pulitzer for biography. Bob Woodward and I chatted on one matter of concern or another, and he was helpful when needed. Carl Bernstein sought me out at the Hearst table at a White House Correspondents' Dinner, and we hugged. Another time, Annie and I ran into him on the street in New York City and again when we were driving in Saratoga Springs and spotted him on a bicycle. He was spending time at Yaddo, the writers' colony.

From the beginning of my days in Albany I reached out to the Capital Region community, an essential and rewarding obligation for a newspaper editor. I accepted speaking engagements at the New York State Academy for Public Administration, the Albany Civic Roundtable, and the Albany and Schenectady public libraries, for which I reviewed books. At the University at Albany I addressed a Phi Beta Kappa dinner and lectured at journalism classes, and I participated in forums at several other local colleges. There were endless invitations, and I accepted many of them over the years. For the Fourth of July 1980, I addressed the role of the free press in maintaining the nation's liberties at the annual convention of the state branch of the American Legion in New York. While we were away, our new home, which we bought after a long search, was burglarized. This served as ironic commentary on the supposed safety of a smaller American city.

The terms of my two-year contract were renewable every year. This gave me a minimum of a year on the payroll to find another job if Hearst no longer required my services. When a new contract was being drawn, I balked at the inclusion of a stock phrase stating the corporation had the authority to transfer me to another of its newspapers. Bob Danzig, head of the newspaper division, wrote me no one was transferred "without his enthusiastic concurrence." He added in his letter urging me to sign the contract: "Further, from what Roger tells me, we could only get Harry Rosenfeld out of Albany by getting Roger out first. We don't intend to do either—you're too good a team." Nevertheless, the contract was amended to satisfy my objection.

My regard for Roger as a good publisher, somebody I could work for with pleasure, had been an important factor in my leaving the *Washington Post*. So before I accepted his offer, I asked how long he intended to remain in Albany. He assured me he was in it for the very long run. In the early months in our association my admiration for him grew. He was indignant when he encountered the kinds of wrongdoing that should be grist for the journalistic mill but are not every publisher's priority. It was too good to last. In less than two years he was gone, promoted to help oversee the newspaper division.

The change surprised me, given the assurances from both Roger and Bob. I had not been alerted. Roger's successor was Joseph Lyons, who came from the Gannett paper in Wilmington, Delaware. Over our years together, we developed a personal relationship with our families and on the tennis court. Our office association differed from what I had with Roger. On more than one occasion, I thought I had worked out an understanding with Joe about the size of the newshole or staff hires, only to find when it came to implementation he had a different recollection of our conversations. Joe had a way discussing decisions concerning the newsroom without involving me in what I considered a timely way, or at all. Among the most glaring was when he did not share proposals for new presses until planning was well along. Our presses were among the more ancient still in service. Replacement parts were hard to get because the presses were no longer being manufactured. In sorry fact, no presses arrived until many years and two publishers later, when George Hearst had the top job. That was not a coincidence. New presses imported from Germany were installed in 2012 and began to print in the spring of 2013, a mere sixteen years after planning began.

In my early career in New York and Washington, I worked for owners who in title or in fact were the publishers. Either way, the paper was their personal possession. It was their money and reputation on the line, and they decided how much they were ready to spend or risk. By contrast, in a large corporation, the publisher is a hired hand impelled by protocol to obedience to orders from headquarters. Corporate publishers' room for maneuver is based on their personal agility and charisma and their inclination to go so far as to entertain questioning their higher-ups, especially when it came to fighting for resources for the newsroom. For them, going along was the more attractive motivator, even to go one better and earn chops for coming in below budgeted expenditures. In this scheme of things, George Hearst was a hybrid—part of the conventional corporate structure whose name, however, was on the front of the store. His was a special status within the corporation, one might say a publisher with privileges.

For each of my first two publishers, my proposed strategies to increase circulation invariably were to deepen and widen the range of our coverage, usually requiring additional editors and reporters. During the first year or so, my colleagues and I closely monitored the capabilities of the existing staffs and shifted assignments to achieve desired improvements. When we deemed we had extracted the maximum benefits, we faced the choice of growth or stagnation. Corporate culture demanded growth but was less ready to increase staff.

By the spring of 1981, among a long list of changes implemented since my arrival, we replenished the middle leadership of the papers. We hired a new city editor and assigned his predecessor to head up investigations. We hired an art director and a new sports editor and created the job of national editor. In the Sunday paper, we launched an op-ed page and strengthened our editorial writing staff. We were making progress in circulation, even though our main competition to the west, the *Schenectady Gazette*, averaged nearly eight pages more a weekday.

Also in the spring of 1981, Dan Lynch urged me to write a column. At the *Herald Tribune* I wrote occasional opinion pieces, usually political analyses. My only day-to-day reporting experience derived from the months in 1969 I spent as a war correspondent in Vietnam for the *Washington Post*. While I liked Dan's idea, I had concerns about bringing it off. I got the feeling Dan wanted to write his own column and thought it best that I go first and thereby clear the way for him. Dan was a thoroughly credentialed writer, as his prior and subsequent journalism clearly demonstrated. Over the years, he also produced thirteen novels and nonfiction books. On one occasion, when both of us attended a newspaper conference in Niagara Falls, we flew separately in very small aircraft, each piloted by a person not long accustomed to wearing long pants. Out of this experience, I quarried a good deal of fright from the bumpy ride. Dan, on the other hand, not only shared the fear, he also extracted a smashing column out of the experience. He had the eye of a natural storyteller.

Anyway, I heeded Dan and began to write a Sunday column in May 1981. At first it appeared every other week. Its purpose was to demystify the newspapers for our readers by explaining how and why they worked. In time, it became a weekly column, stretched across the top of page 2 of the Sunday paper. Joe Lyons objected more than once because I consumed valuable real estate, but I did not want to displace any other regular commentators, local and nationally syndicated, on the op-ed page.

The column was a place to engage reader complaints and to explain the traditional and sometimes arcane values of mainstream journalism. Frequently, it defended the papers against allegations of conspiracy made by critics whose own good cause was not receiving what they considered sufficient recognition in our pages. In the first column, beyond announcing the reasons for its creation, I explained a major change in how we presented local news. A portion of that, politely known as community news but frequently answering to the name chicken dinner news, had been presented in three separate regional weekly tabloids inserted into both broadsheet papers. The tabloids, however, covered all areas except the one in which we had the densest penetration—the city and most of Albany County.

From then onward, we incorporated community news into our daily newspapers, making locally focused presentations. These were zoned, that is, distributed in editions targeted for different counties, taking in the bulk of our total circulation. Over the years, we modified the scope and method of presenting community news, responding to various production and cost-control imperatives.

I used the column to explain why we moved *Doonesbury* from the comics page to the op-ed page (it was getting too political) and why we continued to publish the Dr. Ruth sex advice column over parents' objections that it exposed young children to inappropriate subject matter (it was a serious column for adults, and the paper was not published merely for children). Parents were responsible for monitoring their kids' reading. I explained how our two separate editorial pages worked with the publisher and the editor serving on both (decisions were made most of the time by consensus arrived at through discussion).

Long before Dr. Ruth became a contributor, another sex column posed a problem. In fact, we purchased Dr. Ruth's syndicated column as the solution to one that preceded her. Both writers were professionally credentialed in their field. One of the difficulties with the first writer was that she presented well-informed and sensible solutions about issues of human reproduction and anatomy in words and phrases that lent themselves to risqué parody. The result was that the headlines placed on her columns could be shocking, read in an unintended way. Never had I seen such punctiliousness by headline writers. They had fun being exactly accurate to a fault. Some readers hit the roof.

The practical solution was to put a standing label headline on her columns. This sufficed until we discovered Dr. Ruth. She was as clinically sound in her writing, but her style did not lend itself to smutty innuendo. Of course, readers had another choice: avoid reading the sex column they found offensive but others valued as informative. Not everything a newspaper routinely publishes is intended for every reader. Take the crossword puzzle. It appeared every day yet had a small but devoted readership.

Over the years, my column caused readers to write to denounce or praise. Most originated locally, but others came from cities throughout the nation where the column had been picked up from either the wire that served the Hearst newspapers or the New York Times News Service that distributed the Hearst wire to its more numerous clients. In 1988, one local critic damned with faintest praise as he or she (it was an unsigned postal card) complained: "Now I know you write that stuff yourself. You used the word 'inferred' with the correct meaning. It has been at least four years since this last happened. What next? Pronouns that agree with antecedents?"

When my days as the editor ended in fact as well as title and my responsibilities narrowed to supervision of the editorial pages, I felt free to comment in my columns on anything that came to mind. After all, I had spent many years as a foreign and national editor. My column then took its place on the op-ed page. This arrangement kept up in retirement, where it remained, and, as editor-at-large, I continued to serve on the editorial board.

I began to write my column when newspaper production technology had evolved from the days of hot type. We wrote copy on IBM Selectric typewriters, a new electric machine in the newsroom. I gave up my sturdy

Underwood as I accustomed myself to the Selectric, on which to produce the perfectly clean copy to be fed into an optical scanner. The process was known as cold type. Instead of using columns of lead, it produced type printed on special paper. This was pasted on sheets in the composing room before being photographed and turned into plates attached to the printing presses. Customarily, I wrote my column on Saturday afternoon, after playing a couple sets of doubles tennis, for publication the next day. Because my copy was studded with strikeovers, it had to be retyped by a clerk before it could be processed. After a time, Eileen Shepard, the news editor who as chief of the copy desk oversaw preparation of articles for production, told me she could not spare a clerk for this chore. From then on, I wrote on Fridays when more help, including my secretary, was available.

As the newsroom technology developed ever more productive functions over the years, I came to serve as a guinea pig. Mike Spain, a *Knick* reporter promoted to city editor, early on displayed comfort with the devices of the new age, so in time he was appointed assistant managing editor for systems. He oversaw the integration of modern systems into our workplace. In part, this entailed getting the staff to accept new ways of doing things. He decided if he could demonstrate to the staff that the likes of me, the Old Man, could learn the latest computer applications, it would be easy for them. The Selectric itself soon enough gave way to ever more capable computer systems to perform functions once done by composing-room workers. Much of that function shifted to editors using computer keyboards. Gradually but insistently, most of this work migrated to the newsroom, including the composition of the pages of the newspaper, the setting of type and headlines, and the correction of errors. We were anchored in the new world.

Early in the new year 1982, there was another major change in the leadership of the paper. One general manager left and was replaced with another, for whom Annie and I gave a welcoming dinner party in our home to introduce him to several important local men and women. We had high hopes for Tom Reeves, but he was not to last all that long. After Tom, there was one other before the last one Joe Lyons dealt with. To me, this reflected Joe's close-to-the-vest management style. He appeared happier without a general manager.

We expanded the scope of our coverage in the growing suburbs when the allotted complement of reporters and editors was in place. We hired not only from smaller papers, but also from the likes of the *Washington Star*, *Miami Herald*, *Bergen Record* of New Jersey, and *Newsday*. Now was the time for me to make a major move. The arrangement of two managing editors for the *Times Union*, one for the Sunday paper and the other for the daily, had run its course. Since his arrival, Dan had demonstrated his valuable skills. I shifted Bernard Zovistoski to managing editor for administration, and Dan became ME for news, overseeing the daily and the Sunday editions.

CHAPTER 6

New York's Unalike Governors

The New York News Publishers Association chose me to moderate a debate in 1982 among the four major candidates, two from each party, for the Democratic and Republican nominations for governor. A strict format was designed and as moderator of the panel of three top political reporters from different publications across the state, I had a major role in shaping it, including contacting the campaigns to sort out who would open and who would close. As the principals were in different locations, we agreed on a coin toss in my office. This required a degree of trust between the camps as no representatives of the candidates were present. John Kutzer of the Publishers Association tossed the coin in my presence. He then asked representatives, each connected by his own phone, to make their calls, after which they were informed of the results. In the Democratic contest between Lieutenant Governor Cuomo and New York City Mayor Ed Koch, the mayor won the toss to make the concluding statement, which was much preferred as it offered the candidate the chance to have the last word.

A ferociously angry Mario Cuomo phoned me to decry the coin-toss process in which his campaign organization had participated. He denounced Koch as underhanded, a manipulator who had to be closely watched. Cuomo demanded a coin retoss. Although his fury unsettled me, I said there was no honorable way to comply. The conversation ended with Cuomo not a bit assuaged. The debates at the Gideon Putnam Hotel in Saratoga Springs went off as arranged; the Democrats faced the panel in the morning, the Republicans in the afternoon. Mario Cuomo won the

Democratic primary in a stunning upset and the general election over Lew Lehrman.

Despite what had the appearance of a personal conflict-in-the-making, the governor and I continued to get on well. From our first meeting at lunch when he was lieutenant governor we had far-ranging conversations. At one, he expressed deep concern about the lack of moral content in public education and the role it played in making ours a troubled society. We batted back and forth the problem of deciding whose views would or should prevail. He impressed me as a man of values. His ability to express his beliefs vividly impacted the state and the nation and helped to shape America's political dialogue.

During his three terms as governor, our editorial pages tended to be supportive of his administration. Nevertheless, there were enough disagreements about our reportage or editorials. The governor was a guest at our editorial board certainly in each election year, but also at other times. Some were a grand occasion for us, and for these we set the best table we could in an upstairs conference room for a catered luncheon served on white tablecloths. Attending, in addition to the regular editorial board, were the publisher, the managing editors and city editors, and several reporters. He proved a riveting guest although not always a charming one. Mario Cuomo sometimes turned hostile when, from his perspective, he was sorely provoked. This did not necessarily take a whole lot. At one point, a city desk editor, Rob Brill, phrased a question in which the governor was posited as being a liberal, quite an accurate observation. The governor expressed outrage. He ranted on and on, insisting he was not a liberal (it was election time and deemed a negative) and drove the stunned questioner into the ground with his vigorous rebuttal. I had to intervene to end the diatribe.

During one of these get-togethers Cuomo from time to time spoke about his childhood in Queens and shared that one of his favorite treats was charlotte russe, a specialty offered in candy stores in New York City. I also very much enjoyed this confection as a teenager. It consisted of a rounded piece of pound cake two inches high, wrapped in a cardboard cup, covered with a spiral of whipped cream a couple of additional inches in height, topped with a maraschino cherry. It was a memorable delight.

As an attentive host, I described the concoction to a colleague and commissioned him to find a local baker to surprise the governor when he next came to lunch. The first time what was delivered bore no remote resemblance to what I had described. A couple of subsequent attempts also came up short. Producing a charlotte russe was beyond the capacity of Albany's bakers, shame on them.

The governor's outbursts also occurred at the Mansion, to which the publisher and I were invited along with our counterparts from across the state. As a representative of the local newspapers, the publisher was seated next to the governor and the editor next to First Lady Matilda Cuomo at the head table for a dinner. The occasion was the presentation of the annual state budget. The company first gathered in the large sitting room, drinks with hors d'oeuvres handy, while the governor highlighted his proposed changes for the better. When one editor or another questioned an aspect of the proposal, Cuomo would quickly personalize it and ask whether Buffalo or Binghamton or Rochester (depending on the home turf of the questioner) would like to take budget cuts instead. This behavior was so much a characteristic of his persona that it was predictable, although that did not deter editors from asking, bless them.

Most of the time the governor was either interesting or entertaining to be with, and frequently both. He generously responded when I was deputized to invite him to various corporate events, in Albany or New York City, as well as to solicit his appearance for the likes of Audit Bureau of Circulation, the National Book Awards, and so on, and he almost always came through. There is not one terribly angry letter in my files from him, but that may be because they are not complete. I do recall several tough phone calls of complaint, but he also praised editorials and revelatory articles. When we wrote one editorial, on a waste bond issue, we agreed with the governor's position and he sent a handwritten thank-you and said: "At least this is one subject we won't have to debate."

The *Washington Post*'s Book World asked me to review his just-published diaries in 1984. In a lengthy article, I wrote, "What we find in reading these diaries is that Cuomo is not a saint, but that he sometimes thinks, however subconsciously, he is in the running." He was a workaholic to a fault and possessed genuine religiosity. I assessed him as surpassing Ronald Reagan's ability to spell out a larger political vision and Jimmy Carter's tendency to wrap "himself in the minutiae of policies, making his administration too much a prisoner of his personal participation." He was potentially either courageous or overly zealous. This drew a handwritten reply that demonstrated Cuomo's hidden lighter self. Two excerpts: "You seem eager to have me move on [to the presidency]. I'm not sure it's prophecy, promotion or preference." And "You're dead wrong about my unwillingness to delegate. I delegate a lot! It's just that I like to check up on the work. I scrutinize it. Then I redo it . . . while praying. What's wrong with that?"

Four years later, I published a column whose headline told the story: "Cuomo's ancient art form keeps today's journalists safe." Playing reporter for a day for the Jamestown *Post-Journal*, he wrote his story in longhand.

I wrote: "In carrying out his role, the governor came to his assignment obviously prepared in the subject matter (taxpayer funding to keep a local business going) and ready to ask pertinent questions. . . . He did most everything more than right, as one can tell from his story—its important elements are logically spelled out in the text. He may have been brand new to the art form, but he had figured out what he had to do and did it."

His was such a good job, I wrote: "It's enough to give all of us in the trade a case of the griefs. Who needs a tyro coming along and doing so well the first time at bat? . . . Our long-guarded secret that newspapering beats working is at risk." What saved us, I said, was Cuomo's Victorian pencil fetish. "Until he learns to type, merely being able to think doesn't threaten us in the newspaper trade. We are safe for another day."

To which Cuomo, in a handwritten note responded: "Harry," it opened, "You have relaxed too soon!" (He liked those old-fashioned exclamation marks.) "It's clear if I wish to move upward and onward into your world of real power, I will have to learn to type . . . on a computer yet. I've started my instruction as of last Wednesday. Someday soon I will be typing my own copy. So hold on to your desk Harry . . . I'm coming!"

After he was angered by an editorial accusing him of being cynical in limiting the number of debates in the 1986 election, he took pen in hand to note that the two scheduled debates mirrored what had been done in other state and national campaigns. "Isn't it possible Harry, that maybe I'm not cynical and that the result is what I promised *plus* unprecedented disclosure? Just possible?" Signed, "Mario."

In that campaign, Governor Cuomo's Republican opponent had trouble raising money from sources predisposed to the GOP as well as from open-handed Wall Streeters. Cuomo's campaign manager and counsel, a former colleague of mine at the *Herald Tribune*, assailed our papers, charging that we had "sacrificed objectivity." The proximate cause was our story reporting the Cuomo campaign raised much more money than his opponent—an incontrovertible fact. The counsel, Martin J. Steadman, my past and future friend, apparently thought it was calculated to make his man somehow look like Goliath for having such a lavish campaign chest compared to his opponent. The reason our paper did the story, Marty wrote, was because the governor turned down our invitation to debate his challenger, Andrew O'Rourke, under our auspices.

The figure we used came from an official campaign report submitted by the Cuomo people. It included funds from the '82 campaign, which according to instructions it should not have. In my view, Marty made this fuss because the governor and his camp did not like our coverage. We did not do the negative stories about O'Rourke they touted us onto because we found no validity in them.

After the election, Mario Cuomo berated the national press for being thin-skinned and running in packs. All too true, but in any hypersensitivity competition, Mario Matthew Cuomo easily won the trophy. He personalized his disagreements and whatever motivated him also may have caused him to be overly touchy about the kind of criticisms political figures routinely engender. Cuomo's counterpunches often were perceived as bullying or arrogance. His poor relations with the press were a concern when his name was in play for the 1988 Democratic presidential nomination.

Better angels also guided Mario Cuomo. When my mother-in-law, Martha Hahn, turned ninety-five in 1992, among presents I wanted to give her was an autographed photograph of the governor, whom she very much admired. I called my Capitol bureau reporter and asked him to set it up. He said the governor did not do that sort of thing unless the recipient was one hundred. I told him to try nevertheless.

Next, the governor phoned and told me that instead of merely a photo, I should bring my mother-in-law to meet him. At the appointed time, Martha, Annie, and I went to the governor's private office and he sat and talked with Martha for at least a half hour. He invited her to sit at the desk that Franklin Delano Roosevelt used as governor. FDR was a hero to Martha's generation, as he was to mine. Governor Cuomo pointed out to Martha the built-in platform that permitted Governor Thomas E. Dewey, a man of modest height, to face reporters at press conferences closer to an eye-to-eye level.

In their conversation, Martha asked why he did not run for president, which she had wanted him to do. He offered no insights beyond the pressures of his gubernatorial responsibilities. Besides the personal talk and an inscribed photograph, the governor presented her with several mementos bearing the state emblem. The next day she went around the house saying, "Not if I live to be a hundred, will I ever forget." When the governor's office forwarded photos of the event, he graciously added: "Your mother-in-law was a delight!" That was the more enduring aspect of Mario Cuomo, along with his impressive eloquence and, frankly, the courage he demonstrated with the explication of how he wielded political power in a democracy where church and state are separate. In his address "Religious Belief and Public Morality," given at Notre Dame in 1984, he described how the issue of abortion affected an observant Roman Catholic governor and his refusal to impose his personal beliefs on those in the public who did not share them.

Taking him as the whole man he was, I had never met an official more genuinely intelligent and eloquent. That was the essence of Mario Cuomo's political power.

I had good relations with Cuomo's successor as well. George E. Pataki was distinctly different, beyond the party affiliation, certainly when we first met him in the final hours of his campaign for governor. He had turned aside four of our invitations before he agreed to meet with our editorial board, and then only for a half hour, far shorter than was customary. He struck us then as being on the stiff side. His coiled defensiveness suggested he considered being questioned by us as inherently hostile.

Even so, he demonstrated an impressive grasp of the issues facing the state. His long suit in his victory was not so much what he was—a state senator—but what he was not—a three-term incumbent governor. After twelve years, Mario Cuomo's public support had worn thin.

At the next election, Governor Pataki was much more at ease with the editorial board. His comfort showed as he sat back in his chair, his long legs crossed, amiable and voluble. He was self-confident and relied on what was stored in his brain to answer specific questions, without referring to notes or his aide. George Pataki was dismissive of his predecessor's fondness for rhetoric and abstraction. His later appearances demonstrated a growing command of the details of governance, along with the ability to deploy heavy irony to make his points.

In my latter years at the *TU*, George Pataki turned out to be a great help in a proposal to develop Albany's riverfront as a cultural park. More than Mario Cuomo, he supported the arts and culture for themselves and for the economic development tools he considered them to be. His door was open when I needed him to hear me out for one reason or another.

CHAPTER 7

The Hunt for Elusive Truth

Local news and coverage of state government were our papers' primary missions but not our only ones. In surveys taken for us by different consultants years apart, out of all the dailies in the wide circulation area only ours were regarded by readers as regional and full-service publications. We committed special resources to create this reality. In addition to the general news services, the Associated Press and United Press International, we carried several others, most importantly both the New York Times and the Los Angeles Times–Washington Post News Services. They were copious sources of first-rate national and international as well as cultural coverage. Our aim was to provide national and world news to make our papers a well-rounded read.

With those resources, we published firsthand reports from the scene when in the summer of 1982 Israel struck against Palestinian forces attacking from sanctuary in Lebanon. Partisans of each combatant were outspokenly critical of the coverage, with the pro-Israeli side deploying concentrated complaints about bias. This afflicted many American newspapers. The Greater Albany Jewish Federation studied how the war was reported in the pages of our newspapers. The federation said it reviewed more than 150 news items. It concluded in general our papers presented "a fair and accurate summary of events" but objected to occasional headlines that suggested "inappropriate" Israeli conduct not supported by the stories. It thought local coverage of reactions from both sides favored the Arabs, and it had trouble with a "less objective" use of photographs.

These findings were far more moderate than the outpouring of denunciations from Jewish readers, whose complaints more closely resembled the opinion of the federation's executive director, published as an editorial in the local Jewish weekly. His comments applied to all local news media—television, radio, press—and concluded "that there remains a dual standard of reporting and presentation of news" suggesting an "open season on Israel and the Jewish people . . . that permits legitimizing anti-Semitism." Unlike the federation's study, specifics were not provided.

I checked into each federation allegation and, on close reading, found no bias in our selection or presentation, although we acknowledged mistakes. The challenged items were for the most part reflections of different points of view and matters of interpretation. The editors who packaged the overseas report did not have—nor should they have had—the raw sensibilities of the people who took offense looking at them through the prism of their own partisanship. The events of that bitter conflict were so categorically disputed that there was no possibility of pleasing either side.

The issue was on the agenda as the National Jewish Community Relations Advisory Council convened its four hundred members in Cleveland the following spring. Along with Martin Peretz, editor and publisher of the *New Republic*, and George Watson, vice president of ABC News, I served as a panelist to speak about media bias as it related to the Lebanon War. During the discussion, I made the point that most reporting is done on the run, even more so in war. What might appear to be bias could be attributed more to the elusiveness of truth. If there was actual bias, it appeared to me not anti-Semitic. More likely, it was the result of cultural leftish inclinations of the journalists or maybe sympathy for the underdog. I said I thought American Jews were "oversensitive to a fault." I stressed journalism was "a limited art form" practiced "under the press of time." I noted the most cited examples of "simplistic" reporting occurred on TV, which was more a function of the medium's storytelling needs to feature heroes and villains than of bias.

All this upset one Jewish woman in the audience, who got on her feet and denounced me as a self-hating Jew, thank you very much. A post-appearance letter from the chair thanked me for a "stimulating and challenging presentation . . . not only because it provided valuable food for thought, but also because you were so wonderfully forthright and candid." This was followed by a letter from my rabbi, who had been in attendance. He was a signatory of the Jewish Federation study of our coverage. At the Cleveland meeting, he was startled by my remarks about truth, which, looking back, I expressed too tersely, saying that journalism is not a purveyor of the truth because it was so hard to grasp. I explained to him it would have been better said that newspapers neither disdain the truth nor tell willful lies. "The point is that the truth is hard if not impossible to know on a day-to-day basis. Daily newspapering is done in a hurry and what we get is maybe a slice of the truth, or a truth one day, and if we're good, another slice the next. . . . We print what we think, believe, and hope is the truth, but it is only such truth as we have managed to find out, much from people with an interest in not telling the truth, all of it subject to later correction."

It has been aptly said that journalism is "the first rough draft of history," an iconic adage coined by Philip L. Graham, publisher of the *Washington Post* and the husband of Katharine Graham. As such it is not history and it surely is not revealed truth. Journalism is information, partial, incomplete, flawed. It must intend toward truth and try to achieve it. Consider that historians, writing years or decades after events, with greater access to data, source materials, and testimonies, can produce no more than a reasonable interpretation of truth—if they are good historians and abide by their profession's standards.

Then what is the value of journalism? Along with its acknowledged limitations, it is highly useful because it provides essential contemporaneous information.

Being a Jew as well as an editor exposed me to charges of self-hatred as out of the mouth of the Cleveland matron. More often the complaint was my pro-Jewish bias, sometimes as part of a conspiracy. When our papers dealt with a Middle East crisis, it resulted in hate mail from people viscerally agitated because the editor was a Jew. On other occasions, no self-evident Jewish connection to an event was needed for an anti-Jewish diatribe, linked to control of the media and finance. When this happened, I tried my utmost to control my emotions, whatever faction launched these assaults, to hold on with all the force I could muster to the values of straightforward, factual reporting. I emphasized the need for journalism to inform rather than incite or placate.

Anti-Semitic attacks occurred throughout my career. I used to keep folders of the crazy mail I received with some regularity. I finally tossed them when thinning my files. I kept a single letter as a reminder, should I need it. This one consisted of two pages of horrific images of Jews murdered in a Nazi death camp. Accompanying text proclaimed God's instruction for Israel and American Jews to REPENT. The envelope, posted in Northern Virginia, bore a shibboleth: JESUS IS LORD! and included the name of the sender, a chaplain with the rank of colonel.

The Lebanon War was the high-water mark for that kind of vituperative reaction, yet it differed from other rebukes mainly in its vehemence. It wasn't only a Jewish or Arab syndrome (anti-Arabism was imputed to our political cartoons). An Irish American delegation trooped into our office to protest an article mentioning heavy drinking accompanying a St. Patrick's Day celebration, a very big holiday in Albany. How could we have been so wrongheaded to allege Irishmen liked the drink? It took resolve not to laugh. Maybe it was advertisements for Irish and other bars on the occasion or the police arrests of more vigorous celebrators. Or maybe it was the words of the cardinal down in New York City calling attention to rowdy behavior fueled by alcohol.

Irish objections did not begin nor end with St. Patrick's Day. They were feverish about how the American media took the side of the hated British in the long strife in Northern Ireland. Like Jews on Israel, they detected bias in our headlines, content, and point of view. They summoned authorities from their own camp to make their point and regarded us as either dupes or champions of their enemies.

When the coordinator of the local Irish Northern Aid committee caviled yet again, this time about how his letter to the editor was edited, which was slightly and according to rules published daily, I replied: "We have presented the problems in Northern Ireland from many points of view. I believe that is what may trouble you. You want us to adopt your point of view exclusively and become your propaganda organ. We will not do that."

My door was literally open unless we had an executive meeting. Everyone in the newsroom could easily see what was going on behind the windowed wall, whose shades were seldom drawn. I made a fetish of welcoming criticisms and critics. Many of those seriously unhappy with our work preferred to go to the publisher—commonly a business or social acquaintance. Any review of a performance—a restaurant, an art exhibit, a play—that did not wholly embrace the effort was reason enough to charge the critic with deep-seated prejudice. This is not to claim critiques were always in every way on the mark, but with the rarest exceptions they were not the product of the malice generally ascribed by complainants. For self-protection, if nothing more, we emphasized to the staffers the need to ensure the pertinence of our criticisms.

Bankers complained of being maligned if the reporting did not make them look good, even though the facts had been accurately recorded. Of course, this could be stated in capital letters when it came to politicians and public officials. Physicians often felt unfairly targeted, and judges considered themselves less respected than their station warranted.

Because of my position at the newspapers, Annie and I came to know many fascinating people and their various ways of work, in addition to those in official public life. As we spent even a little personal time with them, we discovered complexities in their character or background. That was true of Marylou Whitney, the doyenne who was a powerful force in the culture of the Capital Region with her support of the arts, the renowned horse racing track in Saratoga Springs, and civic and charity activities.

Surely, among the most notable people we met and broke bread with were two especially celebrated artists. Isaac Bashevis Singer, winner of the Nobel Prize in Literature, was a dinner guest at the home of a University at Albany professor. Annie and I were invited to join a group to meet him before his lecture the following day. He and I talked quite a bit, and a common political sensibility emerged as the first days for both of us in America began as immigrants. He left Poland in 1935 and my family left Germany four years later, though both my parents were born in Warsaw. In the talk after dinner we sat around, and the professorial collective espoused the left-wing certitudes that Singer did not share. Neither did he bother to disguise his disagreement with their political assumptions, which aroused their anger. Singer persisted and held on to his views although he could see that his audience was hostile to them. It was a night to remember.

The sculptor Louise Nevelson came to Albany accompanied by her companion for some high-level appearance with which Governor Carey had an association, the particulars of which no longer lodge in my memory. At the last minute, the governor was detained and unable to entertain the visitors at dinner, so Annie and I were enlisted to fill in as hosts at a downtown hotel. It turned out to be an exceedingly fun evening as Ms. Nevelson, her head swathed in a black turban as always, was entertainingly down to earth as she held forth not only about her art and her life as an artist but also about her childhood, which turned out to have transpired in the Bronx. We got along splendidly.

My relations with animals were not so good. In the 1930s, when I was a very young child in Berlin, still in the high-chair stage, I had a pet canary I named Hansi. The bird died, and I was sad. In my forties, living in Kensington, Maryland, our family had a dog, acquired when our girls were teenagers and younger, rescued from the pound as a reward for one of them doing well in summer school. I did by far most of the cleanup and we spent a goodly sum shoving penicillin into him because of distemper. I took him for walks, but we finally had to give him up after he nipped one daughter and got aggressive with her younger sister. We were all in tears. Who needed any of this?

With rare exception, I have found animal stories boring. I resented them because devoting scarce space and reporter and photographer time meant matters of consequence remained unreported.

That's just me. There is another world out there that melts at the prospect of reading about critters. At the *Times Union* Joe Lyons made a deal with an animal shelter. Our promotion department would run a story with a photo on the most adoptable pet of the week. Managing Editor Dan Lynch instructed editors: "Every Friday, a photographer will be occupied for a brief period taking a picture of that week's beast, and it's not an assignment that can be killed without my specific okay, or Harry's, and don't even ask unless it's a crisis of monumental proportions."

The best newspaper animal story I ever came across was told by one of Albany's most famous novelists, if you count, as you should, Herman

Melville and Henry James. William Kennedy, a Pulitzer Prize winner for his novel *Ironweed* and a former *Times Union* reporter, recounted the tale of the circus coming to town in his collection of nonfiction stories, *O Albany!* The annual event was marked by a parade of the elephants through city streets. In those days, the circus encouraged newspaper coverage by giving out free passes to the press corps. One year following routine, a photographer snapped the elephants lumbering through the streets and photos were dutifully published. The very next day, those same elephants, no longer docile, broke their tethers and rampaged through the city until with great effort they were rounded up. The *TU* photographer captured the live action and brought it to the editor who barely looked at the photos before rejecting them. "We had elephant pictures yesterday," he said.

CHAPTER 8

Ends of Life

My father Sam died in January 1983, a few weeks shy of his ninetieth birthday. His health had declined steadily over his last years. Glaucoma narrowed his sight and he lost virtually all peripheral vision. Arthritis increasingly plagued him, though he kept up his daily walks. He insisted on staying in his one-bedroom apartment opposite Poe Park in the Bronx, to which my parents moved from our three-bedroom residence in a more downscale neighborhood after I had left home. My mother died years earlier while I was working at the *Herald Tribune*. After we moved to Washington, attempts to convince him to live near us were rejected.

Once in Albany, we saw him more frequently in visits to the city, where both Susan and Amy, our older daughters, out of college and working, lived at the time. Following the close of the fur retail business he had begun in his first month in America, we wanted him to move to Albany. My routine was to phone him Sunday evenings to check how he was doing. After Susan graduated from Boston University, he worried she seemed to be enjoying single life too long for his liking. That was his running complaint with me during our Sunday chats. Finally, in exasperation, one night I all but shouted: "Just what do you want me to do?" My father was calm when he replied: "I would find someone for her."

Annie and I found an apartment in a retirement community very near us and got his name on the waiting list. On a visit, we took him to inspect the place. Although he had no more than tunnel vision, he noticed from the window of the apartment a cemetery a fair distance away. The vista did not please him, and he turned it down. Only if he could move in with us would he agree to come, something not practical with

Annie and me both out of the house during the workweek. Many years earlier he had firmly rejected my sister's invitation to join her family in Florida.

As his illnesses intensified—he developed congestive heart failure—Annie and I rushed down to the city. For us it meant driving to New York, thoroughly anxious. One time my father fell as he came to open the door in response to our ring because I had forgotten to bring his house key. He could not get up. I ran to the nearest busy street to look for a locksmith. When I returned, unsuccessful, we had had better luck. His next-door neighbors, two elderly women, had come home from shopping. He had given them a key.

We phoned for help. Annie rode in the ambulance to the hospital. I followed in our car. He was then, and would be again and again, hospitalized briefly before returning home.

My father was a man well groomed and dapper. He developed the taste for good clothes in his youth in Warsaw, living in tight quarters with his parents and numerous siblings in the poorest section of town. Although he could not have made much money, he patronized high-toned custom tailors. I cannot recall seeing him unshaven. His suits and shirts, ties and shoes were well made and neatly placed in his closet. You could say he was fastidious without the prissiness the adjective can imply.

On one of his hospitalizations he was in a large ward with many occupied beds. The nurses were overworked. When we visited, he had not been shaved for many days and was upset. I located his toilet kit, scrounged up soap, a pan of warm water and paper towels, and shaved him. His mood noticeably improved as he appreciatively ran his hand over his freshly shaved face. The physician who was treating him looked in while I observed. That's all he did: stood in the doorway and looked in. He did not come near his patient.

During this period, I suffered a mini-stroke, which brought my physician, Dr. Richard Propp, into our home in the middle of the night. He sat at my bedside for hours until I recovered enough for him to return to his bed. I had at least one other transient ischemic attack, years earlier in Washington. There were no noticeable aftereffects, except to retain an awareness of my vulnerability.

While my father was in the intensive care unit another time, connected to all sorts of tubes and monitors, he asked the young medical intern attending him why was he wasn't at home with his wife on a Saturday. The doctor replied he was unmarried. My father asked him whether he would like to meet "my granddaughter, a lovely girl." The doctor had come to like my dad and thought he had nothing to lose, and so he said he would. When soon thereafter Annie and I visited, Susan was with us. My dad had made sure the doctor would stay beyond the end of his Saturday shift and introduced Susan to Stuart Wachter. They began to date.

As my father's condition worsened I no longer accepted his refusal to join us upstate. I forced the issue, and he finally agreed and was brought to the Albany Medical Center Hospital by ambulance accompanied by a private nurse and placed in the care of our physicians. At this stage, he was bedridden. The doctors wanted to begin a series of invasive and painful procedures. I asked them what the quality of his life would be after treatment. They said it would be pretty much what it was, but their mission was to try to extend life. I said they should make him comfortable and shield him from pain—no more. Annie and I sat at his bedside and soon he went into a coma. We held his hand and talked to him and told him we loved him. After some hours, we took a short break. When we returned to the hospital, the door to his private room was shut. It was a stab to the heart. I opened the door, looked down at my father, his body covered with a blanket, only his head showing. He had seen me safely through the dangers of my childhood. For the last time, I kissed him. He had not lived to see his granddaughter marry the man he found for her, but he made the *shidduch*, the match.

When my father's obituary appeared in the morning paper, Mayor Corning immediately sent his condolences. It was written in the shaky hand of a man suffering a debilitating illness, noting my father's immigrant beginnings in this country and comparing it to the Vietnamese immigrants of the day. Complexity reflected our relationship. Under my editorship, we took on his administration and most particularly his political organization and its corrupt or dubious practices whenever we found them.

On a personal level, our relationship was at least correct and on many occasions several degrees warmer. Still, Erastus Corning knew how to throw his weight around. One Yom Kippur I was absorbed in day-long prayers at temple. I received word that the mayor urgently wanted to speak with me. As such an intervention was a first, I quickly left the synagogue to phone my office—against the strictures of abstaining from such activity on the Day of Atonement—thinking it had to be a matter of great moment. Instead, it turned out to be a complaint about a low-level article that could easily have waited a day or two. You could argue that Mayor Corning did not know it was Yom Kippur or that I was sufficiently observant to be spending the day at worship. I think he was much too smart to be unaware and that he had another purpose in mind: to demonstrate he was indeed boss.

He was a close and intelligent reader of our papers, even of our separate editions, as letters from him querying changes from one to the other showed. He spotted a headline in the early Troy edition: "Corning friends/considered best bets/for county surrogate," which was changed in the Albany edition, and he had a complaint. I explained in a letter to him: "Friends" was saying a bit more than warranted and we substituted "associates." As that was too long, "cronies" was selected. And that was worse than what we started with. "We apologize to you and your associates. . . . And we pray that our mistake does not impair your electoral support."

Despite the *Sturm und Drang* over political issues, his most enduring problem with us was that we published his name as Erastus Corning II. The roman numerals were the way that designation was prescribed by our stylebook, a compilation of rules to help maintain coherence in our newspapers' pages. He insisted on the arabic 2nd. I moved heaven and earth to get our copy editors to let him have his way—and that worked for a time, only to yield again and again to the overriding authority of the stylebook.

He complained that we logged heating days in our weather report incorrectly (something that defied our best efforts to get permanently right) and messed up regularly with rainfall reports as to deficiency and excess.

Although we clashed with him on a range of issues, at times we backed him, even if his stand was unpopular. When the South African

Springboks rugby team was invited by a local club to play a match in Albany's Bleecker Stadium, a huge outcry arose from people and organizations opposed to the apartheid regime. Corning thought he could not ban the game, as demanded, because of First Amendment protections. Our editorial page agreed and the game went off, under heavy police guard that proved unnecessary.

When illness caught up with him, he was taken to the same hospital where my dad died. I visited his bedside twice at his invitation before he was transferred for specialized care in Boston. The second time I showed up after I had received two letters from him. He was in a room with three other patients and was hooked up to an IV and was on oxygen. To speak, he needed the nurse to insert a plastic tube in his throat. He was thin and frail. We spoke briefly. His labored words focused on mutual efforts to make Albany a better place. He looked forward to the future, to fishing and to fixing Albany. His final words to me were: "Harry, we're going to have some fun together."

On a subsequent Friday afternoon, I heard his illness had reached its crisis. At Sabbath services that evening I shared with the rabbi what I learned and suggested he offer a congregational prayer for the mayor's recovery. When he died in May 1983, many attributes of the political organization he led along with Dan O'Connell also succumbed. A legacy of Democratic Party rule survived as far as the eye could see, but the curtain had fallen on an era. During his forty-one years in office, Corning's door was always open and he answered his own phone. He fixed problems large or small if you were a loyal Democrat. When petitioned over a controversial issue implicating his administration's performance, he did not reject it. Instead, he said, "I'll look into it," although that was highly unlikely.

The Saturday he died in the Boston hospital, I wrote in my column for Sunday: "To us in Albany, he has given texture to our lives, as much or more than any other political figure, including presidents and governors. . . . Today, as we mourn Erastus Corning, we celebrate a famous life and praise a famous man. Some of the salt and the savor has departed from this community."

At the urging of my staff, I wrote the University Hospital director in Boston to thank him for its people's extraordinary cooperation responding to our daily and nightly inquiries about Corning's status. We were not accustomed to receiving such detailed and helpful information in a timely fashion.

The sweep of our coverage of the mayor's death stemmed from his historic impact on the community. We prepared articles beforehand to be appropriately updated and reserved large amounts of space for them. By far, most readers who responded were complimentary. A smaller group dissented. For decades, they fought the man and his machine and lost. These people were affronted by our coverage. They could not understand how newspapers so specifically critical of much of Mayor Corning's rule could at his death review him the way we did. They rejected our rationale that our obligation was to convey the full measure of the man and his regime, and the setting in which they flourished for so long. I said flatly we felt no compulsion to dance on a dead man's grave, although we had not hesitated to expose his misdeeds in life.

CHAPTER 9

Standing Up to City Hall

Four years later, Erastus Corning was still on our agenda as the *Knickerbocker News* pursued a court case under the Freedom of Information Law to keep open to public scrutiny his letters, part of 900,000 pages of documents and personal papers included in the official record. After the paper published some articles, further examination of the files was halted. We lost our legal argument at the first appellate level but the state's highest court overruled, deciding unanimously that "personal or unofficial documents which are intermingled with official government files and are being 'kept' or 'held' by a government entity are 'records' maintained by an 'agency' under Public Officers Law, and therefore, are subject to disclosure." The ruling defined the core of the press's relationship to American democracy: "[T]he public is vested with an inherent right to know and that official secrecy is anathematic to our form of government." In enacting the Freedom of Information Law, the decision went on to say, "it specifically declared: 'that government is the public's business and that the public individually and collectively and represented by a free press, should have access to the records of government in accordance with the provisions of this article.'"

While the case was under judicial consideration, Corning's successor, Thomas W. Whalen III, responded to a *Times Union* editorial. He argued that government, like the press, had a need for "a reasonable amount of confidentiality" to do its job.

Courts over the years affirmed freedom of the press in this regard so that the public may be informed about what its governments were up to. I rebutted Mayor Whalen's claims, pointing out that the press's rights derived from the First Amendment, and there was not a word in the Constitution construing such a right for the government. The Founders had established the rights of the Constitution to offset the powers of the government. I wrote: "Government seeks to maintain its privacy in order to keep information from the people. The press seeks its privacy to make information available to the people."

Tom Whalen was a party loyalist and Corning protégé, a lawyer with a prominent local firm. Thankfully, he had no problem with the roman numeral appended to his surname. While he was very much a creature of the Democratic machine and had been president of the city's Common Council for two years, his ascension to real municipal power reflected a generational shift. He began to weaken or discard some of the more ham-handed policies inherited from the Corning and O'Connell years. On occasion, he took the initiative and we backed him on our editorial pages. At other times, we revealed that some of the egregious purchasing practices of the ancien régime were still alive and well, and he shut them down or amended them in ways more congruent with the public interest.

In the early days, he acquired on loan a car from a local auto dealership long connected to City Hall to be used as his personal official vehicle. When Whalen viewed our reporting and editorial comment as an attack on his integrity, I pointed out to him: "We're not against your having a new car. But we really do believe it will be better for you and for Albany that the city pays for it." He responded: "I feel better about the entire matter after having your thoughts. I might also add that your points are well taken."

Quickly enough he devised written policies to set performance standards for municipal employees, including probationary periods and performance evaluations—all new to the city's administration. With the help of a former state budget director, Dan Klepak, major changes were on the drawing board to lower the cost of government.

With these reforms, Tom Whalen ran into trouble with the party cadre from the old days. There were fewer no-bid, noncompetitive contracts handed out. Some experts were hired for important positions, although they lacked Democratic Party connections. Long-established obligations to the party machine were by no means abrogated, but they were attenuated. When he felt the heat too much, he made sure to consult party bigwigs on appointments.

We had good relations personally at the start of his mayoralty, although his administration was from time to time disturbed by our revealing his reformist plans before he was ready to share them. He asked me not to call him Mayor or Mr. Mayor, or he would have to counter with Mr. Editor or Mr. Rosenfeld. He felt comfortable enough to approach us and convinced Joe Lyons to raise funds through our newspapers for the reconstruction of City Hall's carillon. Over the years, it had fallen into disrepair and was no longer functional. The original carillon had been erected with the help of an antecedent of *The Knickerbocker News*, and so I conceded we had a proper role in helping in its refurbishment. I drew the line at Mayor Whalen's suggestion that Joe and I, along with the mayor and Lew Swyer, a politically connected private citizen and community personage, constitute a committee to oversee the rebuilding. Helping to raise funds was okay with me, I advised Lyons, "but to go any further than that specific role gives me pause. I think it will help to confuse the public and our staff about which side of the footlights we are really on."

However much we cooperated and promoted in our pages the various civic activities sponsored by City Hall, our hard-nosed coverage of his administration, which on balance we supported more than opposed, resulted in sharp conflicts. In May 1987, I focused on yet another complaint, this one by Budget Director Klepak, going over each alleged violation to sort out whether we had in fact made errors or indulged in unfair characterizations. "Over the months," I wrote Dan, "I have seen a pattern emerging. You complain about reporters, at least from Capital Newspapers, the papers that don't limit themselves to explicating and regurgitating your agenda. . . . Fair enough, that's part of the game. . . . But as for your persistence of invariably detecting an editorial vendetta against the Mayor and his administration, it is not only absurd, it is demonstrably not so."

I concluded in words I found myself applying to all sorts of self-righteous petitioners: "What we have not done, and what I will endlessly repeat we will not do, is to enlist in the Mayor's camp, as much as you might wish to sign us up. We will not lay off; we will not suppress news or news leads; we will at all times conduct ourselves as newspapers dedicated to serving our readers. We are not your public relations firm."

A follow-up a half year later came in a personal letter from Tom to Joe Lyons, in which he said more than one source advised him of my interest in "negative news relating to the Mayor's performance in the snow emergency." I had not said nor suggested any such thing. He bemoaned "the continuation of an adversarial relationship." He cited his spouse, a journalism major in college, who was taught newspapers needed to "build community." In response, Joe Lyons and I visited Whalen in City Hall to run down the details of his complaint. Tom made a heartfelt proposition to me: I should advise him privately on city policies and if he opted not to follow it, then the papers should feel free to take him on. I was stunned into silence; the very idea was outrageously absurd, yet I recognized his sincerity. I waited for a moment and more to give Lyons the chance to speak up, but he remained silent. I knew I had to respond. The only way I would or could advise him, I said, was through the pages of our newspapers. I could hold no confidential brief with him as this would undermine my integrity and that of the papers.

After the meeting, I reviewed the articles the mayor cited and those he had not. It was quite a bundle. I reported to Joe: "My conclusion is the mayor would have much preferred that only a minimal number, if any, were written. I would in his place. But the stories are relevant and fair, and I think his reaction is by a politician who is not comfortable with the issues raised by being in public life."

Despite the recurring clashes, I lunched more regularly with Dan Klepak than any other public official, to the point that critics of the mayor, ignoring Whalen's by then well-known resentment of the *Times Union* and *Knickerbocker News*, ascribed our public meetings to the fact that Dan and I had married sisters, as much fiction as my ordering negative Whalen articles. (At most, the ladies shared a vague physical resemblance.)

The major crisis of the Whalen administration occurred in 1989, when he and his executives were subpoenaed to appear before a state Commission on Public Integrity. For him, the basic problem was his receiving for years a partner's share from his private law practice while in office. The firm was involved in numerous associations and relationships and deals that amounted to conflicts of interest for the mayor. He underwent a rough two-and-a-half-hour questioning. He evaded answers and was admonished by the presiding chairman not to meander in his responses.

In what had become a pattern, the mayor complained that our reporter was told by his editors how to write his analysis of the hearing. Obviously, Tom Whalen did not like the specific citations of his evasiveness and other behavior included in the piece. Too bad for him, these were on the record. Unable to contradict the facts, he sought to discredit our coverage by alleging bias. No charges were laid against him in the final report. For one thing, he had resigned from the firm the year before the hearing, citing the amount of work required at the jobs did not permit him to hold both.

The mayor had a staunch ally in denouncing the newspaper for "slanted, editorialized reporting in the news columns" as part of an effort "to drive him from office." So wrote Daniel Button, a former executive editor of the *Times Union*.

When I came to town and encountered Dan Button at the home of new friends, I had tried to reach out to him. He was abrupt and walked away from me without showing any interest. Now I responded to his criticisms, acknowledging that we make mistakes. As to the allegation of trying to undermine the mayor, I asked for citations for the charge. "Contrary to your assessment, we have backed him on a spectrum of issues, ranging from the reforms he instituted in the wake of our reporting of municipal malpractices, to the redevelopment of Albany, the budgetary discipline, through the campaign to restore the carillon. . . . However, editorial support does not mean we will pull our punches in our news coverage." I pointed out one subject on which we "consistently disagreed with the mayor—ethics," from the freebie car through his keeping his law partnership while holding office.

Shortly before his time in office ended in December 1993, the mayor took his staff to an exurban retreat for a final meeting. It made for a modest inside story, but Whalen remained in his defensive crouch. He wrote to complain about the reporter: "Poor Jay Jochnowitz. He still doesn't get it." I responded in my Sunday column: "In fact, every *TU* reporter who covered the mayor during his decade of incumbency has made that particular honor roll. This catalogue suggests something else besides failure of reporters to comprehend or a particular personality clash. Rather, it signals that the mayor neither understands nor supports the role the *Times Union* plays as the city's and the region's largest newspaper . . . to tell the public what is happening as it happens, to put it in context and to try to explain why." Tom Whalen believed the press should be supportive of his policies, "even promote them," I wrote, "and should accept his administration's rationale for its actions. After all, they are all honorable, so why fuss about how much things cost or about procedures? The *Times Union*, he says, is negativist."

I thought such an attitude was even more perilous to the public weal when held by a federal judge, the post he was heading to in retirement from City Hall. His nomination, though sponsored by Senator Moynihan, stalled in the Clinton administration. Whalen withdrew from consideration as a judge on the federal district court to rejoin as a senior partner his old law firm, reconfigured under a different name. In subsequent years, through the intermediation of a mutual friend, he invited me to lunch at his country club, where we had a friendly enough discussion of events in our common past.

CHAPTER 10

Scandal and Methodology

While the accomplishments of Whalen's tenure were notable, his deficiencies, rooted in a lack of vision, were hardly comparable to what happened at the county level. The government there was also controlled by Democrats, and its executive, James J. Coyne Jr., attained notoriety when he pleaded guilty and was convicted of conspiracies to violate federal statutes on bribery and mail fraud as well as of extortion.

Coyne was popular, a machine cadre and a man of the people. He was educated as an elementary school teacher. He was a regular at the Saratoga Race Course and a horse owner. Federal district Judge Lee P. Gagliardi, in his sentence, stipulated Coyne had to undergo treatment for both his gambling and drinking. Coyne acknowledged these failings. As he said at the time, "Both had an influence on my life in a negative way—sure, I have to admit that. But that was not a crime."

We began to reveal Coyne's dealings in 1983, with investigative articles about his manipulations of the bidding for supplies for the county's nursing home. The following year we reported on his firing of a county employee who blew the whistle about Democratic Party favorites filling up the tanks of their personal cars at pumps intended for official use. After we exposed patronage hiring at the nursing home, Coyne withdrew the county's advertising for professional positions from the *Times Union*. That amounted to some $60,000 annually. When Lou Boccardi, executive vice president of the Associated Press, read about that in the *New York Times*, he wrote me: "I noted Jon Friendly's item about how the honesty of your journalism affected the quantity of your advertising revenue. May the good Lord bless and keep you. I know the whole profession feels that way."

Coyne's misconduct up to then was in harmony with Albany tradition. Big-time opportunity came with the construction of a county civic center in downtown Albany, an enterprise the *Times Union* supported on its editorial page. This multimillion-dollar project deserved scrutiny by our newspapers. Our investigative reporters closely examined contracts, relationships, and other undertakings.

We found out who owned the land around the proposed center and who might benefit from its construction. We broke the story of Coyne taking $10,000 from one of the owners of the pro basketball franchise that would play at the center, calling it a scholarship for his daughter. We reported Coyne getting a free car from a dealer who got county business through rigged bids.

During construction, the cost of the center soared from $35 million to $69 million, in part because specifications were tailored to qualify favored suppliers. When a new agent took over the FBI operation in Albany, a lagging federal investigation took on new life. In time, Jim Coyne was indicted and tried. He was not convicted in the first trial but subsequently pleaded guilty to three federal felonies for lying on bank loan applications by hiding hundreds of thousands of dollars in gambling debts and business losses. He avoided trial on twenty-one felony counts by taking a plea. In the end, he stood convicted of nine felonies, six of them counts of corruption, including taking a $30,000 payment from the architect of the center.

His last trial and conviction came after he declined to run for reelection in the face of his legal troubles. He had served as county executive for sixteen years. He asserted his innocence in court, and Judge Gagliardi concluded he had shown no remorse. He was sentenced to forty-six months in prison and on release encountered rebuffs as he sought public office again.

Coyne complained the *Times Union* was to blame for his winding up in court. He was right when he said I brought Watergate investigative habits from Washington to Albany. He was wrong when he declaimed to George Hearst that the Hearst Corporation had hired me for Albany just to get him.

Still, newspaper life was not always lived at the high pitch of investigating nefarious enterprises. Because of being there, in 1983 I was elected president of the New York State Associated Press Association. An intermediary seeking new leadership for United Press International, the general news service increasingly losing subscribers, journeyed to Albany and at lunch explored my interest in heading UPI. I did not as much as agree to think about it and left him clearly aware that he had to continue his search.

Throughout the years, working to improve the quality of writing was a priority. On the one hand, we encouraged bright writing to overcome the dullness of newspaper prose, inclined to adhere to the inverted pyramid format: most important fact at its apex and other details presented in descending order of newsworthiness. Too many of the ground-out, formulaic stories were easily overlooked as a reader scanned the pages. On the other hand, enlivened writing needed to be executed with care so as not to distort the facts to produce a more readable narrative.

Unfortunately, there were misfires. One that stood out for me resulted in a libel suit, which in the end we settled because fighting it in court would cost more. The problem arose when New York State issued a press release to warn against contaminated clams sold by a local business. In writing it up, we made two important errors. The reporter misstated the reason for the civil conviction of the business, saying it pleaded guilty for having sold contaminated clams. In fact, the plea was for not having a required tag on the baskets of clams it sold—which turned out to be contaminated. Compounding this careless error, the supervising editor wanted to jazz up the lead. He fancied himself a bit of a wordsmith. He rewrote the lead to say that this was a story about greed on the half shell. Certainly, more attention-getting; unfortunately, not provable in court. The worthy attempt to boost readability did not compensate for the failure to get the facts straight.

Getting facts straight for many of my days in newspapering was routinely avoided when it came to obituaries. It was striking how few causes there were for death. To judge by what our newspapers printed, our local population mainly succumbed to one of two illnesses: a brief one or a long one. Most always, the cause of death was supplied by the mourning family, which shunned naming the specific malady. This reflected the cultural temperament of our community. It was an intention to disguise the cause of what is the second or third most important event in life, as if there were something shaming or infectious about the actual cause of death.

These absurd euphemisms were standard in the newspapers of the twentieth century. Public opinion appeared to insist they treat death as if it were a social disease or a character defect. Readers certainly broke the code and understood brief illness usually meant a heart attack or stroke, while long illness stood in for cancer. Clarity sometimes emerged when the obit information supplied by the family suggested memorial donations be made to cancer or heart funds.

Obituaries made for other problems. Some mourners stipulated inclusion of the phrase "please omit flowers" for cultural, aesthetic, or religious reasons. That seemed to be fine with almost everyone except florists, who lobbied the newspaper advertising staff to ban that phrase. They suggested citing specific charities for memorial contributions instead.

More serious objections arose about death notices warranting a news article. They stemmed from a misunderstanding among readers of what they were. For many readers, especially for families and friends of the deceased, the expectation was the account in the newspaper would be a eulogy. That was true as far as the classified announcement, written by the family, usually with the assistance of the funeral home.

However, the obituary in the news pages was a news story, written by a reporter and governed by general rules. While a news story of a death did not go out of its way to dredge up minor indiscretions, it was obligated to tell the pertinent truth. Therefore, the notorious bookie had his occupation recalled (even though he was the uncle of a high Hearst executive). As did the town justice who was dismissed from office for cause after twenty years' service. For a prominent obstetrician-gynecologist, a laudatory recitation of his career included deep into it his conviction in a malpractice case. His family protested to Hearst headquarters, and New York's inquiry supported how we handled it. On relatively rare occasions when it was necessary to refer to matters in their loved one's past the family did not want to be mentioned, it was not done out of mean-spiritedness. It was done to meet requirements of relevance.

A long time later, in 1999, when Jeff Cohen was editor and I was not, another aspect of the departed troubled the *Times Union*. It occurred when a man wanted to mark the anniversary of his father's death years before, to appear as a paid item in the In Memoriam section of the classified ads. As submitted, it read: "In loving memory of Leo Balint, considerate son, wonderful husband, father, brother and uncle, murdered on this day [April 22] in 1945 by the Nazis and their willing executioners on the death march from Mauthausen to Gunskirchen in Austria. Your goodness and bravery saved us. We will never forget. The family."

The son, Peter, as he subsequently explained, was born in Hungary and lived until the age of thirteen with his parents in Germany. His mother was a German gentile, his father a Hungarian Jew. He immigrated to the United States in 1957, became a citizen, and served in the US Army as an officer for three years. His ad was rejected by a series of advertising personnel, finally reaching the top rung, for being inappropriate to the assumed In Memoriam rules because the proposed ad was "accusatory" against a "race." The ad supervisor suggested an alternative eliminating the word murder and the references to Nazis and willing executioners, resulting in "passed away on this day in 1945" before picking up the rest of the original.

Mr. Balint would not accept the revision and pointed out he was not accusing anyone, simply stating incontrovertible fact. Nor had he mentioned race, only Nazis and willing executioners. He emailed the publisher, the editor, and the ad director and copied me.

Jeff Cohen reached out to Mr. Balint, which he very much appreciated. Jeff lobbied all the others, who through a swift but intense argument, including research of other newspapers' practices, held their ground. The *TU* would not publish this ad as submitted because of policy.

Jeff argued strongly with everyone on the business side to publish what Balint wrote, to which Publisher David White replied: "Jeff, you sound as though you feel the decision should be different in this situation because it relates to Jews and the holocaust. What if it were a different circumstance? I know this is radical, but I use it to make a point. How would you feel about running the ad if it was one being placed by a member of the KKK stating that his father had been murdered by Jews or blacks, especially if they were to use some derogatory label to describe Jews or blacks. I'm certainly not defending the KKK, or the Nazi cause, but perhaps there are valid reasons for the policy. Once the exception is made, where is the line to be drawn in the future?"

Although I was by then way outside any chain of command, as emails circulated with different rationalizations for refusing the ad, I felt compelled to weigh in with a memo.

Frankly, it is extremely hard to take that the *Times Union* proposed to the potential customer that the death of his father in the Holocaust should be described as having "passed away." Just whose sensibilities are supposed to be protected by this sort of evasion?

Second, the *Times Union* policy of requiring verification of the atrocious actions of the Holocaust, in effect asking the customer to supply a death certificate for the sort of mass murder that took place, is absurd. Why would the Germans have confirmed their murders in writing. . . . We should not permit this policy to become known in the present context for it will surely hold us up to scorn and ridicule. . . . the question posed about the ad involving the KKK as a sort of rough equivalence to deaths in the Holocaust is neither fitting nor appropriate. . . .

My own, all too bitter, experiences with so-called policies in the newsroom for nearly fifty years may be quite different from what happens on the business side of newspapers. All too often, matters that were laid off on policies were less a policy than a past practice, established in the first instance to grapple with one particular set of circumstances. Over time, it became entrenched as policy, to bedevil future decision-making.

Rex Smith, at the time the managing editor/news, messaged: "Please, please don't stop this ad. We would deserve whatever onslaught and ridicule that the community would heap upon us for our insensitivity. . . . We should be flexible enough in our application of the rules we have made to make sensible exceptions."

Dave White's resolution of the dispute in time for publication April 22 was embraced by Peter Balint. In Memoriam ran the ad as rewritten, but the *Times Union* published Mr. Balint's full version elsewhere in the paper that day and agreed to review its policy.

Expressing his thanks, Peter Balint captured the solemnity of the matter. "The importance to me and my family cannot be overstated. You see, my father has no grave, no spot to mark in remembrance. This ad acts as a tombstone and an epitaph, a permanent record to show to a visitor to your paper's archives, that he lived, that he was a hero, if only to his family, and that his death was an unfathomable obscenity."

J. Roger Grier, publisher of the *Times Union* and the *Knickerbocker News*, shows off the opulent appointments of the office to his new editor in 1978. Roger hired Harry to make the two newspapers among the best in the nation. Harry and Roger worked well together. Photo credit: *Albany Times Union.*

Hugh Carey was a robust chief executive during New York's fiscal crises. The governor was newsworthy for his accomplishments and his foibles. He and the newspapers stayed on good terms even when he was the subject of critical articles. Photo credit: *Albany Times Union.*

Mario Cuomo was eloquent confronting daunting issues and could turn hostile when, from his perspective, he was sorely provoked during his twelve years as governor. He became a leading Democratic prospect but chose not to run for president in 1994. Photo credit: *Albany Times Union.*

Three Albany Power Brokers join in a public event. Former **Governor Nelson Rockefeller** stands at the podium with **Hugh Carey** immediately behind him as **Mayor Erastus Corning** is all smiles at the far right. Photo credit: *Albany Times Union*.

Senator Edward M. Kennedy at the editorial boards of Capital Newspapers seeking support in his bid for the Democratic presidential nomination in 1980. Photo credit: *Albany Times Union*.

George Pataki unseated Mario Cuomo and also served three terms as governor. He supported Harry's vision to develop Albany Riverfront as a cultural park with a re-creation of Albany's Dutch colonial settlement, Fort Orange, as the centerpiece. Photo credit: *Albany Times Union*.

Walter Mondale makes a stop on his run for reelection as Jimmy Carter's vice president in 1988. *Knickerbocker News* reporter Lise Bang-Jensen stands between the candidate and Roger Grier. Photo credit: *Albany Times Union.*

Daniel Patrick Moynihan, at right, at an editorial board meeting. With the senator and Harry, from left, are Managing Editor Dan Lynch, National Editor Paul Gibbons, cartoonist Rex Babin, City Editor Dennis Michalski, reporter Harvy Lipman, Managing Editor Bill Dowd, and Chief Editorial Writer Howard Healy. Photo credit: *Albany Times Union.*

Erastus Corning 2nd was the longest-serving mayor in America and ruled Albany's Democratic machine. His word, spoken softly, was law. He stands with **Thomas M. Whalen III**, who became mayor on Corning's death, oversaw municipal reforms, but lacked a strong vision for the city's future. Photo credit: *Albany Times Union*.

Alan Miller, Harry's first reporter hire, covered major stories for the *Times Union.* He won the Pulitzer Prize in 2003 for national reporting while a member of the *Los Angeles Times* Washington Bureau. Here he stands tall between Jack Nelson, his former Bureau Chief, and Harry at a celebration of his prize which he shared with Kevin Sack, an Atlanta colleague. Photo courtesy of the author.

Joseph Lyons was publisher of the *Times Union* for ten years. He had a close-to-the-vest management style and never accused Harry of seeking too little in resources for the newsroom. Out of the office, they were frequent tennis partners. Photo credit: *Albany Times Union*.

Timothy White replaced Joe Lyons in 1989. Here he shares upsetting news with the staff during difficult economic times. The editor and publisher were increasingly in conflict. Photo credit: *Albany Times Union*.

George R. Hearst III joined the *Times Union* as director of operations in 1989 and became publisher a decade later. Among his signature accomplishments was the purchase of a new printing press. He is a great-grandson of William Randolph Hearst, founder of the Hearst media empire. Photo credit: *Albany Times Union.*

Three Hearst executives look over new equipment at the *Times Union*. **Frank A. Bennack Jr.**, right, was CEO for twenty-eight years, leading the company to unprecedented growth. Beside him is **Gilbert Maurer**, chief operating officer. **Robert Danzig**, left, was a native son who rose from office boy to head the Hearst newspapers division. In the background is Mike Spain. Photo credit: *Albany Times Union*.

February 23, 1980
SATURDAY
Albany, N.Y. 12212
20 cents

TIMES UNION

Capital City
ALBANY
Albany County

U.S. 4, Soviets 3

LAKE PLACID JOURNAL

Hockey triumph fuels gold hopes

Associated Press

LAKE PLACID — Mark Johnson and Mike Eruzione scored goals in a 1:21 span of the third period Friday, giving the determined United States hockey team a stunning 4-3 upset triumph over the Soviet Union and keeping alive hopes of the first American hockey gold medal in the Winter Olympics since 1960.

The triumph before a frenzied crowd of 8,500 moved the United States into first place in the medals round. And a Finnish victory in the second medal round game later Friday could assure the Americans of no worse than a bronze.

The loss, the Soviets' first since a 5-4 defeat by Czechoslovakia at Grenoble, France in 1968, did not ruin Soviet chances for a gold. But it also left them in danger of missing a medal completely if Finland wins twice.

President Carter called the dressing room to congratulate coach Herb Brooks and the team after the victory.

Brooks quoted Carter as saying "we had made the American people very proud and reflected the ideals of the country."

Soviet coach Vladimir Urzinov said, "Everybody knows the game will be upset in the Soviet Union with the result of tonight's game."

Finland tied Sweden 3-3 in the second game. If the United States beats Finland on Sunday, the Americans will take the gold medal.

Mahre nosed out for slalom gold

Phil Mahre came within 10 one-hundredths of a second of an incredible upset victory in the slalom Friday, but settled for second place and the silver medal, when Ingemar Stenmark of Sweden edged all his coming and will to capture the gold on his final run. Mahre, a 22-year-old twin from Washington, was the first U.S. male skier to win a medal since 1964 when Billy Kidd won a silver and Jimmy Heuga a bronze. It was the second gold medal for the invincible Stenmark, who won the giant slalom Tuesday.

Complete Olympic coverage on Sports Pages 11 and 13

From far-off Tibet, two brothers have their wares. Page 3

More stories, photos on Page 11

AMERICANS DELIRIOUSLY HAPPY — Members of the United States hockey team throw their sticks in the air after upsetting the favored Soviet Union team, 4-3, in final-round action of the Winter Olympic Games at Lake Placid Friday.

Americans jubilant over upset

By CAROL DeMARE
Staff Writer

LAKE PLACID — They were screaming in the streets here Friday night. Cars horns blasted. Fireworks lit up the skies.

"U.S.A.! U.S.A.! U.S.A.!" they chanted.

Minutes earlier a jubilant, almost hysterical U.S.A. hockey team threw itself into an emotional embrace up in the air at the Olympic Ice Arena time and time again after defeating the Russians in a stunning upset, 4-3, keeping alive American hopes for a gold medal.

The American players threw themselves on the ice — 10, 15, 20 of them falling on top of each other, hugging each other, grabbing their goalie, their hero, Jim Craig.

And the more than 8,500 fans in the arena wouldn't quit screaming, waving hundreds of American flags, big and small, kissing each other, raising clenched fists of victory.

The game was over, but they wouldn't leave.

And at center ice stood the Russian team in red uniforms, staring in bewilderment at the American players throwing themselves at the greatest American hockey win in 20 years.

Some of the Russian players actually had their fingers in their mouths in shock as they gaped at the Americans.

Only one fan made it from his seat to the ice, a young man carrying an American flag. His shirt was up in the back and his pants hung a little low, exposing his chubby upper derriere.

The Russians waited for what seemed an eternity of celebrating, and finally the Americans skated over and the two teams exchanged the traditional after-game handshakes.

The fans spilled onto the streets of Lake Placid in a

See AMERICANS, Page 4

Soviets tie strings to pullout

By STEVEN R. HURST
Associated Press

LEONID I. BREZHNEV
... asks U.S. "guarantee"

MOSCOW — President Leonid I. Brezhnev declared Friday that the Soviet Union will pull its troops out of Afghanistan if the United States and Afghanistan's neighbors guarantee an end to "outside interference" in that backward Moslem nation.

The statement, in an otherwise toughly worded speech, came three days after European Common Market foreign ministers proposed that the Afghan crisis be cooled through international guarantees of the country's neutrality.

It was difficult to assess immediately whether the Soviet president's call for U.S. guarantees was intended as an endorsement of the "neutralization" idea and an overture to the Carter administration, or simply as a

ploy to deflect international pressure onto the United States.

In Washington, Carter administration officials said privately that Brezhnev's remarks on Afghanistan may be an effort to split the United States and its European allies on the issue.

Publicly, however, officials took a more cautious stance.

Brezhnev's remarks "will have to be examined all the way through before the administration will issue a statement," said State Department spokesman Hodding Carter.

See SOVIETS, Page 2

Anti-Soviet protests intensify in Kabul; martial law is reportedly declared. Page 2

Day 112

U.N. shah panel leaves for Iran today

Associated Press

The five man selected to hear charges against the deposed Shah of Iran will leave Geneva for Tehran at noon today, the United Nations announced Friday. But after days of uncertainty, the tie between the commission's work and the release of the American hostages being held by Iranian militants was still not clear.

In Tehran, Iranian President Abolhassan Bani-Sadr delivered a hardline law and order speech, blaming the Revolutionary Guards for providing some disturbances in northern provinces and vowing that disturbers of the peace "and all other troublemakers will be dealt with with no mercy." He said maintenance of law and order is the most important problem facing his revolutionary government.

All but two members of the international commission on the shah were in Geneva waiting for their already-confirmed departure for Tehran, U.N. chief spokesman in Geneva, Tony Curnow, told reporters that the two-assent commission members, Mohamad Bedjaoui of Algeria, who met with U.N. Secretary-General Kurt Waldheim in New York on Friday, and Louis-Edmond Pettiti of France, who went to Paris on Thursday, would return to Geneva in time for the Tehran flight.

Andres Aguilar of Venezuela, Hector Wilfred Jayewardene of Sri Lanka and Adib Daoudy of Syria, held further meetings with U.N. officials in Geneva to prepare for their work, and met representatives of organizations involved in past studies of Shah Mohammad Reza Pahlavi's regime.

The commission had been scheduled to leave for Tehran on Wednesday morning. But Waldheim announced a delay until the weekend because the Iranians will reach 18 percent this year if prices keep advancing at the same rate.

A top government inflation-fighter warned of an "ominous trend" with no relief

See U.N. PANEL, Page 1

January price surge: Largest in 6½ years

By WILLIAM J. EATON
Los Angeles Times

WASHINGTON — Consumer prices exploded in January, rising 1.4 percent for the biggest monthly increase in 6½ years and signaling that inflation is all but running out of control.

In another jolt to the economy, major banks raised the prime lending rate for their best customers to a record 16.25 percent, with one New York bank lifting its rate to 16.5 percent.

The result will be even higher interest, raised on many types of consumer loans.

The Department of Labor report on consumer prices, released Friday, showed that the inflation rate climbed to 18.6 percent on an annual basis in the last three months and will reach 18 percent this year if prices keep advancing at the same rate.

A top government inflation-fighter warned of an "ominous trend" with no relief

in sight, and there were fresh expressions of support for wage-price controls from liberal politicians and a labor leader. A White House spokesman, however, rejected controls or gasoline rationing as possible solutions to the inflation spiral.

Gasoline prices, rising at the fastest rate on record, accounted for a large part of the January increase, but every major component of the Consumer Price Index except food advanced sharply.

With the average across-the-nation price of gasoline increasing by 8.9 cents to $1.11 a gallon last month, the transportation index leaped upward by 3.1 percent, the biggest monthly advance in nearly 20 years.

The rise in the prime bank rate was the second increase in a week, reflecting the Federal Reserve Board's decision last Friday to lift its discount rate to 13 percent, also a record. The bank rate immediately affects other short-term borrowing charges, all

though it has only an indirect influence on home mortgage costs.

The January surge in consumer prices followed a 1.1 percent increase in December. The 1979 inflation rate was 13.3 percent, the highest in 33 years, and Carter has forecast a 10.4 per cent rate for this year.

"The underlying rate of inflation has started to explode," R. Robert Russell, executive director of the President's Council on Wage and Price Stability, said before the Joint Economic Committee of Congress.

"I fear it [the January increase] is consistent with the ominous trend that has taken place over the past year."

Russell added that an "explosion of wage increases" was probably inevitable, and he

See JANUARY, Page 1

Credit card users face interest rate rise. Page 1

INSIDE

Automotive	14-16
Classified	11-13
Comics	14
Death notices	19
Editorial	6
Financial	18

Living Today 2
Obituaries 19
Religion 2
Sports 11-13
TV 14
Theater 14

To call us:
[phone numbers]

WEATHER

Cloudy with occasional flurries through Sunday. High today in the low 40s, low tonight about 30°. Max. details on Page 13

Coming tomorrow in the SUNDAY TIMES UNION

Literary gatherings

Literary clubs once thrived in Capitaland but today their numbers have dwindled. Several clubs still exist however, for fortnightly discussions of literature, the arts, and contemporary topics. Mary Anna Leonard takes a look at the clubs in this week's Living Today section.

Capitaland in the '80s

Capitaland Report, the Times-Union's annual economic survey, looks at the coming decade and what it holds for the area. What's ahead in the fields of economics, technology, education, health, environment, the arts? See this special section with reports from staff writers and outside experts about what to expect from the 1980s.

Another special Olympic section

The excitement of the 1980 Winter Olympics comes to a close this weekend and the third in a series of special magazine sections, Lake Placid '80, will provide a wrapup of all the week's action, plus features and profiles of the people involved.

XIII OLYMPIC WINTER GAMES LAKE PLACID 1980

For the 1980 Winter Olympics at Lake Placid, Capital Newspapers deployed a large contingent of reporters and photographers. This front page records a historic hockey game. Photo credit: *Albany Times Union.*

CHAPTER 11

Medical Examinations

Over the years, our enterprise reporting met some of its toughest challenges writing about doctors. Judging by the usual indignant reaction, the medical community was not comfortable having its work scrutinized when the result was not laudatory. Frequently, physicians and administrators resented being questioned and deemed themselves above reproach by ordinary people. It sometimes seemed self-righteousness was taught as part of the medical school curriculum, somewhere before or after suturing. Dr. Kildare could do no wrong.

The *Times Union* published a series of articles on the dubious quality of New York State's system for regulating doctors, using the records of physician misconduct to show the impact on the public. "Examining the Doctors: New York State's Ailing System" took Alan Miller a month in 1981 to investigate and report. The finding: New York, in comparison to other states, disciplined very few physicians.

Among the examples we used from throughout the state was one involving a physician from Albany. We identified the man by name and recounted the charges against him. His case illustrated one aspect of how long a doctor continued to practice while under investigation for serious offenses. He did so without his patients becoming aware—for years—of what was going on. The doctor was charged in 1976 with being a habitual user of morphine and other substances and for prescribing speed and then obtaining six thousand pills "from a non-licensed distributor." He continued to practice until his license was revoked in 1981.

The former doctor asked our reporter not to use his name in the exposé because he was trying to get a job relating to medicine. We received phone calls from another physician and from an eminent cleric, speaking on his behalf. The clergyman did not know him personally but was enlisted by the man's pastor.

Despite these pleas, we published his name, and a woman wrote she and her neighbors felt, as they had two years earlier when the case first became public, that use of the doctor's name was not necessary and certainly not so long after the fact. She asked: "Where does it end? The physician has paid a very high price for his mistake."

When we received requests not to use the name, several editors and the reporter discussed the issue. First, we considered the seriousness of the offense that caused the doctor to surrender his license after resisting for three and half years. Then we weighed whether we needed to use any names in the articles. We decided we had to invest the important public issue with credibility. Anonymity detracted from it. Furthermore, the offenses were committed by real people against real people. The public account of these events had been too skimpy. Our series years later found little public knowledge of the doctor's wrongdoing.

We also decided it would be unfair to name doctors from distant cities but not our local one because he and his family would again suffer from the recital of his misdeeds. Next, we dealt with the argument that our doctor deserved exemption because he had influential interveners. Should someone well connected receive anonymity denied others whose condition in life meant they had no one to speak for them? Was it okay to name a burglar but not a doctor who committed malpractice? Whose wrongdoing was more devastating? A doctor who betrayed his trust did far more damage than a petty criminal.

The most compelling argument against the use of his name was its possible interference with his genuine efforts to make a new start. We also needed to consider what withholding his name would mean to the local families afflicted by his actions.

If there was a clincher to help us decide, it was the former doctor himself, who for years after he had surrendered his license continued to advertise himself as a doctor practicing internal medicine. He did so through a special listing in the yellow pages, which had to be purchased each year. When our reporter called the phone number, the answering service identified itself as the office of the local doctor. In fact, the misconduct had not entirely ended.

Our next notable confrontation with the medical community occurred in 1985. This time it was because a medical center withheld the names of two doctors who incorrectly injected a cancer patient, who died. The story did not stem from our initiative. Rather, people employed by Albany Medical Center contacted reporters at the *Times Union* and *Knickerbocker News*. They said they were impelled do so because they believed the hospital was trying to cover up a grave mistake.

The incorrect treatment occurred on February 27, but the medical center did not make a public announcement until more than a week later. It came after a *Knick* reporter asked the Health Department about the case. Obviously tipped off, the next day the medical center, rather than responding to the reporter, held a press conference to announce what had happened to Lillian Cedeno. She was five-and-a-half-months pregnant when she checked into the hospital earlier that month for treatment of sinus cancer. During her care, her spine was injected with a drug intended only for intravenous administration. This was done by two doctors, one a first-year and the other a third-year resident. One observed as the other took the bottle, clearly marked for intravenous application only, to extract the medicine into a syringe. An hour later, a nurse discovered the mistake. Within days, Lillian Cedeno fell into a coma. In the middle of March, doctors delivered her daughter by cesarean section. The child died twenty-four days later.

We pressed for identification of the doctors, and the hospital steadfastly refused, on grounds of guarding their privacy. A drumbeat of articles, as well as editorials, kept the issue alive in the pages of our newspapers.

Some of the stories dealt with the number of hours residents were compelled to work on their shifts, perhaps leading to fatigue and errors of drastic magnitude. Albany Med's leadership maintained silence as their best defense. Lillian Cedeno's parents supported us in our quest as the hospital refused their request for the doctors' names. One letter to the editor asked whether anyone could imagine that sort of treatment being inflicted on a better-connected family than the Cedenos.

There was much interest among the public but also vigorous criticism of our intense presentation. The hospital's firm stand resulted in news articles offering revelations bit by bit. Most of the objections came from the medical community or those associated with it. They took it personally and wanted us to lay off. They argued our coverage undermined an institution serving humanitarian needs. At a Sunday afternoon cocktail party at a friend's home, a medical center board member and his wife were guests, as were Annie and I. They ostentatiously ignored me, but the wife took on Annie, berating her for what I was doing. Eighty-six days after being injected, Lillian Cedeno succumbed. She was twenty-one.

In the middle of the unfolding of these events, the chief executive of the hospital phoned me at home to ask us to halt the unrelenting coverage. I was sympathetic, although it was his refusal to respond to obvious questions that fueled our persistence. Considering that Albany Med was a singularly important local institution, I offered advice. I told him he should jump into an icy bathtub—hold a press conference to fully address the outstanding questions.

That, I said, would result in a major story on Page 1—but it would largely mark the end. The bloodletting, as he saw it, slice by daily slice, would be over. He replied that his lawyers would not let him do so because of the risk of lawsuits.

After an autopsy, the Albany County coroner ruled Lillian Cedeno died from her tumor, not the toxic injection. In rebuttal, lawyers for the Cedeno family cited the pathologist's ties to the medical center and its efforts to diminish financial liability. For its part, the state Office of Professional Medical Conduct cleared the doctors of professional misconduct. A committee of the group criticized the hospital for "an over reliance on medical residents for critical patient care procedures." It summed up: The "tragic accident was the combined result of human error, inadequate drug controls and the administration of a toxic drug by residents not sufficiently supervised, trained in or knowledgeable of its potential lethal effects."

The *Times Union* reported that "largely as a result of the Cedeno case, the Health Department directed hospitals across the state to ensure that resident and intern doctors are supervised by senior physicians during delicate chemotherapy procedures." The Cedeno family settled their legal action for the wrongful deaths of their daughter and grand-daughter out of court for $400,000, up from an initial $100,000 offer. If the newspapers had not engaged public opinion with their reporting, it could be asked whether the reforms would have been as extensive.

TU reporter Robert Whitaker delivered our next significant encounter with the medical community. This time it resulted not from a tip but from his own curiosity. He was working on a story in 1992 about trauma surgery. He picked up hints that something was not as advertised about what then was a radical improvement in medicine: laparoscopic surgery. It was a wonderful development. No longer would patients with gall-bladder disease have to endure invasive operations. Instead, laparoscopy combined video technology and fiber optics to provide surgeons with an astonishing new tool. They could insert the device through a small incision, view the infected organ, and extract the gallbladder. No longer was it necessary to cut the abdominal muscle. The patient got to leave the hospital after one day as opposed to the five it took with the traditional treatment. It was so much easier on the patient—if the surgery was done correctly by a well-trained physician.

Whitaker discovered traditional safeguards were sometimes by-passed in the rush to adopt the new procedure. Some surgeons trained as little as one weekend and practiced on one pig before operating on humans. Along with overwhelming success, there was a rash of bungled operations.

The three-part series, "The Hidden Perils of Video Surgery," followed by two additional articles, angered and upset some doctors and patients who were grateful for their successful laparoscopies. Others wrote that the articles nearly dissuaded them from taking advantage of the new procedure. We also heard from patients who had bad experiences and wished they had chosen the old though more painful operation instead.

Our purpose in pursuing this story was not to frighten people, but to inform them so that they would be aware of the possible risks and could make a thoughtful decision. Readers were also alerted to question their prospective surgeon about the training he or she had in this procedure. We hoped our reporting—which other media subsequently followed—encouraged health departments and insurance companies to mandate comprehensive training in laparoscopy. Many doctors Whitaker interviewed shared the sentiment. We thought doctors who wrote off the harm to patients as a routine part of a learning curve missed the point: More demanding training increased successful outcomes.

Our three emblematic encounters with the medical community revealed inadequate state oversight of malpractice, insufficient supervision of new doctors, and what can happen in a rush to apply radical technological advances without requiring essential practical education. This work reflected basic aspects of good journalism. Two were the product of reporter and editor curiosity and initiative, and one came from a tip from insiders wanting to right a perceived wrong. The circling of the wagons, as occurred on all three of the enterprise assignments, was in no way unique to the healing arts. Bankers did it; politicians refined the tactic into a high art form. No one enjoys having a failing exposed to public view. When it counts, the responsibility of the press is to do exactly that.

CHAPTER 12

Heavyweight Advice

I first met Seymour Hersh when I was on the foreign desk of the *Washington Post*. As a freelancer, he broke the My Lai story of the massacre of South Vietnamese villagers by American troops. Ben Bradlee, miffed that his own people did not come up with the scoop, bought Hersh's work for the *Post*. Before publishing, he wanted Hersh's sources thoroughly checked. It was my assignment to see to it. The exposé earned him the 1970 Pulitzer Prize in international reporting.

At the *TU* and *Knick*, we were committed to a continuing effort to enhance skills and morale by inviting distinguished journalists to share their insights. Among the best known was Hersh, who had become the iconic investigative reporter of his generation. He spent a day with us in March 1984. He was more than worth his $1,000 fee as our reporters and editors enthusiastically participated in his two presentations.

Over the years, others came as well. In the spring of 1993, we hit a jackpot. Within a span of two weeks, we were fortunate to snare Haynes Johnson, my colleague from the *Washington Post*, by then a columnist for the paper and a writer of books. Donald Barlett and James Steele of the *Philadelphia Inquirer*, famed investigative reporters, followed. Then came Jack Anderson, the nationally syndicated columnist.

With newspapers under extreme economic pressure, each of our guests in an hour or two reminded us in their distinct voices of the basic rules to produce effective journalism. Haynes, who won his Pulitzer in 1966 while at the *Washington Star* for coverage of the civil rights movement in Selma, Alabama, underscored the need for reporters to "get dust on their shoes," going to see for themselves whenever possible in place of reporting what others saw.

Don and Jim, who won two Pulitzers, shared their enduring enthusiasm for in-depth reporting. They urged us to write and rewrite and to make our work lucid for readers.

Jack Anderson, whose stock in trade was uncovering the best-kept secrets of government bureaucracies, stood conventional wisdom on its head and told us that anonymous sources were more credible than officials speaking on the record. Those named will share only what they are paid to say, which time and again does not correspond to the truth.

These celebrated veterans of our craft, in their persons and accomplishments, provided the best kind of encouragement for our staff, many of them young, who had a long career journey ahead into a media world in flux and waiting to be defined.

Another element in the process of upgrading the quality of our work was to stress accuracy. This imperative weighed on my mind when our people strayed from basic precepts. In January 1984, I felt compelled to issue a memo to the staff. Attribution was extremely important, and I stressed the need to make it as detailed as possible. "If we interview the author of a document, from which we then quote or paraphrase, the attribution is not to the document but to the author. Only if we had read the document ourselves can we accurately and reliably quote from it."

Maintaining standards had its comic moments. A sports reporter wrote "Vunder Kint" to describe an impressive young tennis player. Apparently, he derived the word from something he once heard but never saw spelled. It is, of course, wunderkind, with the German W sounding like the V in English. I reminded the sports editor that we had agreed only days before this bit of embarrassment was published "that reporters would not use foreign words if they did not know how spell them and editors would not permit them into the paper if they did not."

I also cautioned against one of the most common of journalistic offenses, mind reading: "One reporter recently wrote that local politicos 'sensed' a mood and then took an action. It is a total impossibility for any one of us to know what another human being sensed, thought, believed, or felt. None of us can read minds. Therefore, we can report what someone said they sensed, thought, believed, or felt. Or we can say what we ourselves felt."

I said certain trigger phrases should be used with wariness, such as "little noticed" and "carefully worded." The same applies to "denied, admitted, conceded," all of which suggest mind reading or conclusion jumping. These expressions lack nuance and lend themselves to going further than fact warrants. Being thoughtful wordsmiths redounds to the credibility of the journalism we aspire to practice.

I also issued instructions about anonymous sources: "These may be used with care and thought when required for a story. The reporter grants confidentiality, not the source. She or he does so on behalf of the newspaper. It is the policy of these newspapers that no reporter may place an unidentified source in a story without sharing that source's name with at least one editor." I clearly had learned my lesson from Watergate, when I did not insist on knowing the identity of Deep Throat from the first.

Mind reading not only tarries as a journalistic temptation, it thrives. It is frequently employed not merely to plumb an individual's mind but to describe what an entire community thinks.

It's quite true that an editor, for example, informed by the people met in his or her work, after a time should acquire a sixth sense about the community. While editors get around more than most people, the environs traveled by many, though extensive, are by no means comprehensive. Editors tend to talk more to people in authority and power, those with better jobs and more education, than to the rest.

Furthermore, you can't make the call based on letters to the editor, because partisans of an issue tend to write disproportionately compared to those not so motivated. Similarly, you cannot really tell from radio call-in shows. To make conclusive judgments from any of these various ways, along with today's whirlwind caused by the internet and social media, would be to impose the views of a few upon the many. Doing so runs the risk of missing the target by a wide margin. A ban on mind reading in journalism should be as inviolate as willful untruthfulness. Instituting such a ban is, of course, not realistic, because mind reading is such a handy technique to bolster a narrative. However, it can be disparaged and discouraged. Tough to do when the best of the best abuses the most basic rules.

In 1984, a *New Yorker* writer admitted altering facts and making up conversations and putting them into the mouths of people he created all for the purpose of finding what he called the larger truth. That made quite a splash and caused me to underline our policy: "There is to be no alteration of fact. Quotes we use are the quotes spoken by real people. Nothing is fictionalized or amended from the information as we discover it. . . . Our policy is to be frank and truthful in our work. We don't lie to ourselves or to our readers."

One of the biggest challenges to credibility of news media remains what since the 1960s has come to be called the New Journalism. It was hatched at the *Herald Tribune* while I labored at the paper in various capacities and reflected that newspaper's valiant, desperate, but finally failed effort to stay afloat. Tom Wolfe, who went on to great fame as a writer of perceptive and relevant fiction, led the charge at the *Trib*. His writing was undoubtedly brilliant, especially for a newspaper. Much of it depended on his intuition and on reading other people's minds to ascribe their motivations.

Since those days until our time, the once-respected values of objectivity have taken a relentless beating. At its beginning, New Journalism's rallying ethos was that desiccated objectivity obscured the truth of the forest because it overly focused on the factualism of the trees. New Journalism relied on the individual writer's viewpoint to reveal elusive truths subverted by straightlaced objectivity. It was a distinctively compelling force because the emphasis on a strong narrative made newspapers more readable.

Objectivity means keeping personal bias out of stories. Bias in this context grows out of looking for facts you are predisposed to find and overlooking those that contradict your suppositions. People used to criticize the press because they perceived its failures to be objective. Nowadays, with our society starkly divided into hostile camps, bias is generally more accepted by the public on the same side but rejected by those on an opposing one.

Many prominent journalists maintain that even if objectivity were a virtue, it would be unattainable. As no human being is capable of being totally objective, especially journalists at their work, why even pretend to try? Those like me who make objectivity a keystone maintain that ours is not an argument for flat, bloodless, boring stories. Nor do we think it is easily accomplished. Indeed, journalists should harbor ideas, theories, and viewpoints. What they also need is self-awareness of those proclivities and not allowing them to distort the integrity of their work.

Objectivity does not signify that context should be slighted. Rather, context itself needs to be reported instead of posited. The complaint that objectivity is useless unless it is perfect is as absurd as pronouncing justice useless unless it is perfect. We have a functioning and effective legal system, which has many faults. Constant vigilance is required for equal justice under the law. The same rationale applies to objectivity in journalism.

It is an uphill slog for those who do not want to settle for the kind of journalism produced by *Rolling Stone* magazine in 2014, when the most basic rules about checking allegations were discarded in service of a most worthy cause. Increasing reports of sexual assaults on college campuses required public pressure for academic authorities to take effective counteraction. To illustrate the problem, *Rolling Stone* published a sensational article describing the gang rape of a college student by seven fraternity brothers. It was too good a story to pass up. It was timely and righteous. Only after publication, through the efforts of other, more punctilious journalists, was it found to be false in its major assertions that could be checked. The *Rolling Stone* story basically transmitted the allegations of a woman who threatened to withdraw her cooperation if the writer and editors attempted to question the people whom she accused. In short, a travesty of an exposé intended to spur reforms.

Not long after that scandal, the *New Yorker* published a review of a biography of one of its writers, Joseph Mitchell, considered among the magazine's revered storytellers, much admired for his vivid portraits of odd but otherwise obscure people. The biography revealed that Mitchell "made things up." This in a publication whose unique reputation was built not only on the quality of the writing in its pages, but also on its scrupulous fact checking, which elevated it to the highest rank in journalism. According to the review, such toying with the truth went further than Mitchell. Additional finagling was not outlawed by those able to know it was going on, including one of the *New Yorker*'s founders. The magazine that to this day labels its fiction failed to tag its suspect journalism. Instead, it tolerated fakery while basking in a reputation its behavior at times tarnished. What a blow to the ranks of ink-stained wretches who over the years yearned for their work to appear in its venerated pages.

Apropos of fact checking, one of the longest talks I had with Bob Woodward, after my *Washington Post* days, occurred in the fall of 1987 and was caused by publication of his recent book, titled *Veil: The Secret Wars of the CIA, 1981–1987*. The claims and assertions made by him in the book drew criticism and rebuke not only from President Reagan but also from colleagues in the press corps. One was Flora Lewis, a *New York Times* columnist and a friend of mine from my tour in South Vietnam as a correspondent in 1969, a couple of years before I met Woodward. So much turmoil afflicted our trade over what he had written, down to questioning Woodward's integrity, I decided to interview him and see what I could make of the matter.

Two questions emerged from the rising storm that implicated the late Bill Casey when he was director of Central Intelligence. The first concerned the integrity and accuracy of the book, which was based on interviews over nearly three years with some 250 sources, many not identified by name. Most controversial of those interviews was one with Casey in the hospital after the CIA chief had undergone brain surgery. Casey's widow claimed the interview could not have taken place because security agents guarded her husband throughout his hospital stay.

The second question stemmed from what Woodward wrote about the interview. He concluded his book describing how Casey acknowledged with a nod of his head that extra money raised through sales of arms to Iran had been diverted to the US-supported Contra rebels in Nicaragua, then battling a communist regime led by Daniel Ortega.

Casey's involvement in the secret funding was one of the mysteries emanating from the televised congressional Iran-Contra hearings. Marine Lieutenant Colonel Oliver North was the only person to testify to the belief of Casey's awareness. Because no one else supported North on this point, by itself it might be interpreted as the colonel's attempt to clear himself of responsibility by blaming a higher official no longer alive to contradict him.

Thus the nub of the second question: Why was this account not published in the *Washington Post*, the paper for which Woodward worked then and now, when it happened the winter preceding publication of the book? Was it withheld so that Woodward could squirrel away his scoop to promote this latest in a series of best-selling books?

For many in the news business this was an important concern. Flora Lewis, among others, thought Bob's reporting was crucial information for the congressional hearings to have. My colleague editors in spirited discussions at the *Times Union* were more concerned about the relationship of a reporter, his newspaper, and its readers.

As far as Woodward's credibility, his record was open for examination. His work with Carl Bernstein to expose the Watergate scandal and cover-up, in the face of daunting obstacles, testifies to his bona fides. As Woodward's editor during Watergate and afterward, I had come to learn, time and again, he was trustworthy. He would not make up a visit and a conversation. It was much more likely security around the bed-ridden Casey was less thorough than the authorities claimed. When I worked with him and afterward, he was a skeptical reporter, even about the reporting his own enterprise turned up. He was not infallible, but his record showed he was very, very good.

Whether Casey nodded affirmatively, only Casey could say for sure, I concluded. What looked like a confirming nod to Woodward might have been a gesture responding to a quite different causation. The nodding of a seriously sick man or his muttering "I believed" in response to the question of why he approved the diversion of the money did not constitute credible, usable evidence. I don't think it would have done the congressional committee any good.

The *Post* was informed of the Casey interview at the time it happened and properly decided not to use it. Although insufficiently lucid for his newspaper, Woodward thought it was appropriate for the book. In the context of the fuller story recounting Casey's activities and his personality and character, he deemed it dramatically relevant.

To those who questioned the propriety of Woodward's visit to Casey's hospital room, Woodward responded that the scandal was no one else apparently tried. He was turned away the first time and succeeded the second time, after Casey's deputy had reported his boss doing well.

After interviewing the principals, including Woodward's chief at the *Post*, my conclusion, which I shared with my editors and our readers, was that the Veil incident, which stirred uproar, confirmed Woodward's intensity as a reporter who brought intelligence to an assignment and the drive and the courage to get the story.

More than twenty years later, Woodward appeared at the Massachusetts College of Liberal Arts in nearby North Adams, Massachusetts. When *TU* Associate Editor Mike Spain found out about it, he suggested I invite him to stop by at the *Times Union* and talk with the staff. He would be flying out of Albany airport to return to Washington. Bob readily agreed and spent an hour and a half with us, talking about the parlous state of the newspaper business ("It's like the polar icecap . . . it's receding") and led a freewheeling "discussion about the inner workings of the president's hubris and the role of a free press in exposing it," in the words of Paul Grondahl's report that appeared in the next day's *Times Union*. He also touched on George W. Bush's reluctance to do his homework, which Bob found as he interviewed the president for the book he was then working on. When pressed by *TU* questioners to describe me, he made me look good, saying: "He's a tough sonofabitch."

That encounter in 2008 provided an opportunity for each of us, Bob and Harry, to define our enduring relationship, much of it long distance. After he spoke to the staff, I emailed him to express our thanks again: "Your words made a huge impact on the staffers." I wrote he gave a generous gift to "some who were kids or who were not born when Watergate happened." Bob emailed me in response: "What an interesting and eventful overlap our lives have had. My gratitude to you will never cease. I have benefited from your toughness and generosity both."

CHAPTER 13

Innards of the Craft

David Laventhol worked with me at the *Herald Tribune* on the foreign desk and at the *Washington Post,* where he played the salient role in the creation of the Style section. He went on to become publisher of *New York Newsday* and the *Los Angeles Times.* Dave returned to New York from LA and volunteered to run the *Columbia Journalism Review* after Parkinson's disease forced his retirement as publisher. The illness struck him at the height of his brilliant attainments. In the opening stages of this degenerative illness, he was as sharp as ever. He proposed I write a piece on the relevance of schools of journalism in the year 2000. The substance of what I wrote then is, if anything, more pertinent these days, as the craft's traditional values over the intervening years have been steadily undermined.

In my day, editors had slight regard for a journalism education. Especially at the undergraduate level, J schools were looked down on at the metros. Instead of a journalism degree giving a job applicant an advantage, those with an English or political science major were preferred. In contrast, journalism schools appeared to be the clear choice of smaller papers not inclined to expend the resources to train newcomers. They sought young people who could (then) operate a typewriter and walk into their first job having been taught enough to grind out work from day one. All the necessary formulas to construct a story they likely would have to report and write, including the number of words in a sentence and the added value of cover provided by the attribution "police said," had been absorbed in journalism school. The metros' dismissive attitude began to change as they became ever more enmeshed with the rapidly developing technologies. They now saw the need for new hires to bring additional skill sets to the job. J school grads had been trained to use computers.

With their reputation enhanced among larger newspapers, to my mind, journalism schools were well placed to perform increasingly compelling functions. They were the handiest places to teach not only technical proficiency but to instill the necessary standards of integrity, then, as now, under much stress. In latter days, that stress arose from the headlong rush to cultivate new sources of revenue with all sorts of cross-the-line accommodations. It blurred the mission to tell the news without fear or favor and make damn sure it's right.

J schools now had an added role: to step into the breach created by newsrooms giving way to opportunism in tougher times. Young men and a growing number of women entering the field needed to understand what was once taught by example on the job: the values that brought credibility to the American press. In addition to instructing students with correct precepts and practices, J schools were the right place to inculcate ethics that ought to govern newspapers. Students needed instruction in how to distinguish between factuality (if truth is too grandiose and elusive) and puffery. They had to be taught the core values of fairness, impartiality, accurate attribution, and a sense of accountability. These go along with the awesome powers to publish. Most important, they should be schooled to stand up to coercion by the expedient and the mediocre. In the words of the Committee of Concerned Journalists, "to provide citizens with accurate and reliable information they need to function in a free society." Were this done broadly, it would infuse the craft of journalism with professional standards to help contain efforts to mingle promotion and advertising with journalism and guard against the assimilation of fiction into what is sold to readers as nonfiction.

A critical aspect of informing readers was and remains the use of confidential sources. As a member of the American Society of Newspaper Editors, I served on its ethics committee, led by a former *Post* colleague, my first metro deputy editor, Andrew Barnes, who had moved on to become the editor of Florida's *St. Petersburg Times*. To contribute to the committee's work, I volunteered to examine how the terms of art involving confidential sources were understood and applied by America's editors and by the public officials and business leaders who most frequently constituted the great unnamed. We devised and sent questionnaires to the three groups. Of the more than one hundred editors and reporters, fifty-one responded. An appropriately adapted questionnaire was sent to the fifty governors, the mayors of the twenty largest cities, the thirteen members of the president's cabinet, as well as to the executives of the top fifty of the Fortune 500. For the nonjournalists surveyed, we stipulated responses had to be by the officials and the executives themselves and not their public relations people. Response from them was skimpy, not permitting any general conclusions to be drawn.

The returns were crunched by Robert Provost, marketing maven at Capital Newspapers. Among newspaper folk, they showed a general agreement about the meaning of "off the record" (you could use what you learned to inform yourself but not publish it in any form); not as much about "background" (differing on the degree of attribution permissible to publish); far less of "deep background." As for "not for attribution," the responses left up in the air how much beyond the source's name was not usable. Each newspaper went pretty much its own way in how it instructed its staff on the definition of the terms. Among journalists, most said the power to grant confidentiality rested with the reporter. On this crucial point, the sources themselves strongly disagreed: they claimed that right for themselves.

The survey's most instructive finding, published as an article I wrote for the *ASNE Bulletin* in the fall of 1988, was the almost unanimous agreement among journalists that the use of confidential sources risked a newspaper's credibility with readers. Officials and business leaders indicated their own disdain for them. My comment was: "If journalists don't like confidential sources and potential sources don't like the role, why are they so commonplace? Somebody, it seems, is not telling it as it is, and there lies one of our bigger problems."

Governor Cuomo was among those solicited. I wrote him: "I am sending you a copy of the study even though you did not participate. That's because I have a sweet nature."

We took a major step to demystify ourselves when we invited the public to sit in on our Page 1 conference at 4:15 in the afternoon. Editors gathered then and there daily to decide what the next morning's paper would look like. Representatives of local, national, and business news, features, graphics, and photography met with the managing editor and editor. All of them were equipped with what we called the budget, a list of the stories being worked on. Each department then argued for the ones deemed worthy of consideration for the front page or for prominent display in another section of the newspaper. The chance of appealing to a large, diverse readership was enormously enhanced by having several qualified staffers stirring the brew to be served. In the end, the managing editor made the final picks but only after full and usually vigorous debate. I reserved and rarely exercised the authority to overrule the ME's call.

Frequently, the discussion about the day's news stimulated ideas for improving how we would report it with supporting articles we called sidebars, as well as for follow-up stories in the days and weeks to come.

The visitors energized our editors, who clearly did not mind being observed as they argued their viewpoints. We got constructive feedback, either immediately or in bread-and-butter letters. We also got criticism, which was a purpose of the enterprise. I received a letter of apology from one man who attended. It arrived many years afterward and took me by surprise. "I came," David Curley wrote,

> hoping to get a better business section. . . . I was assured by you that the change for the better was in the works.
> I then started to berate you, picking on your tie, and just about everything about you; I was completely wrong and I don't know to this day why I was that way. . . . I am sorry for insulting you that day. Please accept my apology.

I wrote back: "I've tried very hard, but I cannot remember being offended by you. Please don't agonize about the matter any longer."

Newspaper work was strenuous and tiring; at times, it was exhilarating. The ever-present tension of having to perform on deadline was compensated by the output of work of consequence, formatted in black and white for the world to read. Almost every day you faced new situations and challenges, which demanded ready access to the best qualities within you to effectively communicate to readers, enabling them to make use of the information. When it came successfully together, it created a powerful feeling of achievement for having bested obstacles.

This made up for the times when it did not work out well.

As a very young editor, I got a nervous stomach when assigned to "run the desk"—on my own oversee a news operation. This was my assignment every Sunday, a day colleagues with more seniority had off. It resembled what one read happened to actors before they went on stage. In time, experience overcame the queasiness. Despite my distress, I did not wish myself someplace else.

With the passing years my responsibilities increased. Many mornings I arose knowing a daunting pile of administrative paperwork awaited me at my office in the newsroom. A newspaper editor risks being overwhelmed. Stuff pours in without hindrance. You can spend all your time on it and be terribly busy. You need to keep your mission in mind, breast the floodtide, to make your way close to the heart of the newspaper, the stories and the people who report, edit, and photograph them. That's where happiness resides, not in the diddly-squat of bureaucratic minutiae. To my mind, good newspaper people never are totally satisfied because they are strivers: Tomorrow's newspaper has to be better than the one just wrapped up.

In the fall of 1984, the Hearst publishers and editors gathered for their annual meeting for the first time in Albany. The choice of location for the meeting was recognition of the performance of the newspapers. A full program was laid out by three editors from the Hearst stable, including me. I managed to get Governor Cuomo to speak to the group. The previous July he keynoted the Democratic National Convention that nominated Walter Mondale. In his address, Cuomo took on President Reagan's depiction of America as "the shining city on the hill." Cuomo's speech was a rebuttal. He said while the view might be accurate from the porch of Reagan's ranch, on the streets of the nation's cities too much poverty endured. With his oratory, Cuomo attained national attention and following.

Consequently, the Hearst editors and publishers made an attentive audience and the governor was a big hit, though most if not all of the publishers and a lot of the editors were not of Cuomo's political stripe. Danny Andrews, editor of the Plainview, Texas, *Daily Herald*, decades later remembered: "During the Q and A Mary Anne Dolan, editor of the *Los Angeles Herald Examiner*, asked something like 'Don't you think Geraldine Ferraro is a bit disingenuous to say she knows nothing of her husband's real estate holdings?'"

Danny continued: "Cuomo said he had high regard for her as a lawyer and went on to say that 'Tippy and I went out to Logan and lobbied Fritz to take her as his running mate.' Not Speaker of the House Tip O'Neill. . . . I thought, 'That's coming straight out of the horse's mouth.'"

During the election campaign, Bill Hearst called to urge me to drop *Doonesbury* as other papers had because the cartoon was too political. I pointed out we earlier moved it to the op-ed page because we decided it belonged there rather than with the comics. I told Bill that if we canceled the strip, one of our competitors was sure to pick it up. In a similar vein, he said he hoped our two papers wouldn't split on their presidential endorsement. To me one of the benefits of having two editorial pages was that our papers could present two sides of an argument if each side had one. Finally, he said: "I don't care what you do, so long as you support Reagan." Interference of this sort by New York headquarters was not unknown but not common.

On October 30, 1984, a select group of Hearst newspaper editors, Washington bureau editors, along with the top Hearst corporate executives were invited to the White House to meet with President Reagan in the Cabinet Room. It was a rather stiff session, with the corporate types sitting on either side of the president, closely positioned to lob him adoring questions as the editors tried their best to get at the substance of issues then under public discussion. My question was based on a recent report on Central America from a commission headed by Henry Kissinger. It showed each year the increase in births there more than consumed whatever economic growth was achieved, only in part because of the instability of prices for their export commodities. The basic problem was rising population. The president's answer was a rambling recital of what had been done, which was to enlist private US investors in the effort to improve Central American economies and a general statement about his administration's support for many family planning initiatives. If countries had a birth rate problem, "they can do it themselves" to find the solution. He did not mention his administration's imposition of more stringent conditions than already were written into US foreign aid law for receiving such assistance if they in any number of ways directly or indirectly funded abortion services. I could see James Baker, his chief of staff, leaning forward with what I took to be concern as his boss seemed to grope his way through the reply.

More instructive was Reagan's attire. He wore a dark brown suit when the political class preferred dark gray, midnight blue, or black. While he might have a problem dealing forthrightly with an issue on which he may not have been properly briefed, it demonstrated the aplomb of a man comfortable in his own skin.

CHAPTER 14

Courts v. the Press

Governor Cuomo, among the nation's foremost Democratic officehold-
ers, in 1985 appointed Sol Wachtler, a Republican, as chief judge of the
Court of Appeals, the state's highest tribunal. Judge Wachtler inherited
a concomitant responsibility as chairman of the Fair Trial/Free Press
Conference, a group of judges, lawyers, journalists, law enforcement representatives, and related social service advocates. Their purpose was to
discuss and attempt to reconcile basic contradictions between the Sixth
Amendment guarantee of a fair trial and the First Amendment guarantee
of a free press. It is a discourse that won't ever end, nor should it. The
conference created a forum for recurring disagreements to be talked out.

The vice chair of the conference was reserved for the press, and Judge
Wachtler asked me to take it on. The secretary was selected from the bar.
When I began my first one-year term, Mayor Whalen was in that post.

Wachtler was an outstanding jurist. His record on the court before
and after he led it was marked by noteworthy decisions, including making
spousal rape a crime and protecting newspapers from undue exposure
for libel lawsuits. He was a person with a brilliant future, prospectively
as governor and in the long term possibly as president (that might have
made him the first Jew to attain the office). His professional attainments
were reinforced by his good looks and an infectious friendly manner.

At the Fair Trial/Free Press annual meeting, the constituent factions
presented their viewpoints on matters then on their minds. It provided
an unparalleled opportunity, for those who frequently disagreed and saw
the world through different lenses, to sit around a large conference table,

getting to know each other as they listened and debated varied concerns. Wachtler conducted these meetings hospitable to all sides.

I could not believe it when in 1992, John Caher, one of our top reporters on state government and courts, reached me with a message late one night while I was at a reception for the Albany Symphony at the Palace Theatre. His astonishing news was the arrest of Chief Judge Wachtler. The charge was harassment of his ex-lover and her daughter, including extortion of money. The scandal and trial led to his resignation and Governor Cuomo's selection of Judge Judith Kaye to lead the court. As with Wachtler, the new chief judge and I developed a close working relationship. She was the first woman to serve on this court and first again to head it. We lunched regularly, frequently in her elegant chambers, on cottage cheese and crackers. It was a treat to be in her company and have the chance to talk over with her one-on-one the seemingly endless conflicts between the news media and the law. Her depth of knowledge and fair-mindedness were widely acknowledged and celebrated. She was a determined jurist and expanded the New York State court system and its ways of rendering justice. Her good name continued to thrive when statutory retirement age forced her to step down. She holds the record as the longest-serving chief judge. In her retirement, governors turned to her to oversee sensitive or potentially explosive investigations, knowing that her sterling character and demonstrated talents guaranteed a good job that would earn widespread credibility and respect among the public.

The annual conference under Chief Judge Kaye during her first years continued in an art deco meeting room on the sixty-fourth floor of Rockefeller Center in Midtown Manhattan, and the discussion generally adhered to the earlier template. At one of the last of these, the usefulness of the conference was demonstrated. The televised O. J. Simpson trial then under way was the focus of our discussion at our May 1995 meeting. The lawyers on the panel were most troubled by what was transmitted. Even those who supported cameras in the courts were appalled. What happened in Judge Lance Ito's Los Angeles courtroom for them was a travesty of typical trials.

In stark contrast, the news media representatives were close to unanimous in assessing the TV coverage as informative and instructive. During the two hours of discussion, it appeared that perhaps the greater irritant was the cameras outside the courtroom rather than the ones inside. Late-night cable specials were deprecated because of their worst aspect, the flamboyant commentators, invariably lawyers, speculating about the impact of the day's testimony on the eventual verdict.

The media members of the panel were more distressed by the tabloid TV shows that exploited each development in the Simpson saga, whether in court or out. The consensus among the larger group was that there ought to be a law—or at least some rules of constraint. They feared the speculation, impermissible in court, would filter into the sequestered jury's consciousness and undermine the very concept of a fair trial. The critics took little note of the gavel-to-gavel coverage and the high quality of the legal commentators on those programs.

The heartfelt and sincere criticism underscored many of the conflicts between press and courts. From the media perspective, the legal establishment sought from cameras in the courts validation of what it does and how it does it. If the camera relayed a picture that did not fit the preferred image, they concluded something must be wrong with the camera. The news people, on the other hand, valued cameras for their ability to record images that might lead to beneficial reforms. The value of the Simpson trial was its revelation of the fallibility of a judge and the role that wealth played to afford a defendant a vigorous defense. Those were important lessons to inform the greater public.

An important consequence of my association with Fair Trial/Free Press began in 1987 when I was selected to serve on an advisory committee on Cameras in the Courts, because as vice chair I'm pretty sure Chief Judge Wachtler wanted me on it, although the invitation came from the chief administrative judge of the state. The committee was to assist and evaluate an eighteen-month experiment having cameras, both still and TV, authorized for courts in selected counties around the state.

The committee comprised twenty-two "distinguished" citizens from journalism, the law, psychiatry, and academia. Richard Heffner, a professor and admired moderator of a highbrow TV program, *The Open Mind*, was the chairman. Floyd Abrams, the esteemed First Amendment lawyer, was on board, as was Kenneth B. Clark, a respected psychologist, educator, and civil rights leader. From the start, Heffner made clear his unalterable opposition to cameras in the courts, probably because he knew television so well.

Over the span of the committee's work it became clear that the preponderant opposition was to TV cameras (the stills of the pencil press hardly came up in discussion). The opponents intended to use the (mostly) sensible restrictions (i.e., don't film jurors and the like) as a way to hammer the experiment into failure. Because the more vigorous opponents were academics teaching journalism, I compared a trivial violation by a TV station to a student not attaining an A in a course and as a consequence failing it. I argued every violation should be noted, but only if it interfered with a fair trial was it pertinent. I held that a lot of distractions likely occur during a trial, but it proceeds nevertheless to a fitting conclusion.

In the end, Heffner, despite his oppositionist views, oversaw a report supporting legislation to permit cameras in courts permanently, albeit under the strenuous restrictions in place and additional ones that would strangle their use in practice. No permanent legislation resulted, only the extension of the experiment for two years.

A second advisory committee was empaneled, consisting of five persons. I was asked once more to be the communications representative. Since it was clear that TV and not newspaper cameras were the true subject under discussion, I argued unsuccessfully for a TV producer to be chosen in my place. I had no higher hopes for the second committee than I had experienced from the first. The result was an advisory committee for the second time recommending making cameras in court permanent. For a year, cameras were suspended before being renewed, this time for a term of two and a half years.

A third committee was formed. This time I was nominated by the Speaker of the Assembly. The chair was a Bronx judge who was quite familiar to the public. Burton R. Roberts was the model for Tom Wolfe's judge in his novel *The Bonfire of the Vanities*. This committee of twelve held its first meeting in New York City in June 1993. Judge Roberts was a forceful advocate for the First Amendment. Less than a year later, we issued our report, to which eleven out of the twelve members subscribed.

The lone dissenter was the prominent defense attorney Jack Littman. The report concluded, "the benefits of New York's cameras in the courts program are substantial [and] serve important educational functions." It continued: "benefits heavily outweigh the minimal, if any, negative effects. . . . Notably, no criminal conviction in New York has ever been reversed on the ground that the presence of cameras in the courtroom interfered with the defendant's right to a fair trial."

Of course, the state legislature, stocked with lawyers, still hesitated, and a fourth advisory committee was formed under the leadership of the dean of the Fordham University School of Law, John Feerick. Fortunately for me, the instructions setting up the fourth committee excluded persons who had served on any of the previous three.

Professor Feerick did summon me to testify at a public hearing at the law school. I noted the obvious: The issue had been "thoroughly examined, tested and retested." The facts were no longer at issue. Over the years of the extended experiment, "the legislature had piled restrictions upon constraint." I added: "What remains intact is the implacable opposition by some under any circumstances." I noted cameras benefited television, newspapers' competitor, much more, but I supported cameras on "the principle of opening up government agencies to fullest public scrutiny. . . . Of all the governmental agencies, it is our courts and our police that require the most openness because they touch the lives of people so directly."

After the four committees held their hearings and issued their reports—all of them endorsed cameras in the courts, although with increasing restraints—nothing permanent came of their efforts.

When the need was deemed great, however, cameras were welcomed into one court. In 1999, Amadou Diallo, a West African immigrant, was gunned down in the Bronx by a four-man squad of civvies-clad police officers. The cops claimed they thought the wallet Diallo reached for was a gun. Daily demonstrations erupted as it became a cause célèbre. A judge rejected a request to have cameras cover the trial. Because of the intensity of pretrial publicity, the state appeals court ordered the trial to be moved to Albany, 150 miles away.

Now it was more imperative than ever to show the public, and especially the aroused minority community, the fairness of the proceedings.

In Albany, Justice Joseph Teresi of the state Supreme Court, disagreed with the earlier decision in the Bronx. He permitted cameras to enter his court and to telecast the proceedings. What apparently had changed was a growing appreciation among the authorities of the value of a camera in court to defuse potential disruptions and allay suspicions by the Diallo camp about any attempts to manipulate the system of justice. As seating in the courtroom was minimal, cameras allowed everyone—in New York City, Albany, and everywhere—to see for themselves.

It was to address these concerns that Justice Teresi issued his ground-breaking decision, saying that a categorical ban against cameras in the courts in place since 1952 was unconstitutional because they were entitled to the same First Amendment access to criminal trials enjoyed by the public and the press.

CHAPTER 15

Unsettling Political Cartoons

It seemed Hy Rosen was the *Times Union*'s editorial cartoonist forever. Without question, his work over the decades made him the staffer most familiar to the public. Out of the office, people approached me, shook my hand, and thanked me for the wonderful cartoons I drew. Obviously, many easily confused our surnames. Attempts to clear up the mistake only compounded the awkwardness of the confusion. In time, I found the better solution was to say thank-you and stuff the praise into my undeserving pocket.

Hy's style was to replicate public figures recognizably. His political inclinations were conservative. He was often at odds with Governor Cuomo, as any self-respecting cartoonist had to be with the chief executive of a state or forfeit his license. Still the paper got into a public dispute because of a matter that involved Hy's speaking up for Mr. Cuomo and others in a cartoon. The person who caused the blowup was one of our syndicated columnists, Joseph Sobran. Sobran's extremely conservative columns were provocative and lucid and a balance to the liberal commentators we also published.

After a while, Sobran turned out to be more malicious than analytical, making ad hominem attacks on people with whom he disagreed. His baiting turned as he took on Jews, blacks, feminists, gays, and liberal Catholics. Ethnic slurs (that's when he maligned Mario Cuomo with a mafia allusion) were not beyond him. He clothed his vituperative arguments in a mantle of Christian doctrine. Those who did not share his political message imperiled it. Joe Lyons was a fan.

Hy Rosen's cartoon of Sobran depicted him as a friend of Nazi ideas after Sobran nastily attacked Elie Wiesel, who respectfully had urged President Reagan not to visit a West German cemetery at Bitburg where elite Nazi SS soldiers were buried. The editors could have killed the Rosen cartoon, as we could have withheld many Sobran columns. After deliberation, we decided to use both. Readers protested the cartoon. They said the editors who okayed it possessed neither journalistic ethics nor common decency. Their language strikingly resembled the objections of those who urged us not to publish Sobran's commentaries. Sobran rebutted in a column.

After the scuffle, I shared my thoughts with our readers.

> Sobran is past master at regularly working over other members of the press in personal terms. The first time he gets in kind what he traffics in, he cries foul, protests that some of his heroes are Jews, and lumps all Jews into his self-serving stereotypes.
>
> In short, Sobran is a bully whose nose for once had been bloodied in retribution. He is also a crybaby.

On a visit to our office, Governor Cuomo complained about Sobran and wanted me to cut him off. I asked the governor not to go public. If he made an issue of it, efforts to solve the problem would be more difficult. In short order, I got the ducks in a row and canceled Sobran.

Sobran continued his old tactics, to the point that he roused his editor, William F. Buckley Jr. at the *National Review*, to conclude, with artful sophistry, that Sobran was not an anti-Semite but his columns were anti-Semitic. In the end, he lost his job and his pulpit and took his Holocaust denial rhetoric to the political fringes.

A couple of years later, in 1987, Hy came under fire for a different cartoon satirizing an African American politician by robing him as a Klansman because he opposed a white man who was chosen as the state's education commissioner, after three black candidates turned down the job. A delegation of blacks and whites hurried to our office to protest the cartoon as racist. Hy was not present to speak on his behalf. In a visit arranged weeks earlier, he was out of town, in Harlem, teaching African American youngsters about cartooning. After three and half hours, he went to Brooklyn where he taught Hispanic kids. Hy volunteered for the project conducted by the Council on Children and Families. He received no compensation and the newspaper took care of expenses normally paid by the state.

Some years earlier, the black community in Albany called on Hy Rosen for help and he supplied a variety of cartoons on civil rights for a memorial observance honoring Martin Luther King Jr. Nevertheless, one of the protesters in the visiting delegation, Anne Pope, president of the Albany chapter of the National Association for the Advancement of Colored People, was sweeping in her condemnation. Rosen, she said, "paraded his racism" for years.

The uproar was understandable. As the editors thought about it after the fact, to criticize the cartoon as offensive, insensitive, or overkill fell into the range of fair comment. However, it was a trifle ironic that a cartoon protesting the imposition of a racial criterion for a state job was itself denounced as racist. The focus of Hy's cartoon was a powerful politician, Arthur Eve, the Deputy Speaker of the Assembly, who controlled a lot of patronage. When he spoke, people listened. Hy's response, when he had the chance to make it, was "a cartoonist may not be robbed of his tool of metaphor." His intention was not to offend Eve as a black man or blacks collectively. He decided to dress him in a Klan robe to dramatize the paradox of Eve and his allies imposing a racial qualification for the office when they, having suffered from such invidious treatment, should have known better.

Hy retired at the end of 1988 but continued to draw a Sunday cartoon for a long time, overlapping with his successor. After an extensive national search, in which the work of 125 applicants was assessed, we hired Rex Babin. Back then, few newspapers held on to their staff cartoonist, an accelerating trend over the years.

Following Hy's dominance was a tough challenge for Rex. Yet he quickly caught on and made his mark and became a reader favorite. Although the diminishing market for cartoonists was ever clearer, Rex's talent someday would make him an attractive hire for a larger newspaper. He was acute and thoughtful in his depictions of issues. It happened when I was no longer in charge of the newsroom. He landed with the *Sacramento Bee*, where his career flourished until his sad, early death at age forty-nine.

In the summer of 1980 the chief editors of the Hearst newspapers were invited to New York City for a nice lunch and a photography shoot for a brochure about the Hearst Corporation. We assembled and posed in our shirtsleeves. After a collegial day together in the big city, we returned no worse off to our home grounds. Then nothing appeared; the reason for delay was not shared with me and I suppose any other editor. Since the end of that year, six editors had left Hearst, creating a problem for the brochure. The remaining editors were not summoned for a reshoot. Instead, crafty art directors cropped the heads of most of the departed and replaced them with those of the still-incumbent, leaving all other body parts in place. Where once I was in the back of the photo, I wound up at its utmost front. Not on my own sorry body, but on that of the lanky Reg Murphy, formerly of the *San Francisco Examiner*. I never looked so good, although at no time more bereft of body if not soul.

Five years later, Hearst launched a nationwide advertising campaign, inserting full-page ads in newspapers and magazines to "the talent and creativity we have throughout to dramatize the size and diversity of the Hearst Corporation." Each ad featured a couple of employees selected because they illustrated "the creativity and professionalism of their co-workers." I was chosen for one ad. The caption read: "Harry Rosenfeld's creative ideas have produced news coverage that has made the Albany *Times Union* and the *Knickerbocker News* two of the most respected newspapers in the State of New York. Whether it's about the aging suburbs, or patients' rights in hospitals, Hearst's Albany newspapers are among the best examples of contemporary journalism." These ads were more promptly published. A copy mounted on an easel greeted me at the home of a new friend when I arrived in Los Angeles for a temporary assignment that summer.

The next time I appeared in a national Hearst promotional ad put me in the very best company. The occasion was the centennial of the Hearst Corporation, in 1987. The copy read: "As a salute to the many thousands of employees who helped us reach this milestone, we have gathered together just a few from the past and the present who, in some special way, represent the achievements of all their co-workers over the past century." A facing page featured fifty-four drawings of the chosen, including Helen Gurley Brown and Mark Twain. I was the only serving newspaper editor or reporter depicted.

CHAPTER 16

East Coast, West Coast Editor

In 1985, the year I joined the Fair Trial/Free Press Conference, Roger Grier from his corporate position enlisted me in a new assignment. Mary Anne Dolan, the editor of the *Herald Examiner*, the Hearst paper in Los Angeles, was on the verge of resigning. She had alerted headquarters, but no successor had been chosen. With her departure imminent, corporate needed to act. In New York's estimation, there was no one on staff ready to take over even as interim editor. Roger decided I was right for the post, basically to hold the fort while Hearst explored whether there was a market for a paper in relentless decline over the years. The task was presented to me as lasting for thirty days or so while marketing surveys were taken. I would retain editorship of the Albany papers and become editor of the *Herald Examiner*.

Being a good company man, I accepted. We canceled a long-arranged plan to take Annie on her first visit to Israel along with close friends. On the flight out to LA, Roger filled me in on what would await me, bringing up almost as an afterthought a long-standing conflict between Dolan and one of her top editors, hired for her design and makeup skills who enjoyed a special relationship with the chief operating officer. He was the paper's top executive in the absence of a publisher. I casually concluded that was one problem I would not have to worry about as it could easily wait on the selection of the permanent editor. Instead, her unresolved status plagued me during my time in LA. Roger also never told me that Chief Operating Officer John J. McCabe had not been consulted on my appointment, merely informed. It did not make for a great start, even for an association intended to be relatively brief.

Annie was not able to join me at first, so I took a room at a downtown hotel. When it proved unsuitable (extensive remodeling was under way, and one room was no more immune to the noise of reconstruction than another), I relocated to the Beverly Wilshire Hotel. There the room was larger and more stylishly decorated, although the commute to downtown took considerable time. It sufficed until Annie joined me, when we needed larger accommodations. Mary Anne strongly urged us to choose Santa Monica. There we found a small hotel apartment overlooking the Pacific Ocean. During our sojourn, the smog lifted a couple of times and only then could we see Catalina Island. Looking north through one of our windows we glimpsed fires fanned by the Santa Ana winds in the Malibu hills.

Coming to the West Coast put us nearer to family. My niece, Janice Kaminsky, lived in Palm Springs and two of her brothers were in LA working in the entertainment industry—Mel Damski, a director and producer with nominations for an Oscar and two Emmys, and Peter Damski, a sound engineer with two Emmy trophies. Through our friends in Albany, we were put in touch with their crowd in Los Angeles. These people generously took us into their lives, which eased our social situation considerably.

It turned out that when McCabe earlier had worked at the *New York Times* and I was at the *Herald Tribune* we lived in the same modest suburban tract development in New Jersey. He was born in the Bronx and I grew up there. We both had come a long way by the time we encountered each other.

The *Herald Examiner* was located downtown at 1111 South Broadway, in a building by the architect Julia Morgan, who also designed the Hearst Castle in San Simeon. The newspaper building was of Mission style with a pink stucco façade, and its large street-level windows had been filled in, a consequence of a bitter ten-year strike that intensified the paper's long and steady decline. The paper's publisher then was George R. Hearst Jr., who later served as chairman of the Hearst Corporation. He was the father of George R. Hearst III, who in 1989 joined the *Times Union* as operations manager and became my good friend almost from the day he started. When I edited the LA paper, George Jr. was no longer formally associated with it, but he regularly shared his conservative viewpoints with McCabe. These sensibilities clashed with how the paper had developed over the years to take a politically moderate editorial slant. By my arrival, the editorial page was more liberal as was its political cartoonist. I did not meet George R. Hearst Jr. during my California tour, although I heard his name invoked from time to time, usually with a complaint about what the paper had done. We met subsequently in Albany and I got a much broader appreciation of the man from the stories his son shared with me over the years.

The *Herald Examiner* building was old. Its presses were antiquated. The staff was young and ambitious, and keyed-up to play in the arena of Los Angeles journalism, matching the titan *Times* against the underdog *HerEx*. As happened when I traveled—to Vietnam, Europe, or LA—a former Tribber was there to greet me. Joe Morgenstern and I hugged when I walked into the newsroom to meet the troops. At the *Trib*, Joe was a film critic, and he was still at it. To make myself known to the others, every day I strolled through the newsroom to chat people up.

The chief editorial writer, Reva Tooley, threw a welcome party for Annie and me at her Malibu home. She was a well-connected local woman, and the guest list was long and prestigious, drawing from the worlds of politics, media, and entertainment. As part of the routine, Reva and I met nearly every morning to discuss editorial topics. In place were Stan Cloud, executive editor, and John Lindsay, managing editor, both experienced and able, as was the city editor, Larry Burroughs. The staff was eager and needed no prodding from me. I made clear my preference for investigative and enterprise journalism and that was fine with them. A couple of major stories broke that summer. One was the renewal of serial murders committed by a man the *Times* and the cops labeled the "Valley Intruder." The *Herald Examiner* tagged him the "Night Stalker," an epithet that stuck. Another was a major earthquake in Mexico. Given the large number of people from Mexico living in LA and its environs, we sent a team to report from the scene despite the strain on our meager budget. We played the story very big. When presented with a front-page banner, I liked it but asked it to be greatly upped in size. Our coverage and display had impact. New York noticed our significant circulation increase, something that had defied earlier efforts by others, including my old boss Jim Bellows.

There were major contrasts between Albany and LA in how a daily newspaper was edited. In Albany, the executive city editor came to work early in the morning, and her most pressing need was to come up with stories to assign reporters because important breaking news usually was scarce. In LA, the city editor faced the exact opposite challenge—what to choose from among a wide range of breaking news stories. There were not nearly enough reporters at the *HerEx* to possibly cover the vast reaches of the city each day. So the city editors picked targets of opportunity. The staff was very quick off the mark to produce a lively and readable, though not all-inclusive, newspaper.

I had to oversee the drawing up of a budget while keeping an eye on the same process in Albany. It was grim drafting a spending plan with so little wiggle room. Somewhere along the line, as the early returns from the market surveys appeared, I began to draft outlines for a future *Herald Examiner*, although I had no expectation of being there to implement it. Observing everything new around me helped. While living in Beverly Hills, on morning exercise walks along local streets, I took my own survey. The *Los Angeles Times* was planted on each driveway virtually without exception. Spotting a *Herald Examiner* was less than rare.

During Bellows's editorship the paper, always highly regarded for its sports and entertainment coverage, shifted from its traditional focus on a blue-collar readership to one written for a younger and more upscale audience. It was intended as an alternative to the staid *Times*. When I took over from Dolan, who had followed Jim Bellows, I found a prototype of a paper that was intended to take the *Herald Examiner* into the black. It featured a gorgeous front page with subtle color graphics, clearly aimed at the upper crust of the metropolitan area. It resembled no other newspaper I had ever seen, which was the point. It was almost too delicate, too fine, too precious, to aspire to a general readership. And it vastly exceeded existing production capacities.

My vision of what a redesigned *Herald Examiner* would be was vastly different. It was based largely on what I discovered as I made my way around town and acquainted myself with more than the elegant high-income areas of the city: the ethnic neighborhoods—Hispanic, Korean, Japanese, African American—as well as less affluent white ones. This exposure informed my sense of the challenge facing the *HerEx* as well as the opportunities. I saw the vibrant Asian business districts, most of the signs in Korean or Japanese, pointing up the coherence of these distinct communities. The point was to build on the *Herald Examiner*'s once traditional appeal to a broad, working-class audience by reaching out to the ethnic minorities that were also blue collar but more. Especially among the Asians, an obvious entrepreneurial component flourished in the many businesses serving that market.

In my vision, the future of the *Herald Examiner* remained as a street-sales newspaper, which it had been at least since the disastrous strike. I proposed shifting it from a broadsheet to a tabloid, taking advantage of its most promising resource, its avid and competitive young staff, and relieving it of any pretense of trying to match the scope of the dominant *Los Angeles Times* with its larger staff and abundant pages. In my vision, the *HerEx* would reach out to all demographics by retaining its superb sports and entertainment coverage and its staff of general assignment reporters. In addition, the new *HerEx* would appeal directly to the area's ethnics, with each subgroup part of constant reportage guaranteed by having a competent and qualified reporter from each community writing columns devoted to its affairs and concerns. There would be one, or possibly two, for Asians; one for Latinos; one for blacks; and at least one for the region as a whole. The numerous and thriving businesses in these communities would be targeted for advertising support. It was conceivable we might have some of the columns published in the language of the particular community.

The future *HerEx* would leave establishment journalism to the *Times* and pick its way into issues that the *Times* was reluctant to take on, despite, or because, of its wealth. It would be highly local in focus and dig deep into endless issues of interest and concern to a mass audience, in other words, doing what it was already widely admired for. An example: During my tenure, a government agency issued a report finding a local supermarket chain routinely overcharged its customers because of malfunctioning scales. We played the story on Page 1 accompanied by a follow-up editorial citing the biblical injunction to deliver honest weights and measures. The *Times*, on the other hand, then in the hands of my close colleague Dave Laventhol, ran a small inside story. On that day, the *Times* management was meeting with representatives from the chain.

This was in keeping with the feisty, underdog, take-them-on-at-all-costs tradition of the *Herald Examiner* going back decades. One result was that the chain pulled its relatively rich advertising contract with the *Herald Examiner* and barred our newspapers from sale in its supermarkets. McCabe was absolutely stouthearted, never complained, because our reporting was factual and fair, even though the paper lost a heavy advertiser, paying a price it could ill afford.

All this transpired in the thirty days, or sixty, or ninety or more that I would spend in LA. I had connected with the newsroom staff and the heads of circulation, advertising, and production. We functioned as an effective team under McCabe and kept in touch with each other. McCabe and I met each morning in his office to go over whatever matters he had in mind, or problems or questions I had. It was far superior to the Albany operation under Lyons, where our meetings were irregular. McCabe and the others kept me connected to what was happening in their spheres, and they knew what the newsroom was up to.

My coming to Los Angeles brought me back in touch with colleagues from yesteryear. There was Tom Huth, who served as chief copy editor of the foreign desk when I was foreign editor at the *Washington Post.* He was outstanding in the role not because he was especially backgrounded in foreign matters but because he understood the elements of clear and descriptive writing. When I moved across the city room to take over the direction of the local news, he joined the Metro staff, where he displayed notable writing talents. In time, he left the *Post* and moved out West to do what he wanted, which was to write novels. When we lunched, he explored a freelancer association with the *HerEx.*

Another colleague was a former *Times Union* reporter, who when we met again in California had that job at the *Los Angeles Times*, which was more than a few important rungs up the career ladder. We had a chatty lunch discussing Albany times. He left me with one earnest message. He urged me to "do something" about Dan Lynch. He felt Dan was too domineering for the good of the newsroom. His criticism was not news to me. I did not follow his advice. Here's why: Among the most useful lessons I absorbed from my newspaper work was that people did their best when free to make the most of their strengths, while I sought to manage their shortcomings.

I knew full well that Dan Lynch was not everyone's cup of tea. He could be heavy-handed. Not only was he often the brightest guy in the room, he also showed it. In his annual reviews, I counseled him about his flaws. On the other hand, Dan was a well-read, energetic, and talented editor, who reflected the highest standards and insisted on them.

I also had a visitor from my days as assistant managing editor/national in Washington. Cindy Kadonaga interned with us then, but she cut the internship short to return to California to marry her sweetheart, to the derision of her peers. We reconnected yet again many years later, when I published my memoir, and have stayed in touch.

Over the months, several times I flew east, either for a meeting at corporate headquarters in New York or for business, personal or professional, in Albany. Steffie flew out in October during a break in her studies at Ithaca College, and Amy showed up with Danny Kaufman, "only a friend" from the University of Chicago Law School, as they traveled cross-country. We saw our niece and nephews from time to time, and we were getting closer to the nice people to whom we had been introduced. Still, Annie's life was more isolated than she was accustomed to. Friends were not around the corner and to get anywhere in LA meant a tedious drive in bumper-to-bumper traffic. Our transience interfered with cultivating relationships. On weekends, she and I walked down steep concrete steps to the ocean and enjoyed beach sitting before I was off to the office. Most people on the beach were couples, like us.

At work, although we had our good moments, McCabe and I began to disagree more and more. I could understand his resentment at having an editor under him who was not his choice. We had a conflict over McCabe's efforts to formally reinstate to her operational status the editor Dolan had removed. I refused to do so because she apparently disregarded me much as she had Dolan. I was not pleased with McCabe's meddling in the newsroom. It got to be a testy relationship.

At the same time, New York saw the notable increase in circulation and how well I melded with the staff. Corporate liked my proposal for the future paper and decided it had identified the permanent editor for the *Herald Examiner*. Bob Danzig talked to me about taking the job. I was interested and was thinking it over. As the weeks dragged on, I received a phone call from Jim Bellows asking me what the hell I was thinking hanging on in LA. From his experience, he saw no hope. Another call came from a close friend in Albany, a successful businessman, who warned me that a corporation focused on its own interests and I should not be sucked into a questionable venture. For my part, there was concern that my Albany salary, even with a substantial increase, would not permit me to live where and how I liked in LA when I was no longer completely on the expense account. That issue could have been overcome through negotiations. Then there was Annie's reluctance, which I might have been able to assuage. What I could not alter was the corporate attitude. It liked my plan to go tabloid. What was not supported was investing money to adapt or replace the existing honor boxes on city streets through which many single copy sales were made. The honor part of the boxes' name came from how a paper in it was purchased. The price of the paper was inserted in a slot, a door opened to reveal a stack of newspapers. A cheater could take more than one paper. Using the existing ones, a tabloid would have to be displayed sideways, hardly an effective sales technique when headlines sell the paper. In addition, there was the customary incantation of having to work within a business plan, which was a given. The question remained: What kind of plan? It indicated corporate was not prepared to make the financial commitment to a redesigned paper, even for a relatively slight matter of new or remodeled honor boxes. On the other hand, I was expected to go from a successful operation to a failing one. It seemed clear the point was to keep the *HerEx* going while not adding to the losses. Without additional resources, I could not see how my proposed plan had any chance of success. I declined the offer and felt that my absence from Albany had begun to undercut what I had built up there over the years.

By late November McCabe and I implicitly had come to a meeting of minds. My interim editorship had run its course; I had held the wheel steady, and the marketing surveys and reader studies were completed. My battle plan was accepted but not funded. The relationship between editor and general manager was at an impasse. I phoned Bob Danzig to ask him to permit me to return full time to Albany, where I knew I was needed. Danzig reluctantly agreed but suggested I simply reverse the program. Instead of working most of my time in LA and occasionally looking in on Albany, I would work mostly in Albany and make short visits to the LA operation, keeping my editor title for all three papers. I could not see how this would improve matters and said to him, "Bob, both your general manager and your editor have told you this is not working out. I think you should listen to them." He did, and my California assignment ended.

Less than two years later, with Maxwell McCrohon, a fine editor in charge, another *Herald Examiner* prototype was presented. I was among those asked to comment on it. This is part of what I wrote: "The prototype lacked court and crime coverage, which all studies . . . indicate enjoy the highest readership. There's got to be a sociological and interesting way to do it without bloodying the paper up."

I continued: "LA is an impossible place to live. Therefore, throughout the sections of the paper, provide stories and graphics to help people cope, whether with traffic, shopping, buying a car or home, whatever."

Then I revived the idea of the ethnic columnists and cautioned: "But the first step is to work out the rationale for appealing to the ad agencies on the basis of higher demographics of present and potential readers, while having to appeal to a comparatively lower strata for actual future readers."

Four years after I left LA, despite the best efforts of Maxwell McCrohon and his staff, the corporation decided to end publication— the ineluctable fate I had feared given the paper's steady losses and the unwillingness to make heavier investment in what at best was a very long shot.

CHAPTER 17

Finding Bits of LA in Albany

Before returning to Albany, Joe Lyons in a memo for discussion with me said communications between the two of us needed to improve. He apparently responded to my description of how it worked in LA and proposed a twice a week meeting. What he didn't pick up was what would be discussed with collegial candor at the meetings, with the parties keeping each other fully in the picture.

The other fallout involved Bob Danzig, who in April 1986, at a meeting in our Albany boardroom, presented me with a gift of perhaps twenty or thirty bow ties, selected by his secretary Marge Murphy. I thanked Bob and wrote to Marge to praise her for her good taste, and I added: "No need to keep my valet any longer." I had begun wearing bow ties some years before and after too long a time learned how to properly tie them.

More importantly, exposure to the *Herald Examiner* showed me that the contentious relationship in Albany's DNA as I found it from the first was not ordained. The genuine camaraderie among top executives of the newsroom, advertising, production, and circulation departments was critical to the publication of the *HerEx*. Everyone in LA worked hard to keep a failing paper alive and collaborated wholeheartedly to make it the best possible newspaper. In Albany, all in all, the newsroom was considered an annoying necessity rather than the focus of our effort.

My return was quickly marked with our newspapers paradoxically finding the kind of stories plentiful in Los Angeles but scarce in the Capital Region. For me it began while I was still at the *Herald Examiner*, when a constant reader in Albany took the trouble to phone me with the message that everyone back home was talking about the troubles that had befallen a respected family business.

It took a while until I was fully back in harness, around the new year, before I was encouraged to focus on the matter by a high public official who said the collapse of the business, Vogel Van & Storage Incorporated, "was the talk of the Rialto." His purpose was not so much to share a news tip as it was an insinuation that our newspapers seemed to be shying from the story. His implication was we were harsher on those in public service than on well-connected business people who were advertisers to boot.

The sad story of the decline of Vogel Van & Storage, the second largest Allied Van Line agent in North America, was a personal tragedy for "a pillar in our community," Thomas Vogel, variously chairman or executive vice president, and his family, long established in Albany. More than that, it was about the vicissitudes that can overtake a successful family enterprise during the stewardship of successor generations. Under Tom's leadership, the company's too rapid expansion to Florida and California resulted in a need to raise financing quickly to deal with a $30 million debt.

Most revealingly, it was about how business got done in Old Albany, where about $12 million was borrowed from the biggest banks in town on a handshake, as long as it involved hands of the right sort, without the encumbrances of documented collateral otherwise demanded from lesser folk trying to get much smaller loans. On those infrequent occasions when he was asked, Vogel made patently false claims about his assets and their value.

When we got ourselves into gear, reporter Ron Kermani spent weeks working with his editor, Lois Uttley, to produce a four-part series that went behind the bankruptcy filings of a venerable business while its executive was on a buying binge of fancy clothes, in which a tony haberdasher was stiffed for $19,000 and another was left with a bill for $43,000 (including the purchase of 173 neckties). All this while his personal bank account increased by nearly a million dollars extracted from the firm for purposes he could not remember when pressed by investigators.

That summer another story unfolded in a local court that, to put it mildly, stirred public interest. In a routine divorce proceeding, testimony described the wife's intimate relationship with the most powerful civic figure in town, a married man. Lew Swyer, sixty-eight, was a renowned and respected developer, a connoisseur and promoter of the arts, a man with a deft touch whose prominence and political and social connections made him a dynamo in the community. He brought people from different dispensations together—the arts and business and politics—and good things happened. When he died, a memorial service was given in the Catholic cathedral.

It was a stunner: This most prominent of men involved with a woman twenty-eight years younger and far out of his social class. Our court reporter learned of the proceeding after it had taken place in privacy at a public courtroom. When we began to report the case, following up on the text of testimony, Lew Swyer came to see me to urge that we not use the story, that it had no public purpose. In fact, Swyer had gotten the woman a job with Albany's Tricentennial Commission, of which he was the chairman. I could not help him, although I knew him personally and lunched with him occasionally. He then took his case to Bob Danzig in New York, a friend from his days as publisher and before at Capital Newspapers. Later I learned Bob, who was not above urging my support for one or another cause on behalf of an old friend from his Albany days, simply told Swyer he could do nothing. Bob said not a word to me. Well done, Bob Danzig. We did not hype the story, as sensational as it was, playing it on the front page of the local section. It took a long time for Lew Swyer to again look at me, much less speak to me, but from then on only tersely.

Before all these stories played out, upon my return from the West Coast, Bob Danzig in January assigned me to head a task force of Hearst editors to find "ways in which the operation of our Washington bureau might be enhanced for the benefit of all our newspapers." Serving on the task force were Gordon Brittan, of the Midland, Michigan, *Daily News*; Ben Hansen of the Beaumont, Texas, *Enterprise*; and Ted Warmbold of the *San Antonio Light*. When confronted by a corporate directive to make major reductions in budget, the Washington bureau was every editor's first sacrificial offering. Each paper was assessed a hefty sum, commensurate roughly with its size, to fund the bureau. Yet everyone without exception believed the bureau did not deliver value equal to its cost. This was a dicey subject because the bureau was the corporate presence in political Washington, and part of its implicit mission was to maintain contacts. Joseph Kingsbury-Smith bore the title of national editor, but he was much more. A Pulitzer Prize winner for an exclusive interview with Soviet premier Nikita Khrushchev in 1956, he was the point man for these much-valued associations. Therefore, closing the bureau was never a possibility. Editors knew this full well but voiced their disdain at times in a sort of pathetic gesture to pull corporate's chain. In practice, as our survey confirmed, the bureau played no meaningful role in the pages of the Hearst papers it was intended to service.

After study and consultations, the task force recommended the bureau abandon its periodic attempts to report breaking news covered by the news agencies and which the bureau's copy seldom matched in timeliness. We wanted the bureau to focus on analytical and explanatory sidebars to the main news. We cautioned this required harder reporting than the news itself. We urged the hiring of qualified reporters and editors to provide a needed service to the Hearst papers and establish a reputation in the trade. We also recommended separating the corporate representational responsibilities from the news bureau, relieving the bureau chief of any role in them and permitting him to devote his total time and energy to the news side.

By July Danzig had our detailed memo in hand and he deemed it "very thorough and thoughtful," providing "a sound basis for improvement." In time, a key editor was hired and other improvements made. Still some bad old habits of journalism lingered, such as greater concern for the needs of sources than for readers. Too much was still permitted to be reported based on unnamed people who shared usually self-serving information that required no cover of confidentiality except to avoid identification.

No sooner was this project completed than Danzig designated me to assess the operations of the New York bureau, in response to suggestions by editors, again as head of a task force. Along with me were J. D. Alexander of the *Seattle Post-Intelligencer*; Carl Green of the Edwardsville, Illinois, *Intelligencer*; and Danny Andrews of the

Plainview, Texas, *Daily Herald*. For the most part, the New York bureau served as a transmission center to move copy from the Washington bureau to the Hearst newspapers as well as for the papers to exchange stories with each other. As far as breaking news was concerned, copy was produced almost always a full cycle behind the wire services because the bureau operated with a limited staff.

Exploring technology at the time of the Washington study, we set up a system for direct transmission from the bureau to the papers, eliminating New York's role. As for the features prepared by Hearst papers and then edited by staff in New York to make them suitable for use by other Hearst papers, New York's handling added no value. We recommended upgrading editors and the swifter transmission of copy. We hoped to establish an authentic New York City bureau with at least two talented correspondents, one for financial coverage, the other for media and political news. These recommendations were not acceptable because loyal old-timers would have to be dislocated. A New York bureau had to be maintained because the city was the seat of corporate headquarters and the source of corporate-produced editorials that were disseminated to all Hearst newspapers. In Albany, we rarely used them.

In the middle of these task forces I was invited by the publisher of the Hearst paper in Clearwater, Florida, to look over his small operation that was squeezed by the metros in nearby St. Petersburg and Tampa. I spent a couple days at the *Sun* and connected with the two top editors. I wrote the publisher that both had a good grasp on what needed to be done and how to do it. When in time the paper folded, I offered the top editor a job, but he declined. We did hire the other editor, who joined our sports department.

I enjoyed these chores and received support from Larry Kramer, the executive editor of the *San Francisco Examiner*. "I can't tell you what a difference it makes to have you with us on all these attempts to move the mountains in this company. You have created a terrific niche for yourself, and the rest of us, in this company. You clearly have the confidence of the big guys, and the ability to convince them to make moves they have never been willing or able to make before. I can't tell you how good that is for all of us."

CHAPTER 18

Momentous Events

In 1987, Annie and I attained a milestone, the birth of our first grand-child. Her parents, Susan and Stuart Wachter, were brought together by my father not long before his death. The baby was named Sarah, in re-membrance of her great-grandfather. When she was born, I wondered whether I could ever match the impact on her life that my father had on his grandchild.

Momentous events also developed at work that year. Whatever our triumphs or setbacks, merging the *Knick* and the *TU* periodically was on our agenda a very long time before it finally happened. It was an un-fortunate manifestation of contemporary journalism. Newspapers com-bined or closed in a chronic decline for the industry.

Early in my days in Albany, publisher Roger Grier had us consider the feasibilies of killing the Saturday *Knickerbocker News* and incorpo-rating some of its salient features into the Sunday *Times Union*. That did not happen. Toward the end of 1980, Roger's successor, Joe Lyons, raised and expanded the idea with me, pointing to the economic gains our op-eration could make if we just shut down the *Knick*. I resisted for years in the face of growing evidence that circulation gains made by the morning *Times Union* were offset entirely or in part by the *Knick*'s losses. Repeated efforts to boost *Knick* circulation through different tactics achieved at most temporal success. By the fall of 1982 we were well into discussions and planning about combining the papers, but still publishing editions for morning and afternoon circulation. Sometime in the process, I de-cided that the *Knick* staff had to contribute to the Sunday paper. A bank was set up into which *Knick* writers would deposit suitable articles for possible use and from which *TU* editors made their selections. The reaction from most of the *Knick* reporters, who were Guild members, was to invoke their contractual right to withhold their bylines. This tactic reflected the *Knickerbocker News* staffers' constant fear of their paper's shaky fate.

A relentless determinism confronted us. Only the when and the how remained to be decided. Reluctantly, I had come to acknowledge there was no way to reverse the fifteen-year decline of the *Knickerbocker News*. Afternoon, or evening, newspapers were a remnant of the day when workers went off to their jobs early in the morning and returned home in late afternoon, before the advent of nightly TV broadcasts. Everything we tried came up short.

Discussions recurred periodically. By the late winter of 1983, we arrived at the point that our several managing editors, supported by key assistants, were given the weighty assignment to draft a plan for combining parts of the staffs of the two papers while both continued to publish. Within weeks the assignment was toughened to drafting a plan to implement the merger of the two papers, keeping only a street sales edition in the afternoon.

According to the publisher's prescription, the 142 total newsroom head count would be reduced to 125. The *TU* would be strengthened with staff shifted from the *Knick*. The planning was thorough and attached names to the necessary cutbacks, as painful as that was. Despite these studies, the merger, different in form, did not come to pass for years.

Nature played its card on a Sunday in October 1987, when an unusually early snowstorm brought destruction and disruption to the region. Branches broke and trees still bearing leaves were toppled by heavy snow, downing power lines. Much of the region was in crisis mode, as were the *Times Union* and *Knickerbocker News* because our plant lost power and could not run the presses. Our general manager turned for help to a competitor, one we had agreed to assist a couple of years before, to produce and print our paper, which under the exigency would be a combined one. The Troy *Record*, an afternoon paper whose executive editor was Kathy Condon, a former executive city editor at the *Knick* and a friend, opened the *Record* newsroom to our staff, moving its people to another part of the old red-brick building. Kathy and her *Record* colleague, editor Roland Blais, through a long day and half the night guided our people step by step through the *Record*'s computer system, which was entirely alien to us. Our *TU* and *Knick* reporters and editors, normally strenuous competitors, worked shoulder to shoulder. The *Record*'s own staff, which came in later in the evening to put out its Monday edition, was shifted to different offices while we finished our work. After a long and difficult day, we made a midnight press start. Plainly said, the *Record* rescued us.

The collaboration underscored the core of newspapering. Its purpose is to publish and to thwart any obstacles that might emerge. Publishing is an obligation and a trust. Twice before in my work, at the *Herald Tribune* in the 1960s and at the *Washington Post* in the 1970s, the papers were not able to publish for one day. At the *Trib*, it was a power failure that wasn't overcome. At the *Post*, it was a strike by the pressmen in which they disabled the presses. Deliberately preventing a newspaper from publishing is like burning a book.

For the first time that Monday morning, the Capital Newspapers bore the flags of both papers. It was not an elegant edition. It was not complete. Despite its deficiencies, it was a newspaper. It was also a harbinger: The all-day newspaper we planned at the beginning would combine the flags of both. Weeks after the snow crisis, we made moves indicating the path that lay before us. We shifted the *TU* executive city editor, Lois Uttley, to head up its expanded state bureau in the Capitol and selected her counterpart at the *Knick*, Joann Crupi, to take over as executive city editor of the *TU* (which in characteristic esprit of *Knick* staffers she said she did only because I made her). The dominant publication of the future would be the morning *Times Union*, published during the night, followed by a street sales edition printed later in the morning. In the planning, we began with hopes for a two-hundred-column paper and were ground down, as was par for the course. So also with the staff numbers.

In the spring of 1988 we went public with our plan to consolidate our newsroom resources into one newspaper. The unified staff and expanded columns devoted to editorial content were the path to a bigger and better newspaper in scope and depth of coverage. No one in the newsroom was laid off; the five-slot reduction was accomplished by not filling existing vacancies.

To merge the two staffs, we relied on the thinking of the senior editors of both papers and asked all staffers to offer their ideas. Bern Zovistoski, the managing editor for administration, plotted a physical layout, locating all news departments, including business and financial news, in the *Times Union* newsroom with Dan Lynch, managing editor for news, in charge.

The features department and sports were set up in what had been the newsroom of the *Knick*, where Bill Dowd, the *Knick's* former managing editor, now led those departments, along with oversight of the photography unit and the library operation. The combined editorial page department was now located on the former *Knick* side that included shifting political cartoonist Hy Rosen, his pen and palette, over from the *TU* side. It was traumatic for Hy, who rarely if ever in his decades at the paper so much as walked through the old *Knick* quarters. Our local columnists—Fred Lebrun from the *TU* and Ralph Martin from the *Knick*—became office mates on the features side.

Combining the staffs of our papers was neither easy nor difficult, but a mix, depending much on the capacity of individual personalities to accept this radical change, long dreaded by *Knick* people, to become colleagues where once they were rivals. Perhaps this was hardest for the editorial writers, who regularly took positions in opposition to each other, with the *TU* slightly more conservative and the *Knick* slightly more liberal. Both were essentially centrist in politics, so putting the writers together broadened their perspectives as they collaborated. As for me, being basically nonideological, I had enjoyed sitting on two editorial boards and would miss having it both ways when either had merit.

It was one thing to sit down with Bill Dowd that late Thursday night in April, to write the last streamer headline for the *Knickerbocker News*. It was another to come in Friday morning and see it laid out in the composing room. It read: "We Say Farewell." For an editor, there can be few occasions more melancholy, and this was the second time in my working life that a newspaper to which I had devoted myself ceased publishing. I had not become a newspaperman to bury newspapers. It was not that the *Knick* lacked competitive spirit. In some ways, it was more intense than the competition I had experienced in Washington. Yet the competition was not an intentional tactic. Rather, it stemmed from the two papers' original separate identities, which were maintained after the Hearst Corporation, owner of the *TU*, acquired the *Knick* from the Gannett chain. It was for real and occasionally hilarious. One time a hustler came to town promising to buy cars for deserving people. Reporters from the *Knick* and the *TU* both got excited. The *TU* reporters secreted this con man in their conference room to keep him away from the *Knick* reporter (and TV types sniffing around). The *Knick* reporter, for her part, stormed through the building complaining loudly and insistently that a *TU* reporter had tried to run her down in the company parking lot.

There are countless anecdotes to illustrate the tenor of the competition between the staffs of the two newspapers. Common ownership never deterred them. At an earlier time, when Roger Grier was publisher, one of the papers, I don't recall which one, came up with a good local exposé and gave it a ride. The other paper all but ignored it, using only the briefest references to the other's achievement. Roger asked how could that happen? If it was such a great story for one, why was it being downplayed by the other? It was my lot to explain to Roger such behavior demonstrated a hallowed journalistic tradition: Unless you couldn't help it, you were dismissive about your competitor's scoop. Far too often, that was standard.

The *Knick* died on April 15, 1988, after nearly 145 years of publication. Truly remarkable was how long we held on to the afternoon paper, keeping its staff substantially intact, as its circulation shrank. At editors' conventions, this was one question I was sure to face: When would we pull the plug?

On April 16, the all-day *Times Union* was published. Soon, the all-day concept was abandoned. The augmented *TU* staff now had the capacity to intensify the kind of journalism undertaken since my arrival. No longer did we need to double our resources against our competitors. Where they sent one reporter to cover an event, customarily the *TU* and the *Knick* assigned one each. Merging the staffs permitted the creation of a special projects unit to produce investigative and enterprise stories, in place of just one editor who scrounged up an occasional reporter. We expanded our Capitol bureau and increased our financial reporters, doubled the number of editorial writers, established a satellite office in Columbia County (in 1983 we had opened a bureau in Saratoga County and expanded our coverage in the cities of Troy and Rensselaer across the Hudson). The merger enabled us to assign specialty reporters in the fields of education, health, and transportation, among other concentrations.

Every senior editor on the *Knick* took on a meaningful new assignment, and each reporter had a full plate within the larger news operation. The only real problem stemmed from cutting some comics and columns that had appeared in either paper because all could not be accommodated even in the expanded space. I told myself no paper needed to publish two daily crossword puzzles. I picked the one I deemed more challenging (neither was taxing) and dropped the other. The reader outcry was substantial. As a result, we went with two crosswords as well as a *Knick* word game puzzle. Its removal aroused much ire, apparently from state workers solving it at their desks, to judge from the complainants.

Out of the depth of our disappointment at the closing of the *Knick*, there arose a sense of expectancy. We marshaled editorial capabilities of a magnitude we never possessed before and which no competitor in the region began to approach. It was the opening move into a world in which we registered the highest circulation in the history of the *Times Union* and achieved the impact and influence that accompanied our extended reach.

It was also the time frame to update the newsroom. According to lore and in practice, a newsroom's looks are at best borderline shabby. Our premises and furnishings were relatively new in 1970 when the papers moved into their quarters in the suburb of Colonie. Nearly twenty years later, in 1989 it was past time to join the present.

While the office furniture had remained static, if not ossified, the tools of our trade transitioned from manual typewriters, through electric ones, to computer terminals. These display terminals and their keyboards were crammed into desk wells designed to hold once ubiquitous and smaller Underwood typewriters. Over the years, the circulation, advertising, and accounting departments had been made over. Frankly, our less than attractive quarters and paraphernalia were not foremost on our minds until the need to accommodate new technology made it imperative.

A committee of reporters and editors was convened. Groups visited newspapers that had modernized. Staffers were interviewed, giving shape to ideas of what was desirable and necessary. Visits to local businesses impressed us with the combination of modern good looks and the increased efficiency of space that would be attainable.

The results were impressive for the aesthetic cohesion as was the speed with which the final pieces were put into place. We wound up with better equipment and increased working space in more congenial surroundings and less distracting noise.

Reluctantly but inevitably, in January of 1988 we came to grips with the need to end an old newspaper custom. No, we did not force people to become teetotalers. Instead, we took the first steps to make our newsroom smoke free. I had spent some of the longest days in my newspaper life enriching the sellers of cigarettes. A butt was most welcome during the tense parts of the day—and much of the day tended to be stressful. Only after a bleeding ulcer laid me low did I give up cigarettes on doctor's orders. Before that, they were a constant companion at work and play.

I completely understood those who resisted change and felt put upon by its champions. At this stage, I had forever quit cigarettes twice and cigars once. The smoking part of newsroom folklore had to give way to the rising demands of others who did not enjoy exposure to secondhand smoke's health hazards. It was a habit whose expiration date had come. This did not keep the local Guild unit from making the point that our reasonable steps were acceptable if there was no authoritarian "you must" attached. Managing editor Bill Dowd informed the Guild officer that New York State law authorized employers to establish and enforce this policy.

CHAPTER 19

Changes and Challenges

In the spring of 1988, Stefanie graduated from Ithaca College and our family gathered for the occasion. Annie's mother, Martha, and Steffie's sisters came up from New York City. That fall, Steffie went on to graduate studies at New York University, to earn a master's degree in studio arts. She remained to become a thorough New Yorker.

Tom Wolfe, my colleague from the *Herald Tribune*, addressed the Ithaca graduates. I wrote to tell him he had done a good job and to praise him for his powerful novel, *The Bonfire of the Vanities*. He replied: "Your generous words have bowled me over. All the more so since it was such a hair-raising struggle to write a novel at this stage of my career." He added: "Congratulations in your command position—after so many brilliant performances in the field. I'm sure you're having a great time." I had last encountered Tom years earlier, when on one of my trips to New York from Washington I stopped in late afternoon at Bleeck's, the bar adjacent to the former *Herald Tribune* building that served as the gathering place for the city's media. Although the *Trib* was by then long dead and buried, veterans of the paper were still drawn to the place to drink, eat, and socialize with old comrades. Tom himself had been a reporter at the *Washington Post* and left it to join the *Trib* because he had wearied of writing about the development of sewer systems in the suburbs. Upon meeting him again as one of the most famous of contemporary journalists, I felt free, in my capacity as a *Post* editor at the time, to offer him his old job back should events ever turn on him.

The 1988 academic season was extra special for our family as Annie and I also attended Amy's graduation from the University of Chicago

Law School and saw Susan awarded her Master of Science degree from Johns Hopkins. That year, too, Annie and I were invited by Howard Simons, then the curator of the Nieman Foundation at Harvard, to attend a seminar on "The Holocaust and the Media." Over two days, we heard panelists—historians, theologians, public servants, and journalists—discuss the reasons the American press for the most part did not convey the extent of the persecution of the Jews in the years it was taking place, before, and during World War II. The seminar posed the question: If more people had been informed, would the dynamics of events have been deflected and the horrors diminished? The profoundly lamentable answer was not likely, given the at best indifference if not hostility to Jews then prevalent in America and Europe.

For obvious reasons, this was a topic with visceral and intellectual significance for me, as a man and newspaperman. The seminar shed a harsh light on the high level of active anti-Semitism in the United States during those times. The credibility of reports of persecutions may have been discounted because they came from Jewish groups and did not attain the credibility of a government report. The Nazis had no interest in reporting their oppression. The world in general, moreover, had no difficulty accommodating the premise that Jews were not entitled to the same civil and human rights as the people among whom they lived.

One example cited was from the early 1930s boycott of Jewish businesses by the Germans. The *Christian Science Monitor* blamed the Jews for being too clannish. This boycott forced my father to shrink his flourishing fur stores and relocate his reduced operation. As for lessons learned, it was surely that the press—in the day of the seminar at the Harvard Divinity School as in our day—remains too dependent on government for the source of news and for vouching for the news' authenticity. This reliance is strong despite the fact, demonstrated again and again over the years, that governments frequently lie, sometimes, it seems, just to preserve the franchise, but mostly to shield themselves from exposure of embarrassing shortcomings.

The November of the seminar was the fiftieth anniversary of Kristallnacht. While journalists and diplomats who were eyewitnesses discussed the plunder, vandalism, and arson, I remembered those terrifying days and nights when my family lived through them in Berlin. The focus on press performance of course made me reflect on how my being a Jew shaped my judgments as an editor. Now I am sure I hesitated to act against the anti-Semite Joseph Sobran because I did not want to overreact to his Jew-baiting. Did this hesitancy reflect on my professionalism? Or would acting sooner have been more an emotional than a proper response? Questions along those lines inevitably arose when issues of special interest or concern to Jews made an appearance. At those times, my purpose was to adhere doggedly to the best standards of my craft, to tell as much of the truth as was discoverable, even when it would hurt my inner or most cherished feelings.

During an afternoon break one day, Annie and I were accompanied on our walk across campus to our hotel by a young reporter covering the conference. As we chatted, he told me I had once turned him down for a job on the local staff of the *Washington Post*. I could not place him as he talked until he reminded me my rejection was based on his being a freshly minted PhD, and I had not long before hired a PhD who did not work out on the beginner's police beat and was not ready to take that chance again. Consequently, I had told the young man at the time of his job interview, I was sure he would not be happy covering a suburban beat. He found work elsewhere and became a successful foreign correspondent, and he made a name writing thoughtful books.

As we walked and talked, he was charming and well spoken. Anger welled up inside me because of my foolish decision. When we parted, the least I could do was to try to make it up to him and myself. I confessed my error and, on the spot, offered him a job on the *Times Union* anytime he wanted it. Richard Bernstein decided to remain with the *New York Times*.

Over the years, our newspaper building had an open-door policy. Anyone could walk in without being stopped and asked what the visit concerned. For security, a competent man, Don Rector, a retired state trooper, was in charge. He was summoned when need arose to deal with an awkward or hostile situation. Too many people entered, found their way into the newsroom, and approached someone they specifically had a problem with or alternatively anyone they selected as the target of their discontent. Rector, a burly man, would escort the person out the door.

This became urgently worrisome one day when a person who had previously phoned one of our women staffers and made suggestive comments showed up at her desk. In late 1989, I sent Joe Lyons a memo asking for permission for the newsroom to take steps to improve security, citing a much earlier proposal not acted on by the second floor. We could not continue to fail to act.

When agreement with the publisher was reached, a team from the newsroom visited other newspapers with established secure office environments. The most instructive one was in Allentown, Pennsylvania, at the *Morning Call*. We adapted its model and limited access to our front lobby, at which point many ordinary chores such as placement of classified ads or subscription issues would be handled. If there was need to visit a business or news department, an escort from those sections accompanied the visitor, eventually through a series of locked doors opened with a special pass.

Once a year, Hearst newspaper publishers and editors met with our corporate masters. It was an occasion to meet old colleagues and greet new ones, swap war stories, role-play, and learn from peers and from programs arranged by New York headquarters. These get-togethers were useful and enjoyable. By illustration, in 1990, we gathered in Columbia, Missouri, site of the University of Missouri's famed journalism school. The program was called New Directions for News and for the first time included two staffers from each newspaper besides its publisher and editor. The criteria for their inclusion were two: they had to be on the younger side and bright. Joe Lyons and I were accompanied by Monica Bartoszek, an assistant features editor, and Bob Provost, director of marketing/research. They and their counterparts energized and expanded the customarily informative dialogue and discussions during the three-day meeting.

Jean Gaddy Wilson, the executive director of New Directions for News, drew out of the enlarged group its wildest wishes and deepest fears. The exercise, conducted in a hotel meeting room, was designed to open minds to improve newspapers and serve readers and communities while becoming better businesses. Cataloguing the wishes (and the concerns they implied) brought out how astutely analytical the participants were about their newspapers and the industry. This collective self-awareness reflected a readiness to make changes rather than to settle for the status quo. The meeting immersed us in the guts of issues confronting newspapers those days.

The exploration of assumptions and behavior for breaking out of the cocoon of habit was a lot of fun. It felt refreshing, even daring, to shed preconceptions and explore radical ideas. We broke up into three panels, where wish lists were discussed and voted on. On the final day, the panels reported to the plenary assembly. What emerged was not a somber recital of how we should mend our ways. Instead, in song and verse, with skits and recitations, supported by props hastily scrounged from scanty supplies, the teams shared their considered findings. Joe Lyons, who had a fine Irish tenor voice, was a big hit. The exercise equipped us to compete with renewed confidence.

Twice we were bussed to the campus for meetings with faculty and students. The contrast between the campus events and the round tables at the hotel was hard to overlook. The university people were unrestrained in their self-praise. Everything they did was the best. They bragged so much it was not credible.

My first private lunch with George Hearst took place shortly after he arrived. He felt the paper was headed for trouble. He asked my opinion about what should be done. I cited the several consultants' studies backing my ideas for strengthening the news staff and enlarging our footprint in the region. During all the years Grier and Lyons sat in the publisher's chair, I strongly argued for specific proposals to assure the paper's future by investing in its growth in staff and the newshole. At lunch with George, I learned Lyons had done nothing to introduce Hearst around town. I had noticed Lyons's coolness to his new colleague from the start. I told Joe he was wrong in his treatment of George. When Annie got to know George, she enlisted him to serve on the University at Albany Foundation Board of Trustees, of which she was a member. It did not take long for his executive talents to take him to the presidency of the board. It was his first engagement of many in varied community leadership and philanthropic roles that made him widely known and sought after in the Capital Region.

This was transpiring in late 1989 when we had to face up to an inevitability that might have confronted us years earlier. The *Gazette*, having dropped "Schenectady" from its flag and in its place put "Daily" to challenge us as a regional newspaper, decided to publish a Sunday paper. It came to pass about a year later. Out of a total Sunday *Times Union* circulation of 150,000, forty thousand came out of the *Daily Gazette*'s main circulation reach in Schenectady City and County and southern Saratoga County, the fastest growing sector in the Capital Region. In Joe Lyons's to-the-point observation, we had been delivering the *Gazette*'s Sunday paper for fifty years. Now the issue was how to confront this serious challenge to our regional dominance.

As almost always, there were two conflicting views: the editor and the newsroom's and the management's. The editorial view was to make our paper better than ever and hold on to as much of our Schenectady readership as possible. This entailed increasing staff and expanding coverage, both large spending items.

Management differed. Historically, even if in sympathy with the expansion of coverage, its mantra was to get it done by increasing productivity, which meant accomplishing the goal with existing if not reduced staff. With conviction, it believed the newsroom was inefficient and underworked. To deal with the *Gazette*'s expansion, management told us to plan for a significant reduction in staff and newsprint to make up for the dollar losses sure to hurt our sacred bottom line, the one by which corporate decided who shall live and who shall die. Our group—the three managing editors and I—heard this from the mouth of the general manager, Bill Clemens. In response to our proposals he said, "You guys just don't get it." Our budget was going to be cut, and our job was to plan to put out a newspaper much reduced in staff and newsprint.

There matters stood as the face-off continued with exchanges of memoranda. Then a miracle occurred. Joe Lyons, who never, ever accused me of seeking too little in resources from him in the way of reporters and space, out of nowhere asked why I hadn't pressed him for more. He proposed we hire. Of course, this was no miracle but a down-to-earth intervention, the direct consequence of the presence of our newly arrived operations manager, George Hearst. George, having taken in what was going on, interceded with the chief Hearst executive in New York and told Frank Bennack how the paper was disarming itself in the face of the *Gazette* challenge. Bob Danzig followed up with a visit to Albany to confront Joe Lyons about his deficient preparation for handling Schenectady's entry into the Sunday arena. This accounted for Joe Lyons's sudden enlightened openhandedness.

We were to get more space in the daily and Sunday papers than ever before, as well as additional staff. Earlier, Danzig strongly urged the creation of a magazine targeted at the most desirable eighteen- to fifty-year-old demographic. His wish was our command. We knew full well that birthing one was an ambitious undertaking for any newspaper but more so for one of our size and Middle American sensibilities. Nevertheless, we turned to Hearst magazine management to help recruit an editor and proceeded to lay the groundwork. We constituted a focus group of fourteen young people who worked for us in all departments of the building. We were intent on meeting the needs of their peers—who, for the most part, were not newspaper readers. We settled on a name, *Personal*, and a mission, to make it a very local magazine focusing on how women and men dealt with all aspects of their lives—their jobs, their finances, their health, their amusements. The articles were primarily intended for the targeted audience but also useful for those outside it.

In addition to working up Danzig's proposed magazine, for which we were allotted an increase of three and a half slots, in June 1990 we launched a weekly entertainment tabloid, *Preview*, published Thursdays. It was geared to informing our readers about what was available culturally in the upcoming weekend until the next.

The Sunday *Gazette* entered the field and we more than held our own. We received word that Frank Bennack said: "The *Times Union* got legs."

CHAPTER 20

New Publisher, New Era

As preparations for meeting the *Gazette* challenge were under way, the Hearst Corporation decided to hold one of its meetings in Albany, in September 1990, bringing along the top corporate executives and several members of the Hearst family, including George's father, George R. Hearst Jr. Governor Cuomo again agreed to meet with the corporate array and once more made a strikingly favorable impression.

The following month the governor returned to our paper for one of his periodic sit downs with our editorial board. Early that mid-October day I had been told there would be a meeting in the publisher's office around noon. No stress for attendance was made nor agenda shared. I thought our session with Governor Cuomo would finish in time. As can happen, our discussion burgeoned. A couple of times my secretary, Beverly Coons, interrupted with a message from the second floor, saying I was wanted. I finally told Beverly the publisher should just go ahead with whatever it was without me and I would join him as soon as I could. Soon thereafter, Lyons burst into our conference room accompanied by a stranger. In front of our visiting dignitary, I was introduced to the new publisher of the *Times Union*. He was Timothy O. White, hired from the smaller *Ann Arbor News* in Michigan, with Joe Lyons named publisher emeritus. It was an embarrassment for me and our organization and stemmed from Lyons's failure to fill me in on what was coming down. This was part of the pattern set when he had succeeded Grier. Then I was told along with other department heads—although there were only three names in the masthead: the publisher's, the general manager's, and the editor's. At that time, there was no high official present to witness Capital Newspapers management stubbing its toe.

Tim was concerned I missed his remarks to the upstairs gathering, so he mailed me a copy. "I assume the governor was worth it," he wrote. In part the new publisher's first words to assembled *TU* executives were: "I am a leader, not a controller. . . . I am a consensus builder, not a dictator. I prefer dealing with individuals face-to-face rather than groups." His behavior as publisher largely contradicted his words.

At the beginning, Tim was scheduled for surgery for which he returned to Ann Arbor. Early on, Annie and I gave a dinner party for the Whites in our home. We invited friends whose standing in the community derived from their contributions to it. They were good people for Tim to get to know.

After the operation, when he was on board, he excoriated the Sunday magazine prototype. It lacked "hipness," irreverence. He questioned whether the editor we hired had the required "it" skills. "Tina Brown of *Vanity Fair* has it," he informed me in a memo. At our salary scale we could hardly afford to hire Tina's housemaid much less Tina's editors, or attract them to abandon big city lairs to come to Albany. Still, his assessment of the prototype was not wrong. We were lucky that with Hearst magazine division help we hired a young and bright editor, Christine Rossell. What is instructive in this context is when the allegedly unhip editor attempted to jazz up her magazine, the advertising department refused to accept personal ads for it "from those with alternative lifestyles." This was not so, claimed the ad director; it was simply about not publishing content that would offend readers of "a mainstream general distribution newspaper." The hipness Tim White ostensibly wanted was rejected by his underling. These ads appeared in other publications whose essence Tim's critique found missing in our prototype.

We did not have the skills—nor the developmental time—to produce the kind of magazine Tim envisioned. Our capacity was limited, so our approach had to be incremental as we found our feet and developed modestly paid writers to produce edgier yet accurate copy. Although long before I had proposed a magazine to bolster the *Times Union*'s reach, I was no longer a fan of the idea, having in the interim learned of the lack of success registered by larger newspapers. Yet once it was decided on, I made it my own and tried to improve it as we went along. Advertising support never materialized, and the declining economy did not give us time to work out the kinks.

Frustrated by lack of front-office support and in the face of implausibly high expectations, Christine Rossell resigned as editor of *Personal*. Her deputy succeeded her, but it did not take Tim long to note that our circulation figures demonstrated our superiority over the Sunday *Gazette*. Tim said he needed the $400,000 yearly it cost to produce *Personal* and asked me to give up my fight for it. This may have been what was behind his initial hostile memo. And so, after six months, the magazine was killed. Tim proposed shifting remaining diminished resources and some additional white space to *Preview*. He observed that attracting younger readers would not be possible without a large dose of coverage of the entertainments they patronized. His observation was much more on the mark than the proposal to build a magazine, especially one printed on newsprint rather than glossy paper, with meager staff and expect it to succeed almost instantly.

On September 16, 1990, we stacked down the left-hand side of our Sunday front page four graphic and disturbing photographs. They depicted a black man being put to death by political and tribal enemies in apartheid South Africa. An accompanying article was published inside the paper.

Publication of the photographs resulted in a storm of reader protests. Most were horrified. They denounced us for sensationalism, for moneygrubbing by trying to sell papers, and for disturbing their day of rest. One woman wrote: "How dare you send this into my home?" A smaller group also regarded the presentation as antiblack or opposed to Nelson Mandela's African National Congress or as serving the interests of the white minority government.

As the editors pored over these unique photographs Saturday afternoon, no one questioned whether we would publish them prominently. The reason was their vivid crystallization of the intensified struggles in South Africa. In our collective experience, atrocities of this dimension seldom were documented on film. The photographs illustrated a conflict we covered for years. They provided a rare eyewitness account of the crosscurrents within the larger conflict.

Previously, we published reams about the tribal slaughter in South Africa and never elicited any noticeable public response. On a recent Sunday, we devoted a full page to the history of the tribal conflicts. We dutifully had recited the number of slain as they mounted, nearly eight hundred in less than two months and almost five thousand in four years. The photographs obviously made a different impact. However sickening, more people now had a grasp on this deep-seated crisis.

We had publicized depredations committed by South African whites against blacks. Our editorials were vigorously opposed to apartheid. Our opinion pages were open for decades to black exiles to make their case. In short, because American public opinion was fully informed by the news media, US national policy shifted into opposition to the apartheid regime. Those who for purposes of supporting a political faction wanted us to withhold or play down or otherwise mitigate revealed themselves as indentured to their ideologies. And we did not play that game. If the photos we published had shown a white man killing a black man, or whites killing a white, they would have received equally prominent display.

Some protesters raised one valid question we could not answer at the time we received the photographs. It was: How can you take photos while a man is brutalized and killed? The answer was provided only when those photos that stirred so much anger and vitriol were awarded the Pulitzer Prize. The photographer, a freelancer working for the Associated Press, said he tried to halt the execution but was rebuffed. The killers ordered him to stop taking pictures. He replied that he would if they stopped the killing. They did not, and he did not. It was personally dangerous for the photographer, Greg Marinovich. His bravery presented evidence to the world of the atrocity.

Important changes in the newsroom leadership accompanied the new year. Bern Zovistoski resigned in January 1991 to join *Stars and Stripes* in Germany. Bill Dowd took over Bern's job with the title amended to managing editor for operations, and Joann Crupi, the executive city editor, was promoted to managing editor for features and sports. She was the first woman to reach that level at the paper. I insisted she move up when others were boosted for the position. During my years in Albany we had women in key management posts—executive city editors, executive news editors, and photo editors, among others. As their presence in supervisory ranks increased, and a number began regularly to participate in our daily Page 1 conference, it was necessary to elevate the meeting's prevailing atmospherics. Editors from various departments competed at this meeting for front-page display of their stories. In the accustomed habits of men, the language at times became more than somewhat foul, frequently the result of excessive tension or bursts of anger. Or it resulted from a relaxed sense of heartiness or an insufficient vocabulary. Whatever the stimulus, gutter language would no longer do. When my instructions to watch the language did not produce sufficient results, Assistant Managing Editor Charlie DeLaFuente suggested we level a dollar fine for each offensive word uttered. It was no more than a crutch, but it helped raise the level of self-awareness in the conference room. I appointed myself as the sole judge of words blue enough to draw a penalty. Fines raised were given to the paper's annual Christmas Fund for the Elderly.

A newsroom is especially dependent on the full collaboration of all staffers. Occasionally, there were complaints I was overly old-fashioned about the use of words that not infrequently the whole family could hear watching television and that were commonplace everywhere else. Yet what are editors for if not to maintain standards? At the time, we also maintained our relatively straightlaced standards in articles we published. When AIDs emerged as a public health crisis, an editor came to me with a wire story that included the words "anal intercourse." My instinctive response was, "not in my newspaper, you don't"—a short-lived decision as the epidemic was explicitly discussed in the media. On the other hand, there were occasions when we used offending words even lacking a clinical context. It depended largely on who said them and in what setting. When presidents uttered them, we used the quotes. For the rest, if a vulgarity was central to an issue, we resorted to ellipses, leaving no uncertainty about the uttered word.

In the early nineties, the souring economy slackened the ambitious spirit engendered at headquarters and in the publisher by the combat with the *Gazette*. Cuts again became the remedy as the business cycle brought on challenging times. It revived concerns, expressed much earlier, about "just how good our paper had to be." The mood was captured in the question I was told Frank Bennack asked Tim White—"What have you done with my $10 million?"—the very ones that had disappeared from the bottom line. Immediately, a 5 percent reduction in expenditures was imposed, followed by severe staff cuts, which fell most heavily on the newsroom. About a quarter of the paper's employees worked for editorial, yet our operation was targeted for 43 percent of the rollbacks. Tim White, speaking in the voice of his marketing background, explained that the newsroom was not a producer of revenue. To the contrary, the newsroom was the primary source of revenue—for what would be the take if people were offered a publication made up only of advertising?

The horrendous cuts fell on our projects team and marked the beginning of a decline in which enterprise reporting that took on special interests faced increased opposition from the publisher. Almost from the first, he and I disagreed about what constituted a quality newspaper. He was strong on allying the paper with the local establishment, whether political or more importantly business, advertisers especially. He was for championing the local repertory company and symphony and public radio network, while I was for informing our readers accurately about how these community pillars were doing without abandoning standards.

Taking Tim White at his word, he truly believed that emphasizing good news over the bad built community. He favored "Golly Martha" stories, the can-you-believe-that school of journalism, easily picked up from the news agencies on any day, over the hard-slogging effort it took to unearth wrongdoing by the people in power in politics or those in business, of whom many used crony connections with government officials to enrich themselves at the public's expense. And he shared the corporate certitude that in the face of falling circulation and declining revenue the remedy required slashing costs to what he and his peers referred to as "the product," by cutting staff and space. From my viewpoint, it made little sense to degrade what you were selling when you were trying to sell more of it.

Tim White had not been our publisher for long when he convened a meeting of the newspaper's managers at an out-of-town resort. During a discussion of what new things might be tried, a proposal to build readership was offered. It was to pick up a version of the trashy supermarket gossip and sex magazines. A shoddy impersonation of such a tabloid was published by our sister paper in Texas, the *San Antonio Light*. I listened as the other managers discussed just how much such a publication would bring into the company till. I said it was not something that would succeed in our market. Whereupon the general manager, Bob Wilson, who had previously worked at the *Light*, denounced me for opposing any innovation ever proposed. It was quite an indictment. In response, I said something along these lines: "We could do that. But wouldn't it be more profitable to sell drugs? Hell, we could open a whorehouse. There's money in that."

Back at the office, I asked White what the general manager's outburst was all about. He said he had no inkling before it happened, something I found hard to credit. In the event, the supposed tabloid lifesaver, *Insider*, did not do enough for the *San Antonio Light*. Hearst ended the paper's problems. It bought the competing *San Antonio Express-News* from Rupert Murdoch and forever doused the *Light*.

A rare picture of the newsroom's managing editors together with Harry. From left are **Nancy Tobin**, who joined the *Times Union* in 1993 and oversaw photography, graphics, and design; **Joann Crupi**, who started out as reporter at the *Knickerbocker News* and held many top jobs on her way up; **Bill Dowd**, an experienced analyst of complicated problems with down-to-earth sensibilities; and **Dan Lynch**, who upheld the highest editorial standards and was also a first-rate columnist. Photo credit: *Albany Times Union.*

Mike Spain is associate editor of the *Times Union*, who for decades spearheaded the paper's technological changes and serves as a walking memory bank. Photo credit: *Albany Times Union*.

Jeff Cohen took over as executive editor in 1994. Cohen served for seven years in Albany until his promotion to editor of Hearst's largest newspaper, the *Houston Chronicle*. Photo credit: *Albany Times Union*.

A city editor, **Rob Brill**'s close scrutiny of reporters' copy gave rise to a new verb in the newsroom: to be Brilled. Photo credit: *Albany Times Union*.

Rex Smith came to Albany to cover the state Capitol for *Newsday*, became the editor of the *Troy Record*, joined the *Times Union* as managing editor, and got the top job when Jeff Cohen returned to Texas. Rex writes an admired weekly column. Photo credit: *Albany Times Union*.

Hy Rosen was without question the *Times Union*'s best-known staffer. For four decades, his political cartoons were a favorite with readers and the politicians he caricatured. Photo credit: *Albany Times Union*.

Judy Shepard, left, was a reporter who produced the kind of copy that Harry sought when he came to Albany. **Lois Uttley** was the *Times Union*'s executive city editor before heading the Capitol bureau. They're with Harry at his retirement party. Photo credit: *Albany Times Union*.

Paul Grondahl was a reporter and columnist before he took over as director of the Writers Institute of the State University at Albany. He edited Harry's first book. Photo credit: *Albany Times Union*.

The daily news conference at the Los Angeles *Herald Examiner* when Harry was editor during a transition period. Managing Editor John Lindsay sits at the head of the table with Executive Editor Stan Cloud at his left and ten of the newsroom's managers, all wearing bowties as a send-up of Harry's style. Photo credit: *Los Angeles Herald Examiner*.

Albany Roman Catholic Bishop **Howard Hubbard** walks with Rabbi **Martin Silverman** at the dedication of *Portal*, symbolizing the passage from fear to friendship, on the grounds of the Cathedral of the Immaculate Conception. Photo credit: *Albany Times Union*.

William Kennedy was a young reporter at the *Times Union* who went on to write fiction that draws on Albany's history and people. He won the Pulitzer Prize for fiction in 1984 for his novel *Ironweed*. Photo credit: *Albany Times Union*.

Bob Woodward talks to the *Times Union* staff in 2008. He inspired attentive staffers with his remarks. Reporter Michael Gormley takes notes. Photo credit: *Albany Times Union*.

Assistant Managing Editor **Charlie DeLaFuente** held several key positions at the *Times Union*. Courtesy of the *Albany Times Union*.

Ralph Martin, was sports editor, provocative columnist and fanatic jogger. Photo credit: *Albany Times Union*.

Roy Goodman at a New York State Museum opening. The Manhattan lawmaker and Harry collaborated on bringing exhibits of great art to Albany from New York City's major museums. Photo credit: *Albany Times Union*.

Judith Kaye, the first woman to serve on New York State's highest tribunal, the Court of Appeals, and the first to head it, poses with two former colleagues, on the right **Sol Wachtler**, a brilliant jurist and her predecessor as Chief Judge, and on the left one-time Associate Justice **Joseph Bellacosa**. Photo credit: *Albany Times Union*.

Martha Hahn has a sit-down with Governor Mario Cuomo in his office on her ninety-fifth birthday. She is accompanied by her daughter, Anne, and her son-in-law. Photo courtesy of the author.

Rex Babin, a gifted political cartoonist, created this cartoon to commemorate Harry's retirement. The depiction recalls the iconic photo of Richard Nixon's departure from the White House in disgrace after Watergate. Courtesy of the *Albany Times Union*.

Rex Babin looks over his last cake at the *Times Union* before joining the *Sacramento Bee*.

A freak snowstorm in October 1987 led to the first-ever publication of the combined *Times Union* and *Knickerbocker News*. Less than a year later, the *Knick* ceased publication. Photo credit: *Albany Times Union*.

A unique banner headline, expressed in three languages, captured a hopeful moment in history. The optimism of that day in 1993 proved transitory. Photo credit: *Albany Times Union*.

College of Saint Rose trustee George Hearst bestows the hood on an honorary doctorate on Harry in 1984. Photo courtesy of the author.

Anne and Harry enjoyed traveling around the country and the world after Harry retired. Here they are in Argentina, the last stop on a South American tour. Photo courtesy of the author.

The Rosenfeld clan—three daughters, their spouses, and seven grandchildren—gathered on a Cape Cod beach to celebrate Harry's seventy-fifth birthday. He and Anne met when they were teenagers and married in 1953. Family reunions on the Cape endured for decades. Photo courtesy of the author.

CHAPTER 21

The Irrepressible Conflict

In preparing to write these recollections, I organized my files. Reviewing them, I found few memos from Tim White commending the staff and many challenging the newspaper's reporting on behalf of complainants or friends. This reflected Tim's basic antagonism to a newsroom he was not able to bend entirely to his will, while I was in place to resist and slow down his efforts that I regarded as undermining journalistic values.

My editing angered him from the start when he vociferously complained before several colleagues in the executive suite over a features article about used car salesmen we had picked up from a Dallas paper. A local dealer threatened to cancel advertising, one of our ad people informed Tim. Tim told his colleagues that would be the last time such a thing happened, or "I'm going to fire Rosenfeld."

Tim White did much to bureaucratize the operation. He wanted productivity charts on each reporter and editor as if they were grinding out a replicable product on an assembly line. Good newspapering takes a lot more time than the routine. You can run up the numbers by doing once-over-lightly work. Among other projects, he established a committee of management and Guild representatives whose ostensible purpose was to improve communications between unionized employees and their supervisors during a period of cutbacks that unsettled the staff. White included himself, his general manager, operations director, and advertising director on this committee, along with a couple of my editors. He excluded me. At the time, I paid it no mind and was not bothered by not having to participate in yet another committee. Looking back, White froze me out of a process to shape the future of the paper.

He rejected my repeated complaints about the proliferation of content that was written by advertisers or special interest types but presented under the pretense that it was the work of the newsroom. These were called advertorials. In addition, columns by industry public relations people were offered as if they were authentic journalist commentators. In this Tim White anticipated by decades the creation of so-called native ads, which unabashedly sold advertisers space to present their message as if written by the publication's reporters. The advantage to the advertisers was the greater credibility their native message would convey. For the publication, these ads were an attempt to compensate for conventional ones that fled the pages of newspapers to go to the internet. It was a tactic sure to undermine the credibility of the papers taking part in this farce.

Conflict between what Tim and I considered responsible journalism manifested itself again, as 1992 was ending, with the publication of a holiday tabloid identified as an advertorial publication. The word advertorial meant nothing to most readers, I protested to Tim in a memo. I added: "It also violated an agreement that advertising supplements, which this is, would be represented as such and not disguised." My protests, though supposedly receiving some support from Tim, did not prevent the recurrence of the same issue. When it happened again, my long plaintive objection included: "What is the reason for the push in recent times, especially to disguise advertising? Are advertisers not proud of their products? Why do they seek to make them appear as something else? Is it because they feel that news coverage has more credibility with the readers precisely because our customers recognize its integrity, disinterestedness, and responsibility? News intends to tell the truth, advertising and/or promotion intend to sell a product." I lectured him: "As publisher, in charge of all operations of the newspaper, it strikes me you are obliged to give voice to the journalistic ethic. . . . Ads exist in order for the newspaper to function journalistically. Not the other way around."

There is no question that advertisements attracted readers. For years, the classifieds, listing employment opportunities, used car sales, house sales, and garage sales attained strong readership before the internet sapped their draw to newspapers. Other ads were attractive, and major businesses had their own followings. These did not supplant the attractions of the journalism; they only augmented them.

Despite the staff reductions during his tenure, Tim insisted we continued to waste resources, for one thing by having too many editors compared to reporters, citing a superficial study put together by the personnel department. A nationwide survey taken by Bill Dowd, with a high response rate (48 percent), showed otherwise. On another occasion, I used our marketing department's analysis in July to point out that the *Gazette* for several weeks was larger than the *Times Union* four days out of seven. Tim responded: "If sheer size were the only (or even primary) way to be the leading newspaper, life would be simple." To underline his reasoning, he for once generously hailed the superiority of our work. He also acknowledged he shared our concern about the size of the newshole.

Tim's complaints about newsroom negativity were frequent, second-guessing often encouraged by the ad director on behalf of a customer or a potential one. It was not easy to tolerate unvarying insistence that anything written by us whenever possible help promote an advertiser. When a features writer did an article on kitchen appliances, the general manager said the dealer cited in the article had not advertised for a year or two and neither had others who were not named. Tim wrote me to protest, saying the reporter had to have gone out of her way not to have mentioned bigger dealers who were advertisers.

This attitude manifested itself strikingly when we looked into the Off-Track Betting operation headed by Davis Etkin. Etkin, an important player in Republican Party circles, operated from his base in Schenectady. The reporting focused on OTB's failure to deliver the promised payoff to member counties, an allegation vigorously disputed by President Etkin. Michael Gormley evolved as the lead reporter on this running story. He repeatedly listened as Etkin, in a transparent attempt to rein in Mike, cited his conversations with White about the matter.

Our early coverage showed Capital OTB had the highest expenses of any OTB operation in New York State and provided the smallest payments to its counties. Spending included jobs for friends and relatives, purchasing deals with cronies, and world travel and high salaries for executives. Before he was through, Etkin made $290,000 a year, counting benefits, or $90,000 more than the governor.

On the whole, Tim accepted Etkin's claim he was operating OTB efficiently and productively. OTB was a steady advertiser. Tim set up a meeting with himself, Etkin, Gormley, and me at the largest OTB facility in town. There the argument was rehashed with no change in positions.

Mike wrote a series on OTB and Etkin's world travel with his wife and top aides on the quasi-public corporation's dime, the expensive lifestyle, and the low profit for the public. As the reporting continued, Etkin and his lawyer increased their pressure to get Gormley to ease off, threatening that Mike's job was endangered because they had Tim White's ear. There were other shenanigans committed by Etkin involving his son. Their revelation in our pages further irritated Etkin and led to the exertion of more coercion. Gormley stood up to it, confident Dan Lynch and I had his back, and he would not lose his job despite insinuations from Etkin and threats from his attorney.

After I was no longer editor in charge of the newsroom, Mike was removed from the story by Jeff Cohen, my successor, and assigned to a suburban beat. Dan Lynch, by then no longer managing editor, had become an impactful local columnist for the paper. When he wrote about the continuing Etkin dealings, he was challenged by Cohen. An astonished Lynch, in September 1997, wrote Cohen he wanted elaboration on "your statement that you will permit no column to appear in the newspaper unless it conforms to yours that Dave Etkin is doing an outstanding job." Etkin resigned in 1998 while under investigation.

The denouement of this sorry tale came in 2000. Etkin, in a plea bargain with the state attorney general's office, admitted to the following: "As president of the Capital District Off-Track Betting Corporation, he utilized and diverted corporate assets for his personal benefit and for the benefit of others, and permitted others to use and divert those assets, while falsely representing that the use of these assets was on behalf . . . and . . . in furtherance of the legitimate business" of Capital Off-Track Betting.

This was basically what Gormley reported years earlier when Tim White insisted that Etkin delivered fair value despite any possible shortcomings. Etkin was sentenced to two one-year jail terms, fined $100,000, and assessed $100,000 in restitution. He served all but sixty-four days of his sentence under house arrest.

In the spring of 1992, we were forced to restructure how we used our reporters and editors because of a 10 percent reduction in staff ordered by Tim White. Tim wanted the newsroom managers to focus on doing more with less. He cited his experience at smaller newspapers—in contrast to mine at metropolitan papers—as showing it could be done. "Harry, you and your management team must accept the notion that your main challenge is to work with me to determine how this can be done. Your challenge is not to figure out how to persuade me to provide more resources." This stated the core of the wide gap between us: He was trained and skilled at making a newspaper smaller; I was hired specifically to enlarge the horizons of the newspapers: to make them better and bigger, not skimpier.

Tim's inclination, if not his instinct, was to respond to a complaint by convicting the newsroom without first looking into its details. I presumed one time to write him that I found it more effective to study a matter before, not after, I reached a conclusion. He was a highly intense booster. When our jazz critic reported an upcoming season at the Saratoga Performing Arts Center was conspicuously comprised of encores from prior years, Tim wrote a memo saying how offended he was by the use of the word "encore" in the headline. "The type of negativism on lead headlines and teasers makes me so angry I want to spit. I want it stopped, and you're the one who's got to get it stopped." He wanted "old favorites" instead.

Later in the year, we unnerved him with a features article about the new car smell no one was sure was safe. The article was balanced but not the headline: "Dashboard of Doom?" with a readout of: "You know that new car smell? It's actually vapors from plastics, and it could be dangerous." It was accompanied by a large graphic of a chemical beaker with a skull and crossbones on it.

This was too much for Tim. "OK, that does it! I'm not going to risk $3 million of auto advertising and the viability of this newspaper just to indulge the sophomoric behavior of overzealous headline writers and thrill-seeking graphics artists," he fumed in a memo. "Henceforth, all challenging articles regarding autos or real estate must [underscored three times] have my approval prior to publication." My notation says we discussed it, but I wish I could recall the conversation. The headline was clearly sensationalist and his remedy, which I don't remember ever enforcing, over the top as well.

In 1993, Tim assigned Bill Dowd to make a pay parity analysis among managerial personnel throughout the paper. Included in the newsroom were those below the rank of managing editor. Their pay was compared to all noneditorial employees of equivalent rank. He found newsroom department heads "lagged behind the rest of the company in all respects, as did those in other categories, except not in all as much."

Not only were editorial supervisors on the short end in pay but also in perks. The *Times Union* for years rented a lakeside house in Lake Placid. It was made available for the use of top executives at the paper and in New York. I found out the noneditorial departments went deeper into their supervisory ranks to permit access to the house. When I brought this to Tim's attention, he agreed this was unfair but did not offer it to two qualified people on the editorial page, as I proposed.

Because of the 1992 cutbacks, Dowd took on restaurant reviews, which had been the assignment of a staffer who resigned. His reviews were in addition to his day job, supervising the preparation and administration of our budget, personnel, training, and new technology ventures. Eating out on the expense account and writing about it was not a stab in the dark for Bill. He had been the restaurant critic at the Baltimore *News American* before he shifted to Albany. I assured our readers: "We would not let just anyone review restaurants. For one thing, Dowd brings to his after-hours chore a well-honed appetite. . . . In addition, he is a dedicated and excellent cook. We know this because he frequently told us so."

Bill Dowd was deeply experienced and useful to have at one's side. He was a skilled analyzer of complicated problems and relied upon to research important data. He maintained calm when crises struck. Newsroom dress was nondescript at its best and rolled-up shirtsleeves and ties at half-mast were the custom. Bill's collar was buttoned throughout the workday, his necktie firmly in place. He habitually wore his jacket.

Senior editors did not relish having to do the heavy lifting of preparing the newspaper's annual budget. It was work for which they had not been formally trained. Yet, each year it was likely the one task with more impact on what the paper would look like than any other thing they did.

When, after years in the ranks as reporter, photographer, or sub-editor, you finally reached a level of responsibility where these chores became your personal property, nothing had prepared you for them. You learned budgeting—as part of management—just as over the years you had absorbed on the job the arts and practices of newspapering. For people probably not much adept at numbers in the first place, it explained why we wound up in journalism rather than finance or the sciences, which required sophisticated math skills. And the reward for good performance as a reporter or lower-level editor was to act, albeit part-time, as an accountant—not certified, merely presumptive. The budget process spelled out our ambitions, and we also tried to anticipate events to provide for emergencies, when additional news pages and personnel might be required. After approval by the accounting department and finally the publisher, the budget was the battle plan for the year ahead.

In the spring of 1992, features writer Paul Grondahl proposed publication of a photographic and word portrait of Albany, hub of the Capital Region, recently honored as an All-America City. He suggested we capture the essence of the city, as its people experienced it on one day. April 15 was the day selected.

Paul's idea underwent discussion. As the outlines of the project firmed up, it was clear it would need to be a hefty newsprint section capable of accommodating color photography. I approached the advertising director with a comprehensive plan, which he enthusiastically bought into and enlarged. From business and editorial viewpoints, advertising argued, the mainly photographic presentation would be most effective published as a glossy magazine. Tim White approved, and we learned how to do it. We had to deal with new issues, such as which grade of glossy paper to use, because it differed from the newsprint we knew well. Our presses could not handle this work, so we contracted with an outside printer and faced a range of other problems. Our assistant managing editor for graphics, Marla Camp, spent long days at the printer, putting out fires and helping to bring the project home.

The actual "shoot," in photographer parlance, was undertaken while we were still sorting out other impinging details. We deployed ten staff photographers and ten reporters. They carefully laid out the strategy to capture the spectrum of one twenty-four-hour day. On the day of the shoot, photographers exposed 109 rolls of film and produced more than 3,900 images. From these we culled the forty-seven photos that appeared in the thirty-six-page magazine, titled: *A Day in the Life of Albany*. It was made part of the August 23, 1992, Sunday *Times Union*.

The magazine vindicated the extraordinary efforts put into it. Our community was served without a resort to boosterism. Pictorially we did not glamorize but let the homely truth speak for itself. There was one major hurdle. The first run off the printer's presses was out of focus, dismaying Marla Camp and all she had worked for. On her behalf, George Hearst intervened and persuaded the printer to reprint the magazine properly.

There was a side of Tim White that came to light when he piloted his private airplane with Joe Lyons and me on board. We headed to Washington for one of our Hearst publishers and editors' meetings. One night there was a formal dinner to which Katharine Graham was invited. She did not appear at ease at the gathering and asked me to sit next to her at dinner. The speeches dragged on past the point of her endurance and I escorted her to her limousine.

On the last day we had a session with President George H. W. Bush. When it was my turn to shake hands for a formal photograph, he greeted me, saying, "How's it going, Harry?" We had met years before at a Gridiron dinner when I was with the *Washington Post* and again when he visited Albany on his campaign for vice president when he was interviewed by our editorial board. That day in the Oval Office, President Bush presented each of us with a tie clip. I wear it to this day, on the infrequent occasions I don a necktie.

The interview with Bush, limited to editors and corporate executives, delayed the flight back to Albany. White and Lyons waited for me as I arrived tardily at Dulles International Airport. It was late afternoon before Tim could take off. By then the sky had darkened and turned stormy. Tim demonstrated his cool and skill as he flew the plane through heavy weather. It was a bumpy ride, but Tim got us home safely.

CHAPTER 22

Deep Cuts, Hard Times

A two-year effort to redesign the *Times Union* reached the finish line in October 1992. Updating the appearance of our newspaper involved the selection of more attractive headline typefaces. It provided additional design elements to ease the reader's way into the paper each day, including how articles were displayed. We implemented the new design incrementally, the previous May, when we introduced a new section, At Home. It was all about housing and was devised by Tim and the ad department to be a good-news-only presentation. Years earlier, I proposed to Joe Lyons a new section to focus on homes and gardens. It was not accepted. I was all for At Home, but I bucked at excluding news appropriate to the subject. Tim dismissed my objection. He said we could handle fault-finding real estate stories in other parts of the paper.

In another design change, the publisher removed the definite article from the front-page flag, making it *Times Union* instead of *The Times Union*. This was only fair, as we had inserted "The" at the behest of a previous publisher. At still another time, the hyphen between Times and Union was removed at a publisher's bidding. It seemed publishers as a breed were tempted to alter the flag, perhaps in the expectation it would perform miracles for the bottom line. It must have been a lesson taught in publisher school.

The redesign was directed by a consultant, Nancy Tobin, who in November 1993, at Tim's direction, joined the paper as managing editor/visuals, overseeing the photography operation and the graphics and design desks. Those functions had already been substantially improved with the hiring of another White protégé, this one from his Ann Arbor paper. Marla Camp was the chief in-house manager of the redesign. When White pressed for the hiring of Tobin, I told him adding another managing editor would not look good at a time when a staff reduction again was under way.

Richard Nathan, director of the Nelson A. Rockefeller Institute of Government, the public policy research arm of the State University of New York, was an acquaintance from my Washington days when he served in Nixon's White House and I directed the Watergate coverage for the *Washington Post*. We reconnected in Albany, and at a 1989 lunch I brought up the issue of regionalization. At the time, a collaboration was mentioned that did not mature. Three years later, Nathan brought the idea up again. He wanted the *Times Union* to sponsor the kind of urban revival project undertaken by the *Dallas Morning News* and the *Baltimore Sun*. He suggested Neal Peirce to handle the project the journalist-urbanist had done for the two papers.

Nathan's idea interested me for here might be a way for the *Times Union* to perform a community service, which Tim White so fervently favored, while doing good journalism. Tim gave me the go-ahead. Talking with Peirce I learned that his methodology involved bringing to town a small team of experienced interviewers to pick the brains of the most informed people in the community to produce a report. For this he charged $75,000.

Tim said the price was too high and told me to find businesses to help pay. I did not see myself going around town soliciting funds to do my job. I read the Dallas and Baltimore reports and was struck by what I regarded as their superficiality. Furthermore, I wanted the *Times Union* to get the credit for rendering an outstanding community service that derived from being the main sponsor. I shared my views with Nathan. He surprised me, agreeing that perhaps the studies cited weren't as impressive as he first believed. I asked him whether one of his people could handle such a project. His immediate response was to suggest a conference, jointly sponsored by the *Times Union* and the Rockefeller Institute. Weeks later Tim, Nathan, and I lunched at the University Club to discuss a conference on regionalization. White was enthusiastically for it. It would explore how the Capital Region could combine the resources of its several municipal and county components to produce a higher level of public services while holding down costs.

I assigned one of my most thoughtful reporters, Harvy Lipman, to work with Nathan and his people. Senator Richard Lugar, the highly respected Republican from Indiana, was invited to keynote the three-day symposium accompanied by extensive coverage in the *Times Union*. As a former mayor of Indianapolis, Lugar was intimately familiar with the implementation of regionalization. In addition to Lipman's extensive coverage, we devoted most of the December 12, 1992, Sunday Opinion section to address many aspects of regionalization. I made sure to use my column that Sunday to spell out the newspaper's unusual role and its responsibilities. On the one hand, we agreed to help explore a matter of potentially crucial importance to the community. On the other hand, I stressed, we remained obliged to report honestly about the enterprise with which we were so closely identified.

Tim was fired up and became a full partner with Nathan in the project. He established a consortium of the CEOs of leading media businesses in the Capital Region, whose primary purpose was to promote the positive aspects of regionalization.

After the successful conference, Tim proposed that the *Times Union* each month run a series of articles on an attribute of regionalization, including to "interview appropriate politicos and put them on the spot and hold them accountable to bring it about." That was his idea of being a proactive force for good in the community. For me, it stepped over an admittedly fine line. Years before Tim arrived, when the *Knickerbocker News* was alive and kicking, it produced a noteworthy series on this issue of governmental fragmentation and duplication. For me, the series, titled "Toy Governments," signified the proper role for a newspaper—to expose a problem and indicate a remedy. I thought sponsoring a conference was within bounds. While supporting regionalization was clearly desirable, imposing a predetermined outcome on the reporting was not newspapering. It was advertising or marketing or promotion—all worthy activities—but not journalism, which is obligated to not overlook the warts on the handsomest visage.

In 1993, we again faced cuts whose effect was more severe following previous heavy reductions. I sent Tim White a two-and-a-quarter-page, single-spaced memo. In later discussion, some of us newsroom managers decided, the memo was the key act hastening the end of my days as editor. I wrote:

> We are submitting to you our studied recommendations cutting expense and space budgets to meet the specifications laid down by you. This means a reduction of 15 columns a day in newshole and trimming $60,000 out of the remainder of this year's expenses, a preview to reducing at least $100,000 more in 1994.
>
> We have done our duty and diligently met those requirements. But I would be neglecting my responsibilities were I not to earnestly protest that embedded in this process are the seeds of present and future danger for the newspaper. These cutbacks are forcing us to take actions that begin dismantling the franchise this newspaper has built up piece by deliberate piece over the 15 years of my editorship.
>
> We are becoming more and more to resemble our main competitors in the market place, surrendering bit by bit the distinguished attributes that have made us what we are.

I went on to recite the different effects that would diminish our paper. Looking back, I inferred that what Tim White did not want was to be burdened with such a specific critique of his policy, especially in writing. Tim, it must be noted, along with his publisher colleagues throughout the chain, was under strong pressure from New York to keep expenses down and the budget lean and positioned to shrink. Do more with less.

Although troubles were ever present during 1993, a bit of relief came in April, when I was selected by Syracuse University to receive the College of Arts and Sciences Distinguished Alumni Award, the first time it was bestowed. The citation recognized "your outstanding leadership in journalism, evidenced, for example, by your distinguished work on the Watergate conspiracy, and the New York State 'cameras in the courts' initiative." Not only was Annie by my side, but Steffie was in the audience with her friend Paul, which made it extra special for me. At the end of the year, I was honored with the Martin Luther King Jr. Commission and Institute for Nonviolence with its Media Responsibility Award for "the promotion of racial harmony."

In October, Tim White copied me with a letter from *Newsday* inviting the *Times Union* to participate in a conference for minority college students and recent graduates for possible jobs at newspapers. Tim was uncomfortable about not attending but wanted to know whether we could find something better closer to home. It was Tim who had forced us to eliminate the summer intern program we had used to recruit minority interns. I or someone else used to attend the *Newsday* forum but stopped when the summer intern program was dropped because of budget cuts.

I replied: "Instead of attending job fairs and doing other things for public relations, if we are serious about committing to minority jobs development, we should recruit in local high schools and colleges for intern or other training programs. AND NOT ONLY FOR THE NEWSROOM. THE WHOLE *TIMES UNION* OPERATION SHOULD JOIN IN THE COMMITMENT." I capitalized and boldfaced the last two sentences because the practice had been essentially to focus on the newsroom to deal with low minority representation, exempting the administrative, circulation, advertising, and craft operations.

For the 1994 budget, we were told to cut not only space and syndicated services but also—again—staff. I spelled out the syndicate materials we would have to eliminate, including two important supplementary wire services. Our main competitors carried one or the other. For shrinking the staff, I pointed out that the labor contract forced us to reduce staff in inverse order of seniority. Among the nine slots we would have to lose, five were filled by women, two by minorities. Once again, I cited our mission to be the dominant newspaper in the Capital Region was being undermined.

To mitigate the draconian changes, I proposed we ask corporate to close the Washington bureau, for which we were charged $195,000. Fat chance of that one flying. The cuts were demanded as competition from cable companies grew. I wrote: "At a time when we should be increasing the intrinsic value of our newspaper, we are withdrawing elements of quality from it."

The corporate creed was to boost productivity (that meant staff and newsprint cuts). Tim in his memo added: "Sooner is better. More is better."

We had lost readers as we raised prices while cutting staff. Our protests about the severe cutbacks led corporate to give back some money in November. At the end of that terrible year, Tim finally conceded: "As you know, we all agree we have gotten too low in terms of staffing and newshole resources."

Amid the concern of cutbacks, we had a big morale booster in the newsroom. When the Israelis and Palestinians reached an accord under President Bill Clinton's negotiating umbrella, Charlie DeLaFuente, our assistant ME for news, had a splendid idea to headline the story of the accord signing with a banner consisting of one word rendered in three languages. The word was peace, centered in English and framed on either side in Arabic and Hebrew. To get the Hebrew right, we checked with a local synagogue. The Arabic took greater effort. Many attempts fell frustratingly short. Finally, as time was running out, a native of Palestine enlisted by one of our Muslim colleagues, Bebe Nyquist, came from his job in the state Labor Department and sat at the side of our art director for more than an hour to get the word right on the computer.

The English we managed without assistance.

This front page was a big hit. I sent framed copies to the three principals involved and received a nice note from the Palestinians, nothing from the Israelis, and a personal letter from the president ending with "I am grateful for your thoughtfulness."

CHAPTER 23

The Inevitable Ax

Tim White took me by surprise one day. As I met with him in his office, without prompting by me he remarked he foresaw a long future for me as editor, provided I did not go crazy. Considering the number of confrontations during our time together, none of which apparently qualified me as being out of my mind, this was nice to hear. Soon thereafter, he insisted on hiring Nancy Tobin as a managing editor. Much later, after Tim had moved on and I had retired, I found out she claimed Tim encouraged her to join the *Times Union* with the prospect of becoming my replacement.

The 1993 publishers and editors meeting took place in St. Petersburg, Florida, in October. For a change, spouses were invited. There I met Jeff Cohen, who had been managing editor of the Hearst paper in San Antonio until it was shuttered. For me it was a routine newspaper division gathering. Annie had a different impression. Intuitively gifted, she read the faces of some of the people and noticed they were going behind closed doors. She told me something was going on. I said I not picked anything up.

Jeff moved to headquarters in New York after the *Light* was closed and spent a year working on special projects to prepare the Hearst newspapers for the rising Digital Age, his putative role at the St. Petersburg meeting.

Additionally, it turned out, he was vetted by *Times Union* executives for the job for which he was already designated by New York—editor of the *Times Union*. If Tim had wanted Tobin as my successor, as Nancy believed, he was overruled.

Back home, my wife heard from a close friend that her husband had been told a new editor was to be appointed. When Annie shared the story with me, I dismissed it as nonsense. It was anything but. The afternoon came, probably at the end of February or the beginning of March 1994, when I was summoned to Tim's office. Never alluding to his previous assurance about my future, he told me that in two days an announcement was to be made replacing me with Jeff Cohen. I would be shifted to take over the editorial pages. I took care to hold my tongue and neither tell him what I thought about his move nor argue with it.

Some days later, he sent me a memorandum summarizing his plan. Instead of engaging with him, I told Tim I needed time to reflect on my course. Meanwhile, I firmly insisted there be no announcement.

Tim first said Jeff would join as associate editor until the end of the year, when he would become editor. Instead, I suggested that I retain my title until then and Jeff come on board as executive editor, an arrangement not unknown in the newspaper trade. After an extended period, Bob Danzig thought editor emeritus would be a suitable title for me, but Tim had another idea: As of the new year of 1995, I would become editor-at-large. Although Jeff was not pleased, after some back and forth it was what came about. My formal retirement date was set for August 1996, my sixty-seventh birthday, with a salary increase and the existing bonus formula intact until then. As the date of my replacement neared, I called Bob, my boss's boss. I pointed out that I had been useful to the corporation in the past and asked whether such a continuing role might be included in the announcement of Jeff Cohen's appointment and my new role. Bob's heavy breathing on the other end of the phone as we talked indicated discomfort. He curtly rejected my request. Although the April announcement did not include any mention of a corporate role going forward, it was in fact an important part of my duties from then onward.

A long negotiation began with a Hearst lawyer. I enlisted my son-in-law Daniel Kaufman to handle my end, which he did with diligence and effectiveness. Shortly before the staff was told, on April 20, 1994, about Jeff taking over direction of the newsroom, I informed each managing editor privately. My greatest unhappiness was telling Dan Lynch, who rightfully aspired to my position. Tim, in his memo of March 4, acknowledged my disappointment at Dan not getting the job. He noted that Jeff was "very different from both you and Dan." The April 21, 1994, front page informed our readers of the change.

The same day a problem surfaced with the agreement Dan Kaufman was negotiating. It was over a section to which I would not agree. It barred me from making disparaging remarks about Hearst. I said that was all right with me if it also provided no one at Hearst could make any about me. It was withdrawn.

Announcement of the end of my job running the paper brought letters from former staffers and incumbent ones. Bob McManus, by then deputy editorial page editor of the *New York Post*, wrote: "Your Mr. Cohen has some big shoes to fill. I learned a lot from you, and never really said thanks. So thanks." Tim Beidel, a former reporter, told me: "I found the news very discouraging. I do not know the circumstances of the change, but I do know that you are too young, vital and energetic to while away time on the *TU* editorial page."

John Caher, who had gone on to write books and work for law publications, recounted a story.

> Now that you are out of the newsroom, I feel I can say something I've wanted to say for a long time: There's no one in the profession whom I respect or admire more. You were not only editor of the *Times Union*, but its moral compass. Sailing in uncharted waters without that compass is a bothersome thought.
>
> You've probably long forgotten this, but about seven or so years ago we had a brief discussion that, to me, was a defining moment, both in my career as a reporter and as an employee of Capital Newspapers. I was working on something that involved the Commission on Judicial Conduct, something that I knew would be very, very troublesome to Mrs. Robb. [She was chairwoman.] I also knew that Mrs. Robb was a close friend of yours. Potentially, this was a sticky situation.
>
> However, you called me in, pointed your finger at me, and said in substance: "Look, we both understand the situation here. She will probably call you and/or me when she realizes what you are doing. You do your job and let me worry about her."
>
> Frankly, that's what I was going to do anyhow. But I can't tell you how important it was to me to know that I had that kind

of support and that your first, foremost and sole priority was in reporting the news, regardless how bothersome in might be to a friend.

Susan Tomer was a reporter and later a local columnist. She wrote: "Working with you gave those who were willing to see it a broader view we didn't know we needed. Your excitement over a story or issue was wonderful to behold; don't ever lose that spark, or your sensitivity and compassion."

Jay Jochnowitz, who as I write is the editorial page editor of the *Times Union*, at the time was a reporter. He told me in a long note:

> You brought balance to the search for news that should be a model of the business—a clear sense of duty to the reader, a firm and consistent demand that public officials and institutions serve well and honestly, and, though harder perhaps for the powerful to recognize, a warmth and humanity that tempered just enough, some of the bloodthirsty instincts of those of us in the field.
>
> On both a personal and professional note, I want to thank you for keeping the first promise you made to me on my job interview seven years ago—that I would never have to fight internal conflicts of interests which I had seen on other papers. I have grown concerned in recent years that there have been pressures of other agendas on the newsroom and I suspect you have been a strong influence in keeping them at bay.

Taken together, for me these sentiments vindicated my editorship. The constant struggle was to maintain journalistic integrity in the face of management's frequent indifference, if not hostility. In the thick of the tumult accompanying newsroom operations and the tensions between supervisors and those they oversaw, at least some recognized the validity of our mission: To publish a newspaper that emphasized our responsibilities to our readers and the wider public. It spoke to what we accomplished, and what we strived for even when we fell short.

With the shift from the newsroom to the editorial page, my relations with Tim improved. He was reasonable in his negotiations updating my contract to reflect the new reality. Moreover, he now had an editor in

Jeff Cohen more attuned to his operational points of view. He was as active as ever pushing his pet policies and people onto the editorial page, generally reflecting his political conservatism. Before him, Joe Lyons also professed conservative views, such as support for a flat income tax favoring his economic class. Yet he never tried to muscle his views onto the editorial page, which opposed the flat tax.

Tim White used me to reach out to the community in my new role, and he was enthusiastic about some of my projects. The tenor of the relationship eased considerably, although each of us remained the person we had been before—but no longer at constant loggerheads. His relentless search for answers to his quest for reshaping the culture of the newspaper resulted in the commissioning of an outside study of staff morale. It was a department-by-department assessment of its leadership and of the top executives. In my report to Tim White, I conveyed the views of the three-person staff I now headed. Communication among us was not a problem because we met every workday. After dragging it out of them, "I was deemed to have been too didactic, and more or less dictated editorial policy. I was described as being better in my new role."

As for their views of Tim White, I wrote:

> There was a different concern involving you in the matter of trust. First of all, trust becomes dicey in the context of the staff reductions the newsroom has sustained. Second, there is suspicion that the emphasis on new ways to disseminate information comes at the expense of practicing good journalism.
>
> There are also concerns about the degree of confidence you demonstrate in the operations, both the newsroom generally and the editorial page specifically. There is the feeling that you adopt criticisms from special interest groups or advertisers at face value without looking into their validity.
>
> That leaves a question lingering whether and to what extent you stand by your people. They are explicitly not saying that everything done by us is not open to criticism or is totally correct.
>
> They do say that critics often have axes to grind and their observations need to be tested for accuracy before judgment is made—or the appearance that a judgment has been made without such due diligence.

My editorial page colleagues' critique mirrored what I had earlier told the publisher but he had not heeded. He was what he was. Even my efforts to connect him more personally with our editorial page staff through regular meetings did not improve matters.

Corporate assessed Tim White's work differently. In January 1996, Tim's responsibilities were expanded to include oversight of the Hearst community newspapers in the Midwest. In his announcement, newspaper division head Bob Danzig said: "Tim White has done a superb job in managing the Albany *Times Union*." At the beginning of 1995, Joe Lyons retired as publisher emeritus (and as assistant to the general manager of Hearst newspapers), having served four years in that role after his years as publisher of the *Times Union*. He had worked out of an office several miles down the road, where Roger Grier had previously set up his Albany office when he joined corporate's newspaper division.

Also, early in January, my wife and I along with the *Times Union* were honored by the Capitol Chamber Artists as "patrons of the arts," Annie especially for her affiliation with a program that sponsored arts education in the public schools, and I for the extensive coverage and support the *Times Union* provided the arts over the years. It was a massive reception for 260 people in the rehabilitated former Union Station.

In February, Annie and I were off to Palm Desert, California, for a two-week vacation. In the second week, I broke my ankle navigating barefoot down a rain-slicked grassy slope toward a swimming pool. It was a severe break, and the EMT could not find a vein to inject painkillers as an ambulance took me to the Eisenhower Medical Center in adjacent Rancho Mirage. There my nephew, Dr. David Kaminsky, the husband of my niece Janice, headed the pathology department. He lined up the hospital's top bone man to attend me. As I lay on a gurney, by then more than an hour later, still without benefit of painkillers, the doctor examined me and decided immediate action was necessary. There was no more time to wait for injections to take effect. He asked me to hold tight to the rail on either side of the bed as he pulled my broken ankle into place. Later that night, it was operated on, and the ankle, now inserted with steel screws, was placed in a cast.

Our return home was delayed for a week until I was fit to make a cross-country flight. Then I was hoisted onto the plane by a hydraulic lift at Palm Springs airport and placed in a front cabin seat arranged by George Hearst. We made it back late that night, after a stopover in Chicago, where Amy and her kids were on hand to cheer me up. On arrival in Albany, there was no elevator mechanism available, so I was carried down the stairs by two very strong men. A limousine arranged by George awaited Annie and me and took us home.

For weeks thereafter, Annie drove me to work and I stayed for several hours a day. I got around in a wheelchair or with a walker. For exercise, I wheeled myself around the parking lot. A colleague from another department remarked that she was unsettled seeing me consigned to a wheelchair. In time, I became more mobile, and a year or so after the mishap, with the bones knitted properly, an operation in Albany removed the steel screws from my ankle.

CHAPTER 24

Milestones and a New Role

According to anthropologists, man and woman play their necessary roles in the evolutionary process by producing offspring. They get to hold on to their usefulness while the children learn to cope with lurking lions, tigers, and bears. Once the kids presumably master the art of survival, Ma and Pa can go sulk in the corner as supernumeraries. Anthropology notwithstanding, before I could consider my parental obligation fulfilled, I had to see my daughters settled in their own lives, with their futures on track, if not guaranteed. I suspect this feeling is not unique to me.

In the fullness of time, each of our three children married in Albany, but only one ceremony took place in the Reform temple the family joined when we arrived in 1978. Susan, the eldest, was first to marry. When she did, her fiancé's Orthodox family found our congregation insufficiently observant, so Susan and Stuart were married in a Conservative synagogue near our home. It had a certified kosher kitchen from which the wedding banquet would be served.

Amy, our middle child, was next to wed, which she did at our Congregation Beth Emeth to the satisfaction of both families. For the Rosenfelds, the event was enhanced because our first grandchild, Sarah, attended as a babe in arms. Wedding photographs captured four generations. Stefanie, five-and-a-half years younger than her next oldest sibling, graduated high school in Albany, and on receiving her BA, continued to New York University for her master's in studio arts. She remained in the city to work in publishing as a graphic designer and art editor.

Over the succeeding years, when her parents initiated talk about her single status, Stefanie fended us off with evasive answers. I feared Stefanie might have thought she was being pressed because I believed she wasn't getting any younger. That did not concern me; what did was the absence of peace in my soul while my baby was out in the world, unanchored, as it seemed to me. I was discouraged, dissuaded, or downright forbidden to speak plainly to my child, lest I distress her psyche or gum up whatever works were actually or potentially in motion. During those times, I remembered the aplomb of my parents as they intervened in my personal affairs as boy and man. However much I may not have relished it, I never thought they did not have standing to do so.

In time, Steffie settled into a long-term relationship with Paul Aiken. Finally, in August 1995, when they married, neither wanted a religious ceremony as they came from different faith backgrounds. The couple planned a small wedding mostly limited to the two families, held on the lawn in our back garden. As our freshly minted son-in-law Paul noted at the occasion in his toast, when first word of their engagement was heard, out came Anne's clipboard and checklist. My role was limited to arrange for my friend, Justice Leonard Weiss, to preside. For most of the rest, I simply said yes to Anne's voice in the matter. Each item was methodically checked off: caterer, florist, tent and chair supplier, photographer, chamber quartet, disc jockey. The countless details were attended to for a celebration set for only weeks after Steffie's phone call that began: "I have some good news."

Anne Rosenfeld's greatest test suddenly loomed three hours before the wedding. She was alerted in the late morning by our next-door neighbor, who would attend. She asked why the caterer's people had not yet appeared. The tent was up and the rented chairs aligned in rows, the wedding bower in place. Anne phoned the caterer, who told her he was busy preparing the feast for the next day. She remained cool, went off to consult with the caterer, while I contemplated imminent humiliation and searched my brain for where to find sixty prepared meals in a hurry.

In the event, the caterer rose to the challenge and produced a delectable repast and fine service. It turned out in so many ways to be a perfect day, including the weather, which made the garden setting ideal for the family gathering. Just before 9 p.m., a couple of police officers showed up to convey a neighbor's complaint about noise. The young people posed with the officers. Those photographs will always cause those looking at them to smile. And I had my own reason.

Dan Lynch continued as managing editor/news after my newsroom role ended. He and Cohen clashed, and Dan lasted only until August 1995. I recommended to Tim White that Dan be assigned to the Washington bureau as a writer-columnist. Instead, he became a popular local columnist.

Tim White asked me for suggestions for Dan's successor. My first pick was Joann Crupi, but Tim showed no interest. Consequently, I proposed Rex Smith, the editor of the Troy *Record*. I had been cognizant of Rex since his days as the Albany reporter for *Newsday*. From what I knew of his work as a reporter and editor, I thought he would be good for the job. Tim White apparently agreed because Rex was selected, although the story was that Cohen had another preference.

As editor in charge of only the opinion pages, I wrote editorials as needed. My topics ranged over local, state, national, and international issues—whatever had to be done when the editorial writers were not available. I experimented with a regular presentation for the op-ed page, which selected a trenchant quote from a person in the news, accompanied by a photo and brief biography. In addition, I was enlisted for special projects for the *Times Union* and for Hearst newspapers.

In 1995 Tim White wanted to establish a Community Advisory Board, followed in 1996 by his desire to set up a Publisher's Roundtable, followed by a Readers' Roundtable in 1997. All were community outreach efforts, including establishment of an editorial advisory board, in which I played a greater or lesser role.

There were so many balls in the air as the retirement date neared that it was postponed. At first it was extended until August 31, 1997, and then to October 31, which would fall on the anniversary of my hiring in 1978. However, when told by the corporate pension executive I would benefit if I worked the entire year, Tim generously agreed.

I had begun to look past my days at the *Times Union* at the end of 1995, pondering what I might do. I sent Bob Danzig a lengthy proposal "to enhance the indelible connection between the House of Hearst and the news industry for all the years ahead." It outlined several approaches for Hearst to undertake to impact the industry and therefrom gain prestige. These ranged from training recent college graduates seeking a career in journalism to one serving the professional needs of midcareer working journalists. It could encompass all media, including the budding internet. It could be established in New York City or Washington, D.C., at a university or as a freestanding venture. "I offer this memo," I wrote, "to initiate a discussion. . . . I see myself playing a major role in the programs after the conclusion of my assignment at the *Times Union*." I said this proposal might be discussed at an upcoming meeting of selected Hearst editors scheduled for January 1996 in Houston.

My memo triggered Danzig to involve his two top aides who were planning future meetings. His initial reaction to my proposal was negative, and he stated to them: "I believe the efforts all worthwhile but the reputational value exceedingly modest." Tim picked up on the Danzig email to message me: "Harry, don't give up too easily. I think the point your memo makes speaks directly to the fact that the Hearst Foundation efforts to date have been unfortunately low profile. . . . On the Editorial side, no one within Hearst with the prominence and stature of a Harry Rosenfeld has yet lent his shoulder to the effort to improve this. Stay the course."

The Houston meeting assigned me to several corporate projects intended to elevate Hearst newspapers as a group. Because I had been chosen more times as a Pulitzer juror than anyone else in Hearst, I was asked to draw up guidelines for the preparation of entries from Hearst newspapers to be assessed by Pulitzer juries. Danzig, in a memo, went so far as to suggest: "The facilitator editor will also provide guidance to encourage placement of Hearst editors on Pulitzer committees and board." When Tim shared that memo with me, I immediately and vigorously protested that it was a very bad idea. Were it known in the industry, it would bite us in the butt. In response, Tim told me: "I kind of agree with your observation regarding campaigning to stack the Pulitzer committee. . . . And I think the very reason that your name has been included and suggested is precisely because you have more experience, more knowledge, and more insight in this whole process than arguably anyone else in the Hearst Corporation. Precisely this kind of input is going to be invaluable as we move forward on this. I appreciate it."

In April 1996, with the help of Chuck Lewis, the chief of the Washington bureau, along with a Houston editor, I compiled a list of the prizes for which the work of Hearst newspapers could reasonably aspire. I urged the submission strictly follow the rules laid down by the contests and provided practical advice, including a ban on hype but recommending a detailed description of the best physical format for entries, making them reader friendly for jurors. These were self-evident suggestions that my experience informed me had not been generally followed by the few Hearst entries I encountered in the three Pulitzer juries on which I served up to that time (a fourth would come later). None was as impressive in its presentation as its content merited.

The Houston meeting outlined my role also as facilitator to produce a project on which Hearst newspapers were to collaborate. The entire bundle of assignments was part of a corporate campaign to focus on Journalism of Distinction for Hearst newspapers. The following May, after consultation with editors, the first Distinction project was launched, including, significantly, the Washington bureau. The subject was: How safe is the nation's drinking water? I solicited the participation of all papers but commanded none. From their suggestions, the elements of the series were devised and articles, graphic, and photographic chores assigned. All copy would come to me in Albany to be processed by *Times Union* editors. When the package was finished, it was transmitted to all Hearst newspapers. A master plan was provided for a three-day series with a main story and sidebars, graphics, and photos for each day's presentation. The four-month effort was ready in late September for publication in early October. Each paper designed its own presentation.

The reporting team comprised reporters from the Washington bureau and the *Houston Chronicle*; *San Francisco Examiner*; *Seattle Post-Intelligencer*; Midland, Texas, *Reporter-Telegram*; and the *Times Union*. Graphic artists from the *San Antonio Express-News* and photographers at the *Houston Chronicle* and the *Times Union* participated. The complex project—coordinating the work of the separate newspapers and developing the ideas of all twelve Hearst newspapers—was edited by me.

After reading my message that accompanied the electronic transmission of the vast project, Tim White emailed me: "Harry, a great note, and most impressive package." Bob Danzig messaged: "Your 'facilitator' hat fits nicely. Congratulations."

Working with Chief Judge Judith Kaye in 1996, I put together a panel on domestic violence. The production of the *Times Union* Community Forum in collaboration with our regional public TV outlet was a follow-up to a series of articles published before the panel was convened. I was coproducer and Judge Kaye a panelist. With her contacts, we recruited experts from the Capital Region and across the country. The moderator was a renowned New York University professor of law, Stephen Gillers. The discussion was taped for use by all of New York's public TV stations and made available to PBS stations nationwide. The program, which took the better part of a year to put together, was broadcast September 29, 1996.

One of the panelists was Joan Zorza, the editor of *Domestic Violence Report*. She turned out to be related to my old friend Victor Zorza, a gifted journalist I worked with in my days in New York and Washington. I lost touch with him over the years and I was saddened when told that Victor had died after a long illness. Only because of Joan's participation on the panel was I able to write my condolences to Rosemary, whom I knew as his wife. I learned from Joan they had divorced, so I also wrote to the woman he lived with the last two and a half years of his life. He was a driving force behind the hospice movement in the United States, following the death from cancer of his young daughter. It was hard to imagine a world without Victor, bereft of his passion, energy, and quickness of mind.

As soon as the taping of the panel ended at the WMHT studio in the deep woods of Schenectady County, I bummed a ride in the van taking the downstate contingent back to New York City. That evening the fortieth anniversary of the closing of the *Herald Tribune* was to be observed and I did not want to miss it, as it would be our last, really our last. Ten years before, Richard Wald, the impresario of the annual gathering throughout the decades, decided that thirty was enough for a newspaper event. The signature reporters typed to indicate the end of their usually too lengthy articles was -30-. It could also be rendered as XXX or xxx.

By the time the fortieth anniversary approached, the City University of New York had acquired the Tribune Building on Forty-First Street and located its new Graduate School of Journalism therein. That sufficed as incentive for other veterans of the *Trib* to take up the cause and summon the lame and the weak, the battered survivors of ancient newspaper battles, to gather again in their old haunt for a truly last hurrah in the building where they labored as their beloved newspaper fought for its life.

Seeing former friends and colleagues after all those years was a mixed blessing. It was depressing how many people were only recognizable by reading their name tags. The famous mingled with those whose later accomplishments did not reach the celebrity status of Tom Wolfe or Jimmy Breslin, but whose attainments were substantial. It was heartening to see them all again and to recall as best we were able the anecdotes of yore that bound us together as we marveled about how much the other guy or gal had changed—for which read "aged."

The high point for me was when a tall blond woman I could not place smiled at me. Not remembering her in the least, I turned my attention elsewhere. She finally laid her hand on my shoulder. As I turned to look at her full face, she asked whether I recognized her. The first name on her tag read Diane. It came to me suddenly. "Yes," I said, "but earlier I knew you as Peter." Now there was someone who really had changed.

It was a night to remember, best summed up by Dick Wald reflecting on why so many had chosen to gather over the years. "We shared something," he said, "that was valuable for us at the time—and since." When the paper closed in 1966, I had been connected to it for half my life, eighteen years, twelve of them full-time (I took four years out for college, working summers, and two more for Uncle Sam). It's where I learned my trade step by step and grew from boyhood to manhood, working alongside accomplished reporters and editors.

CHAPTER 25

The Homestretch

In my final two years working full-time, I also took on long-range civic projects that I pursued into my retirement years. The origins of these had come to me long before. When I was still editor, on occasions when the weather was nice and absent a working lunch, I drove to the Hudson, parked underneath the elevated Interstate 787 highway, changed into sneakers I kept in the trunk, and took a walk along the riverside. Especially at those times, the separation of Albany from the Hudson River by this otherwise useful interstate was too obtrusive to overlook. Between the highway and the river remained a narrow strip of land, wide enough for a bike and walking trail and some other minimal uses. On my walks, I passed the handful of exercise workout stations set up at intervals along the pathway. One chap grew rice in a patch of land. Here and there was a park bench. Discarded trash was everywhere.

The site called out for improvement. I envisioned an ambitious venture to reconnect the people to their river. These thoughts became more focused in my thinking when as editor-at-large I was relieved of the responsibilities of running a newsroom. The centerpiece of my plan was to recreate Fort Orange, the longer lived of two early European settlements (circa 1640) where Albany would be established along the littoral of the west bank of the Hudson River. The strip of publicly owned land would be available virtually cost free.

Authenticity was essential for the riverfront project. Fort Orange should be built to resemble as close as possible the original, whose plans, however, were nowhere to be found. The location of the fort was unearthed during archeological digs in the early 1970s before the completion of the six-lane 787 over it. Restoration in its exact original spot was not possible. The dimensions of the original fort were a modest 120 by 140 feet, surrounded by a wooden stockade and a not highly protective moat. The fort was small enough for an accurate copy to be built on land available nearby. Archives, diaries, and ancient maps could provide additional guidance to what it looked like.

Rather soon my vision came to include construction of a Dutch settlement attached to the fort, just at it had been historically. The next step was to erect an Indian village of the kind local tribes would have inhabited. A copy of Henry Hudson's ship, the *Half Moon*, which had been built in 1989, plied the river that bears his name and other waters, could be permanently berthed at a pier. A museum would house the many artifacts dug up every time a shovel was stuck deep enough into the flat ground of downtown twentieth-century Albany.

To make it visitor friendly, two restaurants would be placed into the scheme, one a cafeteria, the other a bit pricier. As for the rest of the narrow littoral, my idea, taken from visits to the Chicago Botanic Gardens near my daughter Amy's home, was to recreate as far as practicable the plantings of colonial times and enlist the various garden clubs of the region in its development and maintenance.

Along the line, I involved two people. John Egan, then the chief executive officer of the Albany International Airport and a former New York State executive, much admired as a builder and manager, was most excited by the plan. We became a team. John also provided the political savvy necessary to leverage government support and funding. Of course, I had to get Tim White to sign off, and he too jumped on board.

I approached Governor Pataki, who became an effective advocate. John and I came up with the idea of integrating riverfront development in Troy, on the east bank of the Hudson, the bailiwick of Senator Joseph Bruno, the majority leader. There we proposed exploiting Troy's historic connection to the Industrial Revolution with some of the buildings from that era still standing.

The governor connected me to his parks commissioner, and there were several meetings. Bureaucracy ate up time with a variety of studies and proposals. At a formal dinner given by the governor at his mansion, George Pataki asked how the riverfront project was going. I said:

"Governor, unless you get on your horse, it's going nowhere." The governor acted, providing a substantial sum for a thorough feasibility study. The final report delivered some bad news. Heavy rainstorms triggered the discharge of sewage into the river. I did not think it meant the end of the world for the project because public health considerations and the recreational use of the river themselves necessitated dealing with the problem, never mind Fort Orange Redux.

Then came September 11, 2001. Afterward, there was no longer any steam in our engine. Potential political supporters suddenly had more urgent priorities. It was a pity. It remains a good way to evoke the culture of the community in a facility integrating and celebrating its history.

I had better success with another major proposal that overlapped with Fort Orange. Over the years visiting New York City, Annie and I usually took in one or more of the city's world-class art museums. It occurred to me that the Metropolitan Museum of Art, especially, was known for storing art it had not sufficient space to display at one time. Wouldn't it be feasible to have some of it taken out of storage to be presented for a temporary but long-running show at the New York State Museum in Albany? It would do much to enrich the capital city's culture. I proposed this idea in Joe Lyons's time as publisher. It went nowhere because of resistance from the state museum director. I tried again with Tim White, who was enthusiastic, and in 1996 I again set about getting it done.

I contacted Senator Bruno, who voiced immediate support. Most importantly, the majority leader encouraged me to call Senator Roy Goodman, who headed the Senate Arts Committee.

Then I consulted Gil Maurer, the chief operating officer of the Hearst Corporation, a longtime trustee of the Whitney Museum. He was completely supportive and outlined important considerations I needed to keep in mind as I proceeded to court the assistance of the museums. The key to opening the doors that needed opening was Senator Goodman, himself a wealthy patron of the arts who represented Manhattan's Upper East Side. The timing was right. All the influential players were Republicans, namely, the governor, who had installed Earle Mack as chairman of the New York State Council on the Arts, and Senators Bruno and Goodman. These people appreciated the arts and recognized them as a valuable tool of economic development. Unlike, for example, Mario Cuomo, who whiffed on both counts.

In November, I went to New York to meet with Senator Goodman and to lunch with the president of the Metropolitan Museum of Art, William Luers. He was agreeable, but he had to make sure any traveling exhibit was properly curated to keep faith with the Met's standards of quality—no small or inexpensive matter.

Chairman Mack told me the governor and Mrs. Pataki were strongly in favor of the project. With the editing help of George Hearst, I drafted a letter to submit for Hearst Foundations funding support. I had to deal with another hesitant state museum chief, finally having to point out to him the panoply of important public officials with power over his domain who backed the project. It was not until the next year, in May 1997, that the inaugural show was presented. It was "Winslow Homer and His Contemporaries," drawn from the Met's collection. The *Times Union* sponsored a grand opening reception. A large turnout of Albany's establishment showed up, including Mayor Jerry Jennings and civic and community personages. Bill Luers was there and expressed his delight and looked forward to future collaborations. It was the first but not the last reception the *TU* underwrote because in the following years prestigious exhibits followed, under the rubric "Great Art Exhibitions," including working relationships with the Museum of Modern Art, the Whitney, and the Guggenheim.

Annie and I were invited to spend five days at a Renaissance Weekend at the Aspen Institute in Colorado at the end of the summer of 1996. We flew into Denver and rented a car. I was on one panel speaking about the *Post*'s Watergate team and a second about how the presidential campaign should be covered. Anne Spitzer was among the designated questioners on my first panel, and Annie and I became friendly with the other Anne and her spouse, Bernard. He was a New York real estate developer and she an English instructor. We socialized a good part of the time at Aspen together, including a whitewater raft trip. The Spitzers' son, Eliot, was then beginning to make his mark in New York State politics.

Anne Rosenfeld appeared on a panel on America's Contemporary Arts (she was vice president of the Institute for Arts in Education) and as a questioner for another panel. After we left Aspen, we took a road trip through the stunning national parks in the region. We hiked through streams in canyons, Redlands, Canyonland, Bryce, and others; visited the Grand Canyon; drove through Navajoland and got to see some of the desperate conditions of reservation life. We concluded our road trip in Las Vegas, where we spent a day and one night in one of the grand hotels. I had made sure to reserve an outfit for the metropolis in the desert, only to find it overdressed me for the occasion.

Bob Danzig nominated me for membership on an external assessment panel for a journalism project to prepare minority students at Florida International University to become candidates for jobs. Under scrutiny was a program on the media. Particularly pertinent for this group of generally at-risk students who lacked basic skills was to focus on the development of good writing before prepping them for journalistic purposes. It suggested the use of computer programs to teach grammar, among a host of recommendations. Integrating minorities into the newsroom is essential to performing our work comprehensively, thereby serving the nation's well-being.

In the middle of November 1996, Jeff Cohen finally got from Tim White what he wanted all along: the title of editor. After eighteen years, I surrendered the position that drew me to Albany. I became editor-at-large, which I remain as I write.

With the title shift I gave up oversight of the editorial and op-ed pages. Joann Crupi, the managing editor/features, was moved out of that spot to make room for her replacement by a Cohen hire, Karen Potter. Crupi became editor of the opinion pages (including the Sunday Perspective section) and my boss, because I continued to write my column, which she edited. I remained a member of the editorial board. Unlike the announcement when Cohen replaced me as boss of the newsroom, this time it was noted that Rosenfeld "will oversee special projects for both the *Times Union* and the Hearst Newspaper Division."

The next year was filled with rewarding activities. Less than two weeks after giving up my title and position, in 1997 I was invited for the fourth time to serve as a Pulitzer juror. I was reelected vice chairman of the Fair Trial/Free Press Conference. For the *Times Union*, I pulled together community outreach programs, soliciting all senior editors and local columnists for their ideas and from them shaping a proposal for Tim

White's consideration. The first *Times Union* Town Hall meeting, staged in a local charter school, focused on an issue material to the very life of the city, the quality of its public school system. Like most cities, large and small, Albany was diminished by middle-class flight, declining real estate values, and underperforming schools. The forum, one evening in May, explored the relationship between discipline and academic achievement in Albany's public schools. Parents, students, teachers, principals, policymakers, and delegates from neighborhood associations attended. More than two hundred participated, and the session lasted an hour past its scheduled time. New York State Commissioner of Education Richard Mills, who took part, said the most significant value of the meeting was bringing together people who in the ordinary course of events would not join in a reciprocal discussion.

I undertook direction of another signature project for the Hearst newspaper division after a meeting of principal editors in Washington, D.C. It was spearheaded by the Washington bureau, under Chuck Lewis and his reporter Holly Yeager. It was titled "Handguns in America."

With participation of the twelve Hearst newspapers, the metros and the smaller ones, a four-day package of articles, graphics, and photographs was prepared. Centerpiece of the project was a national survey. It found most Americans "think the average citizen should have the right to own a handgun, but they also want the government to regulate gun ownership," and half of those wanted it to be on the federal level. A full page of the answers to the survey was published. Holly Yeager, among her other heavyweight contributions, detailed the money being made in the handgun trade.

The Hearst papers began to publish the series in their Sunday, October 26, 1997, editions. In Albany, two major parts of the first installment were spread over the front page. Another story was in the lower right-hand columns of that Sunday *Times Union*. Its headline stated: "A legend of journalism/opts to retire—sort of." The subhead explained: "Harry Rosenfeld, the man who brought you Watergate, leaves daily grind after 5 decades."

Thus had it come to pass—publicly though not formally.

CHAPTER 26

Poignancy of the Finale

In the days leading up to my retirement, Jeff Cohen asked me what would happen when the date came. Would I simply walk out of the door? I said that was just about it since New York had not supported my proposal for a Hearst journalism program in which I might play a major role. Cohen replied that wasn't right. He thought I should remain connected to serve as an all-around adviser and he discussed it with the publisher.

A while later, Tim White said he wanted me to remain active on the editorial board because my experience would back up Joann as she grew into her new role. I was expected to come to the office twice a week, for a couple of hours, and also when important people appeared before the editorial board. He proposed I should continue to be listed in the masthead as editor-at-large. He set me up with an office in my home, with a phone connection that also rang in my new cubicle of an office at the paper. If not answered there, the call would be relayed to the home office.

I was provided a fax line and a computer setup. I was paid a modest retainer. Nothing was said about my column, and I continued it throughout the years until I decided to concentrate on writing my memoir. Either party could withdraw from the arrangement at a month's notice. The agreement remained intact through three succeeding publishers—as I write this book twenty years later—down to the starting fee.

Tim not only wanted me in a continuing public relationship with the *Times Union*, he insisted on giving a big retirement party. Annie and I demurred when we sat with him in his office during the weeks preceding my public retirement. I had attended too many retirement parties with their faux expressions of mutual devotion and admiration, accompanied by a surfeit of studied insincerity. Better just to say so long and leave it at that.

Tim would not hear of it. An elaborate dinner party was planned and a date selected, September 19, 1997, a Friday night. At the time, it did not strike me as it should have, for it was Shabbat and meant my rabbi and some observant Jewish friends would not attend. I became aware of my gaffe only after mailed invitations to them were declined.

Tim White was the only suitable master of ceremonies, though he tried to avoid the role. He was finally convinced to take it on and performed outstandingly, as Dave Laventhol later wrote him.

Some 170 guests attended the dinner at the Albany Marriott and others came to the opening cocktail party. From the past colleagues from the *Herald Tribune*—Bill Miller and his wife Barbara, Mike and Thel Kandel, Erik Lars-Nelson and Dave Laventhol—traveled to Albany. Alan Miller, my first reporter hire at the papers, came from Washington, D.C., as did a delegation from the Hearst Washington bureau, including Chuck Lewis, Susie McBee, and Victor Ostrowidzki. Former governor Mario Cuomo made a video appearance. So did Katharine Graham, Ben Bradlee, and Bob Woodward, videographed by Chuck Lewis. Mrs. Graham, responding to Tim's letter of invitation, wrote: "I would give anything to be at dinner for him and with him," except that very night she had to leave for her book tour promoting her Pulitzer Prize autobiography and was flying to South Korea. Jim Bellows was kept away celebrating his daughter's birthday. Along with his best wishes for the occasion, he responded to Tim, "Some of us have to keep working."

Our Albany friends turned out in force. Also there were the Roman Catholic and Episcopal bishops. Then-assemblyman, later congressman Paul Tonko presented a citation in my honor voted by the Assembly, and Roy Goodman sent over one issued by the state Senate. Chuck Schumer, then a member of the House of Representatives who would rise to be minority leader of the US Senate, came up to Albany that night to attend. Among the guests were local politicians and state officials. Newspaper executives turned out as well as many key staffers.

Chief Judge Kaye spoke, as did Clifton Wharton, the former chancellor of the State University of New York. Bob Danzig represented Hearst Corporate along with George Irish, his successor-in-waiting as head of the newspaper division. Dave, Eric, Alan, and Chuck all spoke. Jeff made gracious remarks.

When my turn came, it was an opportunity to thank the people I worked with in Albany and to take note of those in my past years in New York and Washington, and of the formative impact they collectively had on my life. It was especially a good chance to hail my *TU* and *Knick* colleagues, noting Bill Dowd's down-to-earth sensibilities, Dan Lynch's enormous contribution, and Joann Crupi's long years of creative leadership.

Tim's main address had been researched and written by Paul Grondahl, who reported the retirement story for the paper (and years later would edit my first book). Tim opened his remarks noting my childhood in Nazi Germany. I also referred to those beginnings. In the audience was our immediate family, including Annie, my sister Rachel, and our children, their spouses, and extant grandchildren. That very Friday night was exactly fifty years to the day since the Friday night I first saw, met, and held Annie in my arms at a high school dance in the Bronx. So much of the carousel of life infused the evening for it brought to the fore the beginnings animating what we became. It brought to mind the connection between what I had lived through as a young boy and the New World that opened for me when I set foot in America, relieved of the dread inflicted on my family in Nazi Germany. I concluded with these words: "A final reflection, hope that my life's work will be accepted as partial payment on the great debt our families owe this country for having given us refuge and permitting us to flourish." This sense of obligation has never left me. It is immovably implanted.

Joseph Bruno sent a letter, saying, "As you leave, do so with the knowledge that you have really made a difference. Through your work, you've done an enormous public service and left a legacy that will educate and inspire others." This from a man with whom our papers time and again had found ourselves in conflict—but never personally. Former reporter Chris Ringwald's note said: "Thanks for being an editor who loved news and who backed up his reporters."

Frank Bennack wrote: "All of us were appropriately proud to have lured you to join us . . . but I think none of us really knew what a sound contribution to the paper, and to all of us at Hearst, you would make in the years that followed. . . . I am genuinely and deeply appreciative of the quality of your journalistic skills and of the positive impact of those skills and your commitment to the *Times Union* and the Hearst Corporation. We've been well served by you."

My longtime secretary Beverly Coons could not make it because of a serious illness in her family. She had urged me to retire when she did years earlier and now sent me a moving letter. "Anyway, I am sorry we can't see you but you deserve the very best. You are a very caring and understanding person and excellent boss and you have a gracious wife."

Howard J. Hubbard, Roman Catholic Bishop of Albany, in a letter extended "an expression of my esteem and gratitude for the sterling quality of your performance and achievements. . . . Your long career has revealed the wisdom and intellectual honesty that characterize your practice. You have shown your balanced vision and unerring sense of Albany's 'state of mind' as you discerned the day-by-day experience of a city so rooted in the early history of our country and in the ongoing complex political life of our Capital."

Michael R. McNulty, who represented Albany in Congress for twenty years, could not attend. "I'll be attending my daughter's wedding rehearsal dinner," he had written. "Let me put it as simply as I can; I hope Harry never *completely* retires. He is a model of integrity, and we need more like him!"

Andrew Barnes, my first deputy Metro editor at the *Washington Post*, then the president and CEO of the *St. Petersburg Times*, wrote: "I'm still learning the lessons you taught me—when in doubt, print; focus everything on your best story; constantly work to respect and understand the readers. Mostly, remember that newspapers are about news."

Bob Danzig presented Annie and me with a week fully underwritten in New York City. We benefited over three years because we used the generous gift in small segments.

Limited seating capacity meant the entire staff could not be invited to the event. A buffet dinner celebration followed October 31, 1997. There were more speeches and tributes. I wanted my last formal words to the staff to be a message urging commitment to our craft in a future already under threat from the internet. There were two especially telling moments. One stemmed from a visit paid to me earlier by a delegation from the local unit of the Newspaper Guild. They handed me a framed citation from the union:

> Whereas: Harry Rosenfeld has not only written that journalists should pursue the truth fearlessly, he has lived those words; and

> Whereas: Harry Rosenfeld came to the *Times Union* as Editor in 1978 and during his tenure fought to maintain the strength and integrity of the newsroom;

> Now Therefore Be It Resolved: The Newspaper Guild of Albany pauses in its deliberations to honor Harry Rosenfeld and to wish him a long, happy, and healthy retirement.

These words need to be weighed in the context of the inevitable and frequent conflicts between management and staffers, whose effects lingered to the detriment of both sides. The Guild's generosity was unparalleled, and I became emotional expressing my gratitude the night of the staff party.

The topper came when Dan Lynch presented me with a copy of the remarks made on the floor of the House of Representatives by Congressman McNulty on the day preceding, October 30, and read into the *Congressional Record*. Reciting my background as an immigrant, army veteran, and journalist, the congressman said:

> For nearly a half-century, he has served as the living embodiment of the loftiest principles of his profession. In his community and in his industry, he enjoys a well-earned reputation for integrity and undying devotion to the highest standards of his craft.
> Because of Harry Rosenfeld's commitment to honest, courageous reporting as the foundation of responsible journalism, he leaves his community a better place. I am proud to salute my friend Harry Rosenfeld for his distinguished journalistic service to the cause of democracy.

Looked at from the memory bank of an old man, mine was the story of a young kid who fled to this country for asylum and found an America that opened its doors not only to life itself but also to the chance to make something of it. To be celebrated at his work's conclusion with tributes in the Congress and both chambers of the state legislature, to have shaken hands with five presidents and several governors and others of high estate—all these were beyond the realm of realistic ambition and even audacious imagination on that sixteenth day of May 1939, when I walked down the gangplank of SS *Aquitania* and touched first foot on America—my America.

Jeff Cohen and his senior colleagues did not let matters rest with the staff party. Afterward they announced the establishment of the Harry Rosenfeld Award for Distinguished Journalism, bestowed each year for outstanding work done by a *Times Union* staffer.

I never yearned for retirement, indeed I saw myself working for another three years, until the age of seventy. For some five decades, daily journalism was my focus, and I did not practice it in lieu of something I would rather have done. Beyond family and friends, tennis and fitness training, I had no hobbies or interests that I just could not wait to get to once I retired.

Looking backward, there was good and bad in being totally absorbed by my work. The good of it was I never resented going to the office. My workplace provided me matchless opportunities. I edited the news coverage of our time's most exciting and compelling events at the *New York Herald Tribune* and the *Washington Post*. And in Albany, I fulfilled what had become a major ambition to run a newspaper.

The bad was not being the involved father I wished in retrospect I had been and left the major burden of the decisions families must make largely in the hands of the woman I was lucky to encounter as a teenager and to convince to marry me. My family's sustained support permitted me to concentrate on the work I loved. It was a gift to find myself in places—New York, Washington, Albany, Los Angeles—to learn and to accomplish. In one sense, reflecting on the beginnings of this work, it seemed far in the past, when enthusiasm outpaced ability.

I cannot resuscitate bygone days and the ambience of my youth—and its physical and emotional attributes. I can only savor them as much as the storehouse of the mind permits. The five decades I spent at work were packed with engrossing events readily recollected. And then, one day, you look up from your desk and you realize that this is the day your career wraps up.

CHAPTER 27

Travels in a Restless World

With daily journalism at its end, I devoted myself ever more to writing my column, venturing farther afield in topics. I kept it up during the varied outside activities I took on. By itself, the column consumed much of my time, because I no longer operated as part of a newsroom but worked at home, researching and writing. I needed to gather string for the current week's column as well as for prospective ones. Deciding on a topic and digging out germane facts ate up many hours. I usually wrote on Friday.

I was also fortunate to become involved with some weighty projects, which helped keep me occupied. I was one of two civilians on a seventeen-member Regents Commission to develop a vision for libraries in the twenty-first century. My lack of specific professional background turned out to be useful because I raised dumb questions the experts on the panel were too informed to ask, but which sometimes clarified discussions. Public hearings were held in cities throughout the state and we met six times over the two-year life of the commission.

A final report was issued in July 2000, with ten recommendations. The first was to create an "online virtual electronic library that would deliver high-quality, reliable, digital information to all New Yorkers." The second, my favorite, for which I pressed, was to "ensure that all New York students are information literate by providing school library media programs." In short, teaching all kids, from kindergarten through high school, how to use the tools necessary to function on the internet while learning to evaluate the quality of information cascading out of it. The third was to create public library districts congruent with school districts in the state, so even the remotest localities would have access to library services.

In 2003, George Hearst, still president of the University at Albany Foundation Board of Trustees, urged me to head up a community board, under the auspices of the School of Social Welfare. I guess my age was one of my credentials. The purpose was to improve delivery of services to the elderly. The method would be creation of "an advisory board of influential stakeholders and citizens," including business people, academics, and representatives of state and local governments as well as nongovernmental organizations. I accepted with a stipulation, which no one challenged: The board would be executive rather than advisory. I recruited top people based on the board's essential executive character.

Probably the most important achievement of what came to be known as the Elder Network of the Capital Region was suggested by George Hearst, himself a board member. It brought together as members of the board the commissioners from the four counties of the region whose responsibility was to minister to the aging population. This permitted a degree of coordination otherwise shunned by the political establishments in the separate jurisdictions. They obsessively feared any intimation of regionalization that might detract from their autonomy.

The Elder Network created a web page with pertinent data and information to connect seniors to specific services their conditions required, social and health related. More elaborate plans to provide information and assistance services through a staffed operation, and efforts to establish the equivalent of a 911 telephone service, were not achieved. After the John A. Hartford Foundation funding ran out, the School of Social Work, the backbone of the network all along, absorbed its functions. Under the bureaucratic rules to which we were being increasingly subjected, options for implementing our ideas narrowed because our group legally could be no more than advisory. It was the effective end of the enterprise as it had been. Somewhat later, the School of Social Work, under Dean Katherine Briar-Lawson, awarded me a handsome medallion for public service.

Deep sadness was occasioned by the death of United States Senator Daniel Patrick Moynihan in March 2003. His meaningful, courageous, and original contributions often violated cherished societal pieties.

Fittingly, Pat Moynihan's most insightful analyses of public policy, denounced in their time as wrongheaded or racist, came to be appreciated for their prophetic acuity. He understood, as few did, the essence of the challenges facing America.

At home, he saw the enduring complexity of a nation of immigrants retaining ethnic distinctiveness as well as the enduring gap between whites and blacks, and the pathologies that fostered disparities. He advocated for minorities and argued for paying attention to the needs of all working people, including whites. In the wider world, he recognized the implosion of the Soviet Union from fatal internal contradictions while others in power spent these United States into debt to confront what they continued to regard as a formidable threat.

In short, the man was amazing in the way he stood up to conventional wisdom throughout the more than four decades of his public life—as an administrator for four presidents, ambassador to India and the United Nations, and for twenty-four years as US senator from New York. My first encounter with him was brief, outside a White House buffered by parked buses to thwart anti–Vietnam War demonstrators when he served in the Nixon administration. I got to know him well during his Senate years, when our editorial boards hosted him once or twice a year, occasionally more frequently.

Moynihan came to Albany not only to call on us. He had political business in the state's capital in which he had labored in Governor Harriman's administration. In addition, his farm sixty-five miles west of Albany, where he did most of his prolific writing, brought him upstate regularly. He dropped in on us to or from his country home, sometimes when he was killing time before his plane departure, but never merely for a chat.

Our minds raced to keep up and to make sure we would not look foolish in his eyes by asking superficial questions. Physically imposing, tall and slender, he was even more impressive for the scope of his widely admired intellect and for his ready wit, which he could flash with a cutting edge, as called for.

Memorable was his contempt for what he regarded as the failure of the Central Intelligence Agency to do its job. The CIA did not comprehend what was happening in the Soviet Union behind the façade of exaggerated power it successfully foisted onto American policymakers. Looking at the available basic data, Senator Moynihan discerned the problems steadily overwhelming Moscow. He thundered against CIA incompetence and blamed it for helping fuel an unnecessary and costly arms race. He recommended abolition of the agency.

Another time, he spoke with us after David A. Stockman, President Reagan's director of the Office of Management and Budget, published his book about the Reagan Revolution. Moynihan discerned the political intent behind the creation of the enormous deficits (the result of cutting taxes while increasing the military budget). It was to circumscribe other government spending. Agitated, he rose to his feet and from his lofty height brought down his fist onto the conference table, pounding it for emphasis as he denounced the deficit as a deliberate creation designed to prevent funding of essential social welfare programs.

He recalled his days in Albany in a letter welcoming the announcement of my appointment as editor of Capital Newspapers, reassuring me of my decision to take the job. In his note, he regretted the building of the Empire State Plaza complex because it destroyed the city's central ethnic enclave. "The city we knew was like an old, fine piece of velvet. Alas, Governor Rockefeller's architects hacked it to pieces." He thought the construction of Interstate 787 an abomination for severing the city from the Hudson River.

In many ways, we were justly awed by the senator. That did not keep the *TU* editorial page from holding him to account when he, as chairman of the Senate Finance Committee overseeing new tax legislation, by letter invited lobbyists to an affair at New York City's Rainbow Room. Our editorial denounced Senator Moynihan's party. The tab was $5,000 a head, up from a "customary" grand or grand a half.

After the brazen fundraiser became public, he canceled it, claiming in a note to our editorial page editor that although he accepted responsibility, he "had never heard of the event, never saw the letter."

Daniel Patrick Moynihan, as we knew him, was an extraordinarily accomplished public servant, comfortable in the world of the powerful. He was eloquent and elegant in thought and word. To me, it matters most that he took his eminence in stride and kept faith with the highest American political ideals, of which he had a clear-eyed understanding.

Relations between Christians and Jews in the Capital Region were especially, if not uniquely, more than good. Two exceptional prelates, the Episcopal Bishop David Ball and the Roman Catholic Bishop Howard Hubbard, in my time, played a large role and encouraged a conciliatory tone, along with other clergymen and laypeople, Christian and Jewish.

Bishop Hubbard lived the message of the Second Vatican Council. He began his priestly service when it was in session in the early 1960s. On Palm Sunday in 1986, he did something not ever done in Christendom. In that night's service, at the Cathedral of the Immaculate Conception, the bishop, joined by two local Reform rabbis, Martin Silverman and Bernard Bloom, participated in a "celebration of healing and atonement." The bishop apologized to Jews for the cruelties inflicted on them by Christians throughout the millennia, especially at Easter. The event was a culmination for the active work of a group of laypeople drawn from the Christian and Jewish communities. Three years after the historic night, a sculpture, *The Portal*, representing in steel the passage from fear to friendship, was dedicated on the cathedral grounds.

Most everyone but Bishop Hubbard understood the critical role his person, his behavior, his early service as a street priest, and his incessant modesty played to bring about this coming together of communities. He was a quiet man and a valiant leader. His exhortations reminded the faithful to bring the teachings of their religion to bear on the troubles and the troubled of this world. He joked that once a bishop, you never had a bad meal or heard the truth. Yet he remained lean and harkened to all voices. At his ordination as bishop, he was the youngest in the country. Had Francis been pope when Hubbard was bishop, his chances of higher church responsibilities would surely have been greater.

Also remarkable was his standing among non-Catholics. We Jews, without presumption, regarded him as "our bishop."

Some years later, in 2004, during a time when newspaper-exposed pedophilia by priests created a national scandal, this noble man was charged with sexual misconduct. The allegations, one by a brother of a mentally ill man long dead, the other by an admitted prostitute, were no more than claims. Neither accuser moved to take criminal or civil action to assess the validity of the imputations, which the bishop denied, saying: "I assure you, if I were guilty I would step down immediately."

The charges made headlines. I was incensed by the bishop being denied his day in court. I devoted a Sunday column to exhort the wider community to stand up for him. With no factual substantiation offered, he stood, in his own words, "besmirched and besmeared" and denied the judicial processes that could clear him. I wrote:

> Others must protest that these accusations cannot be permitted to hover in the air, forever unproven. . . . He needs the support of people who recognize the depth of the unfairness of his situation.
> The entire community—not only Catholics—should find its voice to speak up.

In the summer of 2005 Mark Felt revealed himself as Deep Throat, the iconic unnamed source who attained fame in the *Washington Post*'s exposé of the Watergate scandal. Soon thereafter, I heard from an old acquaintance. He was Paul V. Daly, in my time the FBI field office head in Albany. We had friendly contact, and in retirement in 2005 he remembered our relationship and gave me a call. What he had to tell me made for startling news when the Felt revelation again put Watergate into the media's focus. I turned the tip over to the *Times Union*, and one of its best reporters, Brendan Lyons, was assigned to report on it.

As Watergate played out, according to Paul, "Felt was part of a clandestine group of high-ranking agents who agreed to leak information about the Watergate break-in so that the publicity would counter White House efforts to quash the probe," Lyons, son of the former publisher, wrote. The group shared their agents' daily discoveries with Felt. Daly discovered the collaboration in 1978, long after it occurred, when he was assigned to assist in the investigation of FBI agents involved in illegal break-ins. This was not something we at the *Post* reported three decades before when we laid out the Watergate story.

Toward the end of my full-time job, we took breaks from the Albany winter. We tried Florida a couple of times; from much earlier visits, we decided we preferred the California desert. At first, we stayed for a couple of weeks. Post-retirement, we rented for a month. At this juncture, our kids told us to snap out of it. We were too young, they said, to be so sedentary. This was the point in our lives to travel. And travel we did over the next decade.

We began our overseas trips in the late winter of 1998 with a month in Italy. In the following years, until illnesses made my travel infeasible, we visited nineteen other countries. Along the way, among a vast number of sights and experiences, we walked through the ruins of Pompeii, tracked wildlife on the Serengeti, gawked at the changing of the guard at Buckingham Palace, snorkeled over the Great Barrier Reef, swam with sea lions in the Galapagos Islands, trod the stones of Machu Picchu, took in the Prado and a bullfight in Madrid, strolled the garden paths at Monet's Giverny, and stood on the Normandy beach sands where our troops landed and saluted the fallen at the great cemetery nearby.

Our major international travel ended in 2009 with a tour of Central Europe, much of it by riverboat on the Danube. We flew to Prague; made a side trip to the notorious Theresienstadt concentration camp; rode a bus to Linz and boarded the boat to travel to Bratislava, Slovakia's capital city; and finished up in Budapest.

Early in our travels I came down with health problems, usually of bronchial variety. On our trip to Central Europe I again was plagued by deep coughing and a renewed difficulty with a painful knee that slowed my walk. Limping through Prague and Budapest was no pleasure and pretty much ended it for me. Our daughters had been on the mark urging us to travel while we were in shape to do so. During the years of our journeys, many with our friends Shirley and Herb Gordon, we were exposed to the beauties and wonders of great cities and countries and to their people and cultures.

Our last overseas trip is a bit of a long story. Annie's maternal grandfather, Moritz Strauss, was born on April 2, 1865, in Gross-Karben in Hessen, years before Bismarck unified the Germanic principalities into the powerful nation they became, for too much ill. Moritz Strauss died on February 4, 1943, and was buried in the Czech city of Terezin, Theresienstadt in German. Once a fortress of the Habsburg Empire, by 1942 it was a Nazi concentration camp. It was generally considered the least atrocious of the numerous death and work camps, Hitler's historic legacy. Least atrocious is likely an absurd characterization because of the cruelties relentlessly inflicted there.

According to a rabbi who survived Theresienstadt, Moritz Strauss was the last Jew buried there in a religious rite. Afterward, Jews were cremated, their ashes discarded into the ground. Many, many years after his death, a great-grandson of Moritz Strauss, Jonathan Cobb, commissioned a headstone. It stands at the far side of the camp's crematorium and marks not his grave, which is unknown, but is a commemoration.

Thus, when Anne and I, accompanied by the Gordons, toured Central Europe in October, we felt drawn to Theresienstadt to honor the *opa* she had last seen in 1936, as a five-year-old when her family resided in their German hometown of Reinheim. Her very last glimpse of her grandfather came at the railway station as Annie, her sister Doris, and their parents, Sol and Martha Hahn, began their journey to America.

At the site of the headstone, the four of us recited the mourner's kaddish and placed small stones on it, as is the custom. Before we left, Anne touched the headstone and said to her grandfather, "We will never forget you, *Opa*." Over the years, Moritz Strauss's stone was visited not only by his grandchildren, but also his great-grandchildren and their children.

From the heartbreaking site, we were driven to Terezin, from which the Czech residents were forced to move so it could be turned into a concentration camp for Jews. At first, it was a transit camp, in which a quarter of its inmates died from hunger, cold, and disease. Soon enough, prisoners were sent off to death camps. It was featured in Nazi propaganda films, for which the town was beautified to influence world opinion. At this, the Germans succeeded.

In a small fortress the Germans installed a large washroom, with individual sinks that all too easily fooled an International Red Cross inspection so cursory as to be complicit. None of the sinks connected to a water supply.

In the town, we entered what had been a secret synagogue, which operated unknown to the authorities and most Jews. It was a small room, in a courtyard behind a high wooden gate. A guide who had been imprisoned in Theresienstadt as a small child translated Hebrew inscriptions artfully painted on the walls of the windowless room. They were quotations from the Psalms. One exhorted the faithful to hold to their beliefs under oppression. Another spoke to the Jews' yearning for their ancestral homeland: "If I forget thee, Jerusalem, let my right hand forget its cunning."

In Prague, we went to the Old Jewish Cemetery, which was established in the fifteenth century and contained some twelve thousand ancient tombstones. Among these, Anne found a stone marking a person named Hahn, her maiden name. In Budapest, we visited the Dohany Street Synagogue, also known as the Great Synagogue, the second largest in the world (exceeded by New York City's Temple Emanuel). It was a reminder of the rich traditions of a once thriving Hungarian Jewish community. The Germans used it as a stable.

As our tour wound up, the guide took us to the Garden of Remembrance in a courtyard behind the temple. There stood a Tree of Life sculpture, its leaves engraved with the names of some of the hundreds of thousands of murdered Hungarian Jews. Near the sculpture were two steles on which were inscribed names in gold, honoring Righteous Gentiles who at the risk of their lives acted to save Jews. Our guide walked over to one of the steles, pointed to the fourth name on it, and said: "That is the name of my father, my Catholic father." Anne hugged her. As the guide walked off to meet her next group, my wife picked up a stone from the ground and placed it on the memorial.

Although in the decade of travel we never went on a tour specifically centered on Jewish life, there was not a country in Europe, nor many elsewhere, where we did not confront the history of the Jews—whether in Spain or Portugal with their expulsion in the fifteenth century, or more contemporaneously in Norway, where a memorial of empty chairs faced the open sea, marking the Quisling collaboration with the Nazis in the deportation of the country's Jews to death camps. The stamp of Jewish contributions was not obliterated by the Nazis, for vestiges of their impact remained in all these places.

CHAPTER 28

A Book Takes Shape

Serious illnesses struck our family starting in 2005. First Susan discovered she had breast cancer and was treated, sustaining a mastectomy. The next year, Annie was diagnosed with the disease and underwent two lumpectomies and a year of chemotherapy and radiation treatments. She and I went to Albany Medical Center each week where she was infused for four hours. She lost her hair and wore a wig that preserved her usual appearance. She endured the pains and discomforts. Perhaps the harshest for her was to keep her distance, as doctors advised, from her youngest grandchildren because of their susceptibility to childhood's infectious germs and illnesses.

After we climbed those mountains, Amy had a routine mammogram that showed nothing untoward. Alerted by her sister's and mother's illnesses, Amy demanded an MRI. The MRI spotted a malignant tumor. Further tests revealed no genetic basis for this prevalence of breast cancer in our family—but we also learned genetic testing was not well developed. Too many potential genetic connectors remained to be discovered.

It was not until well into my retirement, April 1999, that I started on a narrative I hoped would be a history of my life and times in newspapering, as well as Annie's and my life as a couple, written for the benefit of our children and grandchildren. This had been my ambition from the time I belatedly recognized my failure to question my parents about their early lives. For the most part, they did not volunteer anything about their upbringing or how they met in Warsaw in the first decades of the twentieth century. I do not recall my father sharing stories from his youth, while my mother was a little more forthcoming. My sister, Rachel, eight and a half years my senior, knew more about those times. She and mother obviously talked about family matters. She also was old enough to discern on her visits to Warsaw, by herself or with mother, something about our parents' early life as well as through conversations with aunts, uncles, and cousins.

It was my wish that my children have available a fuller account of their parents' early days. Even so, my first ventures into autobiography remained sporadic.

In May 2005, Mark Felt revealed himself as the Mother of All Unnamed Sources, Deep Throat, leading to a widespread retelling of the story of Watergate. Most of the attention focused on the two reporters who spearheaded the investigation, but it also renewed interest in the part I played. I was the editor at the *Washington Post* in charge of the daily coverage of the exposure of the affair, the boss of Bob Woodward and Carl Bernstein. Our coverage was awarded the Pulitzer Prize Gold Medal for Public Service, the most coveted of journalistic honors.

Because of the renewed interest in things Watergate, Deputy Education Commissioner Carol Huxley proposed to host a discussion on the topic to be staged in the auditorium of the state museum. The format was a talk between Rex Smith, the editor of the *Times Union*, and me, about those bad old days in our nation's history. The evening of June 22 fulfilled Carol's expectations. The auditorium was fully occupied, all the fixed seats taken, and supplementary folding chairs brought in. Rex's astute questions guided our discussion that concluded with the audience rising to its feet to applaud.

The Watergate revival impacted me in another important way. I received more and more encouragement and pressure to tell my part of the story in a book. For many years, my friend Bernard Conners urged me to write my story. I always listened to his advice but did not follow it. I was fully occupied by my Sunday column whose production consumed the week. There was no way for me to take on a book project while I produced a weekly column. I also harbored doubts that I could bring off a book of interest to a public audience. So much had been written about Watergate, and I questioned what I could add.

At this point, George Hearst encouraged me to write. Even so very late, he thought it was a good time to share my story of Watergate and newspapering. Nevertheless, my procrastination persisted for years until George renewed his push. When he held out the possibility of research assistance, I finally decided to go for it. George agreed to the suspension of my column, which occurred in February 2010. Upon Annie's and my return from our winter sojourn in Palm Desert, I sat down to begin to write seriously. In the early stages as a hedge I told myself at the least it would result in a record for future generations of our family.

Book writing at the age of eighty was a significant challenge because the mind's facility was not as it had been in earlier years. At times, I sat immobilized at the computer keyboard, a fleeting remembrance of a word lurking in my mind that would exactly depict the thought, and I was not able to dredge it up. Little wonder that professional writers like Philip Roth and Alice Munro stopped at the age that I began.

Sitting for hours in front of the computer was an added difficulty. A once mild back problem eventually was diagnosed as spinal stenosis. The discomfort has never gone away, only gotten worse or better.

Three years of work followed before I had in hand a manuscript that needed editing. It also lacked Celebrity, Scandal, and Sex, all capitalized, for commercial presentation. With the help of friends, I took my work to State University of New York Press, which agreed to publish it.

At the heart of the memoir was the connection between my childhood in Nazi Germany—in 1938 I saw my father taken from our home by the Gestapo in the dead of night for deportation and witnessed the burning of my synagogue—and my coming to America, where I found my new life and my future in journalism.

From Kristallnacht to Watergate: Memoirs of a Newspaperman was published in September 2013. An hour-long interview on local public radio launched it. Appearances followed in New York and on a national tour. Friends were closely involved in getting me many of these gigs. A personal appearance was standing room only at the College of Saint Rose in my Albany neighborhood, arranged by George Hearst, a college trustee, along with Joann Crupi, in retirement from the *TU* a college staff member. Down the road, Saint Rose chose me as the commencement speaker at the June 2014 graduation. As is customary, before the address I was awarded an honorary degree, Doctor of Humane Letters. The program noted I spoke as Dr. Rosenfeld. My mother's ambition for me was to become a dentist and, so, in her son's mid-eighties, she got a doctor, albeit *honoris causa*.

My son-in-law Paul, then the executive director of the Authors Guild, helped set me up with a national tour. I was booked into three sites in Florida, two in California, and others in New Jersey, Pennsylvania, and Atlanta. Friends arranged for two appearances in Washington.

My daughters set up presentations where they lived near Boston and Chicago and in Manhattan's Greenwich Village. My niece Janice Kaminsky worked diligently to negotiate appearances in Southern California.

The bountiful and thoughtful help of my family and friends, for which I was endlessly grateful, was an unexpected bonus from having published the book. This was true also for the indelible impressions made by women and men encountered in the places we visited. There were many large public audiences and exposure to people—people who related to the story of my childhood, my Americanization, my army service, and my newspaper work—and to their lives. In one way or another, some passage in the book encouraged them to speak to me about their own experiences and ambitions, some of their suffering or of terrifying histories.

In Tampa, it was the woman who survived the Holocaust as an infant. Her father was in a concentration camp. Her mother worked in a hospital for orphans that operated under Nazi supervision in Vienna. After the war, the husband, who survived, rejoined his wife and child. He then became a smuggler to sustain his family until they received the permission to immigrate to America.

In Tampa, too, we met a young man, tall and handsome, who used a motorized wheelchair. He was gravely injured taking photographs, when to steady himself, he grabbed with his bare hand an electrified power line. He lost the use of one arm and was rendered a paraplegic. At dinner before my talk, I learned he was a college student pursuing a degree in social work. He was active and forward looking, not permitting his disability to hold him back.

In California, at the Rancho Mirage Library, a tall, elderly man approached the table where after my remarks I autographed books. As I signed his, he told me, in what I recognized as a faint trace of a German accent, he had also lived through Kristallnacht. He said at the time he was five years old and resided in a small town in Germany. He was not Jewish but saw with a child's eyes the brutalities the Nazis inflicted on Jews. In a voice so low I could barely make out his words, he said he wanted to apologize. For a moment I could not grasp what he had in mind. When I figured it out, I told him I could not accept his apology because he had no cause to offer it.

In Boynton Beach, Florida, a couple of women told Annie they had known my father. One of them remembered him from Germany. It turned out that their uncle and aunt had been guests at our wedding.

At my appearance in Washington, at the Newseum that houses an interactive presentation of the history of the American press, Len Downie, my former deputy on the *Post*'s Metro desk, interviewed me. He wound up his illustrious career as no one's deputy, rising to managing editor and then Ben Bradlee's successor as executive editor. Gina Logue, of Middle Tennessee State University, was in the sold-out audience. After the conversation, she invited me to speak at her campus in Murfreesboro. This last stop of the book tour would stir one of my most poignant and deeply emotional memories.

It took me back to a phone call from a stranger in August 2005, which I wrote about in my first book. The man who contacted me turned out to be a cousin of a childhood playmate in Berlin. My friend's name was Gustav Loewenstein. Although I remembered him, I had forgotten his name. I saw Gustav last in Berlin in 1939, days before our family left for America. Gustav's cousin, Roger Lowen, the man who called, said he had a letter written by Gustav to his uncle and aunt, Roger's parents, in America about the departure from Berlin of his last friend, Harry Rosenfeld. Mr. Lowen said he had wanted to contact me years before, but those efforts fell short until his daughter, back from Israel and a visit to Yad Vashem, the Holocaust memorial, helped him.

Roger restored Gustav's name to my memory and I learned of the fate of my friend and his father. They died in a Nazi work camp in

Estonia. Although I was fully conversant with what happened during the Holocaust, hearing of the death of my boyhood friend caused me deep anguish. I wept when Roger told me and howled in agony after the phone call ended. This had to be, in part, because I had the good luck to evade the Hitler killing machine. My family arrived in America 107 days before the outbreak of the Second World War. Despite the attempts of Gustav's American relatives to rescue him and his father, they failed to secure the necessary papers in time.

I vowed never again to forget Gustav's name as long as I retained the power to remember. He is often in my thoughts and certainly during the Day of Atonement memorial service. I wrote his story for the *Times Union*. It was prominently displayed with photographs provided by Roger Lowen and the Rosenfeld family album. Gustav's story resulted in the strongest reader reaction created by any of my writings. My granddaughter Dana Kaufman, while on a Fulbright Fellowship in Estonia in 2012, went to see the prison grounds where Gustav and his dad likely were confined in their final days.

Our friendship began in comradeship and ended in suffering for him and in life for me in a country that provided greater opportunity than I ever could have had in a normal, non-Nazi Germany. This is my burden, if not precisely of guilt, then surely of sorrow. His story frequently plays out in my head as I reflect on the slim margin by which I survived. Inevitable questions loom to rebuke and shame me: Did I do enough with the life that sheer luck permitted me to live? Should I have tried harder to accomplish more? Posing the questions was to answer them.

Four years after Roger's call another Lowen relative contacted me. His son, Simon, was to become bar mitzvah under a twinning program commemorating Jewish children slain in the Holocaust. Simon wanted to share the rite with his cousin, something Gustav did not live to experience. To prepare for the ceremony, Simon asked me to tell him everything I knew about Gustav, who was the first cousin of Simon's paternal grandfather. Simon's thoughtfulness touched me, and I shared all I knew with him.

While Simon was undergoing instruction, another relative phoned to pose a question. Since Gustav's mother had been gentile, was Gustav an authentic Jew qualified for the religious ceremony? I was the last person to consult on a matter for which an answer steeped in Mosaic and Talmudic law was required. I knew Reform Judaism accepted Jewish descent through the father along with the traditional matrilineal criterion or by conversion of the non-Jewish mother. My definition was framed differently. I said: "Gustav was killed as a Jew by the Germans. His identity card was stamped with a huge J for all the world to see. Gustav was a Jew."

Some sixty-seven years after his murder, Gustav became bar mitzvah, Son of the Commandment, alongside Simon on July 11, 2009, at Congregation B'nai Emunah in Tulsa, Oklahoma.

At my talk in Tennessee five years later, Gina Logue interviewed me in front of sixty or so townspeople and students. Gina and I talked for about an hour, and then I shifted to a hall table to sign books. First in line was a young man and his mother. He identified himself as Simon Lowen. When he spoke his name, I instantly rose to my feet to hug him as if he were family. Simon was a college sophomore. A few years earlier, the Lowens moved from Tulsa and now lived about an hour distant in a suburb of Nashville. They had spotted a notice of my appearance in a newspaper and drove to Murfreesboro to see me. Our meeting was brief, but in some ways, I suspect, everlasting because I embraced a familial heir of my childhood friend, parted from me by his death.

In writing so much about my life, in my mind I returned to those early years to see if I could garner insights into the why of what happened to me. Different occasions have triggered these introspections, one of which, of course, was learning about Gustav's fate, and another was the same year when I was given an award. In May 2005, I was honored by the Maimonides School in Albany, a vibrant sector of Orthodox Judaism, with the Dr. Morton Berger Memorial Award. Dr. Berger's memory resonated with the strong humanistic traditions of a Judaism observed not only in the synagogue but practiced as well in the transactions of professional and civic life. The award impelled me to examine how being a Jew shaped me to be the person I became. When I did, I found, as I said that night: "Circumstances forced me to understand from the first moments of understanding, who and what I was. . . . I was a Jew and I lived in a country where to be such was to be despised." The lesson I drew from the pervasive racism of Nazism was:

> When an entire society bears down on you to define you in its terms, you must struggle to define yourself in yours.
> I recall from those years that I would attend synagogue—I must have been seven or eight—on Friday night by myself in the temple that during the day served as the Jewish Community School. I learned to love Friday night services in that time and place and I collected money for the Jewish National Fund.

In short, the more I was reviled for my Jewishness, the more I valued it. As a grown man, I better understood how Judaism embodied precepts of righteousness and justice. Those teachings were intrinsic to my work as a newspaperman. They mated well with the imperatives of the free press to foster a democracy whose calling card is equal justice under law, inscribed on the façade of the United States Supreme Court building.

My book, which recounted this story, brought me modest honors, bronze medallions from two independent publisher groups. It was State University of New York Press's best-seller for the season. Much more was the full-hearted support, practical and emotional, provided by my wife, my daughters, and their husbands; by my grandchildren, my sister, my nieces and nephews; and by my friends. They are the gold medallions I will forever cherish.

The end of the book tour freed me to sit again in front of the computer. This time, equipped with a more ergonomic chair and an effective back brace, I undertook writing about the final period of my newspaper life and the retirement years. Anne and I are in the seventh decade of our marriage, and it has not been nearly long enough for us. We have a full measure of the joys from having lived our lives in tandem, from the caring, thoughtful mothers and accomplished adults our children grew up to be, and from the attainments of our grandchildren with their hopes and aspirations.

During these later years, our family continued to endure the usual and the unusual afflictions. There was no surcease as our son-in-law Paul Aiken bravely battled the ravages of ALS for three years, dying two days before his fifty-seventh birthday. His contribution to protect the copyright of authors distinguished his score of years leading the Authors Guild, where he dedicated himself to preserving the written word. The death of my sister at ninety-four was hard for me to bear. Our oldest daughter had a second mastectomy. Time after time we as a family rally when in pain and need. We put one foot before the other to try to keep our balance as we make our way in the world. We will do it as a family that, above all, cares for one another. This is our fulfillment and, we pray, our legacy.

Epilogue

Before I wrap it up, a final word.

In the prologue of this memoir I invoked the promising days of the 1970s when newspapers, abetted by new technologies, raised their standards and sights to reach a higher level of journalism. I conclude concerned about the uncertain future of newspapers as we know them, challenged today by forces unleashed by the internet in its varied guises. Newspapers' role in maintaining our democracy is threatened.

During the epic events of my life and career, the centrality of freedom of the press to the vitality of our political system was firmly established in my mind. Experience teaches that authoritarian nations universally lack a free press. Without one, countries posing as democracies might acquire some of their trappings but not the substance.

Under the umbrella of the Constitution, the press possesses its special protections for one reason: to hold to account the accountable, by serving as a check on the powerful, and exposing corruption and other abuses.

More than ever in many generations, these days the nation stands imperiled. The press is under calculated political assault from an ascendant right wing for its very independence at the same time that its strength is sapped economically.

I write these words in a day when the president undermines the press because it has the temerity to decline participation in his amen chorus.

The contentions of my later years as an editor began to illustrate the enormous business pressures brought to bear by the Digital Age on the viability of newspapers and all other traditional media. Internet alternatives enticed away readers and advertisers. Staffs were reduced; fewer pages were available to publish their work. The newspapering the First

Amendment is purposed to encourage and shield inevitably suffered because the best reporting, the hardest to do, takes time and money. This is today's ineluctable challenge. How to overcome it remains unclear.

I spent my life doing journalism in black and white and on paper. For me the tactile newspaper was the way news of the day was conveyed. So it was with strong reluctance, gradually over time I acknowledged the dislocation of the printed page. With misgivings, I accommodated to the realities of the new age. Compelling journalism no longer has to be produced by the traditional newspaper, magazine, or book. It comes down to content more than format.

Since communication is their business, how and in what form can newspapers survive? After a slow start and some early faulty decisions, newspapers slowly integrated the web and other internet forms to present information to the public. A serious mistake was to offer their content online for free. As the readership shifted to a variety of social media, accessed on the screens of smart phones, tablets, and other devices, it was difficult to convince the public to pay for a service initially provided at no charge. Monetizing the new ways of presenting news is necessary to raise revenues the producers and deliverers of news require to do their work. Allied with the papers, digital media don't need printing presses and other costly accoutrements necessary to publish and distribute newspapers.

Before the day comes that journalism on the internet makes enough money to pay for itself and entirely supplants newspapers, we need to confront the chill of the long and dark shadow cast by the internet here and now. Along with its vast reach and connectivity, its very ubiquity empowers once scattered and fragmented fringe political upstarts to coalesce and establish themselves in the public arena, giving voice to radical and racist factions. Web pages convey comments anonymously and brazenly. Along with linking a universe of like-minded friends, they equip the ill-intentioned and haters with huge power to viciously cyberbully.

Furthermore, the 2016 presidential election brought into the open the exploitative possibilities of fake news, that is, fabricated stories, to attract or distract a distressingly large part of the population. The campaign again demonstrated the insecurity of the internet to tampering.

Any transmission is vulnerable to hacking, including the most sensitive government communications or, for that matter, financial and personal transactions. As of now, no impenetrable protective barrier exists. When one is hailed as such, its code is broken. Hostile nations, criminal gangs, political factions, and economic competitors are capable of boundless tinkering with the instruments of the internet. Journalism reliant on it is not immune. Distinguishing between the false and the factual is the job of writers and editors. It was trenchantly described in the old days as having "to pick the fly shit out of the pepper." Only today there is vaster abundance of both. Information pouring out of Facebook, Twitter, and the tsunami of social media, not to mention talk radio and cable news channels, demands an enlarged skill set to differentiate the valid from the deceitful.

Identifying the solution is simple, its implementation complex and pricey. The desire to acquire the aptitude must come first. That is not a sure thing at a time when too many people prefer to get their information from sources championing their entrenched beliefs. Senator Moynihan's profound insight that people are entitled to their own opinions but not to their own facts holds true in a rational world, though not so much in one increasingly tolerant of alternative facts.

What's needed is a major cultural shift, reversing what occurred when the public's preference for objectivity in news gave way to clearly partisan interpretations of it.

We as a society must decide what is meant by a basic education. The current bias against national standards needs to be overcome. Civics and American history should be mandated courses to buttress citizenship. The curriculum of every classroom from kindergarten through high school has to provide grade-appropriate information tutorials, including scrutiny of good and bad examples. This would equip pupils with the essential facility to assess the authenticity of information.

If the United States is to preserve its constitutional framework and maintain the ideal of equal justice for all, then Americans confront a weighty task. It is up to the collective will of the people to decide. The shape of the future is within reach. We must be willing to seize it and hold it fiercely tight. The haters, self-dealing political hacks, and opportunists will not cease in malversation of government and its far-reaching powers. We must, in short, become full-time citizens, taking an active role by voting and by stepping up as informed observers and participants in government at all levels from local to state to national.

Thomas Jefferson's epic instruction—"Eternal vigilance is the price of liberty"—must be firmly fixed in hearts and minds and affirmed by behavior.

Index

Note: *Italicized page numbers indicate material in photo captions.*

ABC News, 56
abortion, 34–35, 52
Abrams, Floyd, 117–18
acid rain, 31
advertising: advertorials, 186; decline in revenues from, 2; ethical issues, 17–18, 185–87; In Memoriam section, 78–80; native ads, 186; in *Times Union* Sunday magazine, 160–61
advertorials, 186
African Americans: and civil rights movement, 99–100, 123; and discrimination, 6, 36; minorities in newspaper jobs, 197, 219; and police brutality, 35–36, 119–20; and political cartoons, 122–23
Aiken, Paul (son-in-law), 196–97, 208, 240, 244–45
Albany, New York: and Capital Newspapers Group, 12–13 (*See also* Capital Newspapers Group); City Hall carillon reconstruction, 71; county civic center, 76; *A Day in the Life of Albany* (*Times Union* special magazine), 191–92; and Democratic machine politics, 5, 12–13, 27–29, 35–36, 65, 67, 70–73, 75–76; description in 1978, 13; Elder Network of the Capital Region, 228; Empire State Plaza, 12, 230; Fort Orange/Dutch colonial settlement re-creation proposal, *84*, 215–17; governors of New York state (*See* governors of New York); Hearst Corporation meeting (1984), 111–12; Hearst Corporation meeting (1990), 159; Interstate 787, 215–16, 230;

Maimonides School, 243–44; mayors (*See* mayors of Albany, New York); New York State Museum collaborations, *176*, 217–18; *Portal* (sculpture at Cathedral of the Immaculate Conception), *173*, 231; relations between Christians and Jews, 231–32; Riverfront cultural park proposal, *84*, 215–17; Nelson Rockefeller impact in, 12, 230; snow crisis of 1987, 144–45, *180*; Tricentennial Commission, 139
Albany Civic Roundtable, 39
Albany County Bar Association, 35
Albany Medical Center, 10–11; and Lillian Cedeno, 95–97; and Erastus Corning 2nd, 67; and Anne Rosenfeld, 237; and Sam Rosenfeld, 65
Albany Times Union. See Times Union
Alexander, J. D., 140–41
Allentown (PA) *Morning Call*, 154
Allied Van Lines, 138
American Legion, 39
American Society of Newspaper Editors, 108–10
Anderson, Jack, 100
Andrews, Danny, 112, 140–41
animal stories, 60–61
Ann Arbor (MI) *News*, 159
anti-Arabism, 58
anti-Irish bias, 58
anti-Semitism: and bias accusations in journalism, 55–58; in Europe, 152–53 (*See also* Holocaust); of Joseph Sobran, 121–22, 153; in the United States, 121–22, 153
Aspen Institute, 218–19

251

Hearst Corporation *continued page 256*